The Cook's Idea Book

The Cook's Idea Book

1001 great ideas for creative cooks

by Valera Grapp Blair

Clarkson N. Potter, Inc./Publishers NEW YORK
DISTRIBUTED BY CROWN PUBLISHERS, INC.

Published simultaneously in Canada by General Publishing Company Limited

First edition

Printed in the United States of America

Library of Congress Cataloging in Publication Data

Blair, Valera Grapp.
    The cook's idea book.

    Includes index.
    1.Cookery.   I.   Title.
TX715.B566   1977   641.5   76-48158
ISBN 0-517-52740-5

RECIPE FOR HAPPINESS

Take 2 heaping cups PATIENCE
One heartful LOVE
2 handfuls GENEROSITY
Dash of LAUGHTER
One headful UNDERSTANDING
Sprinkle generously with KINDNESS
Add plenty of FAITH *and mix well*

*Spread over a period of a lifetime and serve
everybody you meet.*

ACKNOWLEDGMENTS

I am indebted to the many home economists and writers on cookery who have, over the years, through magazines and recipe books, contributed to my knowledge of cooking, as well as to my mother, my aunts Florence Meade and Antonia Hoffmann, and many friends who have shared their prize recipes with me.

Since I have read cookbooks as assiduously as I have read legal journals and case reports, it would be impossible to give individual credit for ideas gleaned from those many friends and writers. I am, however, grateful to all of them for their excellent and stimulating thoughts about food. Our camaraderie in sharing a love of cooking is one no bar association could hope to match.

V.G.B.

Contents

Introduction

Hundreds and hundreds of cookbooks are brought out each year and all of them have one thing in common: Recipes. All assume that a dish prepared by the book, as dictated by the author, will please everyone. This cookbook, however, is different. It is a cookbook *for cooks*, to give them, not more recipes, but new ideas, new ways of preparing old favorites, bringing together unexpected ingredients, spices, or flavorings, and presenting foods in different ways for home meals and for parties.

Most of the women and more and more men in this country have become experienced cooks, preparing several meals a day for their families and frequently entertaining at home. Most are able to make juicy tender meats, fish and chicken. They know not to overcook vegetables; they can make smooth sauces, crisp salads, light cakes and flaky pie crusts; and many bake their own tender bread and rolls. Many hosts, hostesses and house-wives have specialties of their own, perfected with practice—dishes that are well loved by their families and friends. Chances are that recipes are something they don't need more of, but a good cook is always on the lookout for cooking ideas.

The Cook's Idea Book is intended to fill this gap and to stim-ulate the art of presenting basic foods imaginatively and health-fully to add excitement and interest to meals. These pages are designed for the busy person, whether homemaking is a full-time career or not. It is time consuming to search out new variations from books or a mass of recipes clipped and saved, stored in boxes, files or the kitchen drawer. You will find here in one place, and in concise form, hundreds of variations on basic recipes.

Some of the suggestions are elaborate and elegant, making use of costly ingredients such as filet mignon or caviar; many use the plainest of foods, cabbage, carrots, peanut butter in glam-orous ways. And the chapter "Instead of Meat" will prove that an intriguing meal can be served without mortgaging your soul to the butcher.

This book circumvents another problem with recipe books—the fact that tastes differ. A perfect lemon pie to one person is thick; to another, runny or sweet, or tart. This book won't tell you how to make a basic lemon pie—make one to your taste, using a mix, your grandmother's favorite recipe or one from a book you have found reliable. What this book will do is to sug-gest tempting variations—such as an elegant meringue crust or folding macaroon crumbs into your lemon filling to make *lemon-macaroon pie* or using your filling to make a *surprise frozen lemon pie*.

Cook your roast beef as you like it, be it prime rib or a lesser cut, rare or pink or crispy well done. But try it with some of the variations here; *chili-glazed apples* or a garnish of *tomato baskets.* If you have some beef left over, you might try a *meat-stuffed potato roll* or make *glorified hash* or serve cold *rare beef vinai-grette.*

Trying out some of these ideas may spur you to new ideas of your own. One of the desserts in this book, *strawberries in the snow,* was born of necessity the day a very special friend was coming to dinner. She preferred fruit for dessert rather than rich pies or cakes, but the strawberries I had bought, to be served with sugar, seemed too simple for the occasion. On impulse, I made a quick butter frosting, dipped the berries in the frosting, then in grated coconut and a new dessert came into being, one that is now a favorite.

From the time I was ten years old, I have read, collected and tried out recipes. I baked my first cake, a chocolate one, in the oven of a wood-fed stove in Grandma Kepler's kitchen in Center County, Pennsylvania. Grandma was known for her fine cooking. She had the advantage few of us have now of fresh garden vegetables raised in her own backyard, plump fresh chickens fed with rich country milk, fresh-churned butter, newly laid eggs, and hickory-smoked hams cured with logs from our own woods, which also supplied hickory nuts and black walnuts. Her raw materials were superb and lovingly and carefully prepared. Her notes to herself were written down in her well-worn ledger with directions like "Mix as butter cake." Cooks *knew* how to mix a butter cake then, so there was no problem. There was often a difference in texture and flavor from one cake to another because the home-grown or home-prepared ingredients and methods varied. These variances were all good and added to the interest of the dishes.

Today we have certain advantages our grandmothers didn't have. We have mixes which take the problems, even for a beginner, out of making a basic recipe. We have frozen, canned and convenience foods. These mixes, standardized for flavor and texture, can get pretty dull, as can frozen foods, vegetables, meat, fish, butter, and poultry which are necessarily produced, graded, stored and packaged to maintain *uniform* flavor. Mixes and convenience foods can be infinitely improved by adding embellishments and variations of one kind or another. I have included many suggestions for them here, as well as variations for "start from scratch" recipes.

Although I was actively engaged in the practice of law for nearly 30 years my avid interest in cooking continued. Relaxation for me, after a day in court, was cooking gourmet dinners for my family and friends. In Pittsburgh where I was raised, I had learned to cook many ethnic dishes from mothers of friends of Italian, Polish, German, Syrian and Greek descent. Through the years I have traveled widely throughout the United States, Europe and the Caribbean, constantly accumulating recipes and ideas.

Seven years ago, I retired from the practice of law and opened my dream gourmet restaurant on a farm in Greene County, Pennsylvania, in a huge brick house with five fireplaces, once a stagecoach stop, called the Ryerson Station Inn. Last year, I opened a natural foods restaurant in St. Petersburg, satisfying my life-long interest in health foods. This interest was sparked by my parents who took me to the health food lectures and classes so popular in the thirties given by such people as Professor Paul Bragg, Elsie Audrey Hiller and Gaylord Hauser. Admiring their principles of healthful natural cooking through the years has made gourmet cooking all the more delightful and rewarding.

Here, then, are the results of my years of cooking, clipping recipes, studying, experimenting, and I might add, zestfully eating. I hope you will enjoy this, my life's work. Good cooking, good health and good fun!

VALERA GRAPP BLAIR

Appetizers

Cold Canapés

Cheese with Red Wine. Mix cognac with Roquefort cheese. Serve with melba toast or butter crackers and chilled red wine.

Cold Meat Pinwheels. Spread a generous mixture of chopped dill pickles and blue cheese on slices of boiled ham. Roll the slices, wrap tightly in waxed paper, and chill overnight. When ready to serve, cut the rolls into thick slices with a sharp knife. Serve on crackers or pastry rounds.

Another combination: cream cheese and horseradish on slices of tongue.

Daisy Canapés. Spread rounds of bread with butter and then lightly with anchovy paste. Garnish with narrow strips of hard-cooked egg white to resemble daisy petals and place sieved hard-cooked egg yolk in the center.

Egg Salad Canapés. Spread rounds of bread with egg salad. Dip edges in minced parsley. Top with red caviar (salmon roe).

Emerald Crown Canapés. Spread rounds of bread with butter and dip edges in minced parsley. Put a small slice of smoked turkey in the center of the buttered round. Place a border of mayonnaise around the turkey and arrange white grapes in the mayonnaise.

Jeweled Crown Canapé Tray. Arrange colorful canapés in the shape of a jeweled crown on a large, flat, round platter. Suggestions: giant pecan halves held together with softened blue cheese; triangular-shaped canapés of red caviar and egg salad; chopped-liver canapés garnished with minced egg white; sharp cheese balls rolled in minced dried beef; cream cheese balls rolled in chopped chives.

Miniature Cold Sandwich Snacks. Butter slices of party rye bread. Top with baked ham, liverwurst, salami, or tongue. Serve on a large platter garnished with a scooped-out cucumber filled with tiny sweet pickles and a green pepper cup filled with a sauce of sour cream lightly laced with mustard.

Old and New Canapés. Bind chopped black olives with mayonnaise and use as a border contrast for such standbys as cheese or chopped-egg canapés.

On-Hand Canapés. Spread thin slices of party rye bread with mayonnaise. Garnish with a very thin wedge of peeled tomato and place a slice of anchovy-stuffed olive or a rolled anchovy sliced crosswise on each side of the tomato.

Pantry Pâté-Stuffed Rolls. Buy crisp, long poppy seed rolls or submarine rolls. Cut lengthwise, not quite through, and scoop out soft inside. Fill with a mixture of canned or homemade liver pâté and cream cheese moistened with a bit of mustard and flavored with chopped chives. Chill. Just before serving, slice into circles.

Party Pie Canapé. Cut a 1/2-inch-thick slice from the widest part of a round rye or white loaf. Trim the crust. Spread the slice generously with a mixture of equal parts butter and mayonnaise seasoned with a trace of fresh crushed garlic.

Mark the buttered round slice in concentric circles (do not cut through bread), using a round cookie cutter for the center ring, and gradually using larger dishes or bowls to indicate the larger rings, until you have 4 or 5 rings.

Fill each ring with a different dip or canapé mixture. The center might be caviar, the first ring clam dip, then egg salad, then ham pâté, mashed avocado dip, chopped olive or pickles, etc. Salmon salad or any variety of cheese spreads may be used. Frost edge with cheese spread or mayonnaise.

Place on a large round platter. Cut in pie-shaped wedges with a sharp knife, but do not separate. Serve cold within a few hours. You may garnish the canapé pie with pickled onions, stuffed olives, radish roses, or sliced pickles.

Red Caviar Appetizer with White Wine. Top a mound of whipped cream cheese with a dollop of red caviar. Or spread red caviar on a block of cream cheese. Serve with dark melba toast (made by double-toasting buttered party rye slices). Serve a Riesling or sauterne, well chilled or on the rocks.

Ruby Crown Canapés. Spread rounds of bread with butter. Roll edges in ground parsley. Place a small piece of smoked tongue or ham in the center. Border it with chili sauce and insert in the border thin slices of small stuffed green olives, slightly angled, next to each other.

Santa Maria Canapés. Peel small, hot Spanish sausages, or boil, cool, and peel frankfurters. Cut into 1/4-inch rounds and marinate in French dressing. To make the canapés, dip some of the marinated slices in finely chopped parsley, some in mashed or grated hard-cooked egg yolk, and the rest in finely chopped hard-cooked egg white. Spread 1-inch rounds of toast with blended mustard and butter. Arrange 3 sausage slices—1 green, 1 yellow, and 1 white—on each round.

Smoked Salmon Canapé. Spread small squares (including edges) of pumpernickel bread with cream cheese and top with a thin slice of smoked salmon. Dip edges in minced parsley.

Hot Canapés

Apartment-Kitchen Pizza. Split English muffins in half. Cover each half with a sprinkle of olive oil, a thin layer of canned tomato paste, and a thin slice of mozzarella cheese. Sprinkle with finely crushed oregano and dot with chopped anchovies or thin slices of Italian hot sausage or pepperoni. Place on baking sheet and bake in moderate oven for 15 to 20 minutes. Brown lightly under broiler, if necessary. These can be prepared ahead of time and baked just before serving.

Bacon and Peanut Butter Canapé. Spread saltines with peanut butter mixed with crumbled cooked bacon. Place under the broiler for a few seconds.

Baked Cheese Canapé. Use a sharp cheese spread, topped with broken (not chopped) nut meats. Spread on bread squares which have been buttered on the bottom and put on baking sheet. Bake in a hot oven for about 12 minutes.

Cheese-Cracker Onion Crisp. Make a crumb crust of crushed cheese-flavored crackers and melted butter. Press half of the mixture into an 8-inch-square baking pan, covering bottom and sides. Half fill the pan with sautéed onion slices mixed with a beaten egg and 1/4 cup of milk. Crumble remaining cracker mixture on top. Bake in moderately slow oven for about 30 minutes. Cut into squares and serve hot.

Cheese Napoleons. Roll pie dough out to an 8 x 12-inch rectangle. Sprinkle generously with grated sharp cheese. Fold the pastry over lengthwise in thirds, like an omelette. Sprinkle the folded dough with more cheese. Fold once more lengthwise. Press the resulting cheese-filled dough strip lightly with your fingers until it is about 16 inches long and 2 inches wide. Sprinkle the top with celery seeds, pressed in lightly. Cut into 1-inch-wide pieces and bake on an ungreased baking sheet in a hot oven for about 12 minutes.

Clam Imperial Canapés. Moisten well-drained canned minced clams with a mixture of mayonnaise, chili sauce, and prepared horseradish. Spread on toast rounds. Brush the top lightly with more mayonnaise. Broil until piping hot and bubbly. Sprinkle with paprika and serve hot.

Exotic Cheese Rounds. Mix 1/2 cup of chopped chutney with 2 small jars of blue cheese spread, lots of chopped chives, and 1/4 teaspoon of cumin. Spread thinly on melba-toast rounds or potato crackers. When ready to serve, broil for 2 minutes.

Filled Cheese Circles. Make cheese pie crust with pimento cheese. Cut out rounds with a cookie cutter. With a thimble or the center of a doughnut cutter, cut a hole out of the middle of half of the rounds and place one on each whole round. Press outer edges together and bake in a very hot oven until a delicate golden color. When slightly cooled, place a dab of deviled ham or peanut butter in the hollow center. Serve immediately.

Ham Sticks. Roll pie pastry 1/8 inch thick. Spread with canned deviled ham. Fold twice and roll again to 1/8-inch thickness. Cut in strips. Bake in a hot oven for 10 to 12 minutes, or until brown.

Hot Cheese Canapé. Mix sharp cheese spread with a little mayonnaise and season with salt, Tabasco, and Worcestershire. Cut bread into rounds or stars, and lightly butter the bottom. Spread the cheese mixture on top, adding an anchovy wrapped around a pickled pearl onion. Bake in a hot oven for 5 or 10 minutes, or until cheese is bubbly.

Jiffy Cheese Puffs. Cut sharp cheese into 1/2-inch cubes. Wrap bits of flattened biscuit dough around the cheese cubes to form small balls. Fry in hot oil. Serve immediately with cocktail picks. These go well with beer, ale, or tomato juice cocktail.

Miniature Cheese Biscuits with Ham. Make biscuit dough, adding 1/3 cup of grated sharp cheese to the dry ingredients. Cut miniature-size biscuits with the inside of a doughnut cutter. Bake, split, and serve hot with thin slices of tender baked ham inside.

Miniature Quiche Lorraine. Bake in small tart pans. Use rich milk instead of the specified amount of water in recipe for the pastry. Dessert tarts can be made richer and crisper this way too.

Monsieurs. Make chicken salad sandwiches with white bread. Remove crust after sandwich is made, and cut each one into 4 triangles. Dip the sandwiches in a mixture of 1/4 cup of light cream and 2 beaten eggs. Place on a buttered baking sheet and bake in a hot oven until browned on both sides.

Nut-Butter Crisps. Mix 2 parts of ground nuts with 1 part of butter. Use sweet butter if nuts are salted. Season well with Worcestershire sauce and a dash of Tabasco. Spread thinly on potato crackers. Heat quickly in hot oven.

Pantry-Shelf Canapés. Spread round crackers with a dab of deviled ham, then a dab of mustard. Top with a small piece of American cheese and put under the broiler until cheese melts.

Sizzling Steak Canapé. Barbecue a juicy strip steak. While guests watch, the host carves, flipping each hot, juicy slice onto a thin round of party rye bread. A crisp vegetable relish tray completes the picture. Worcestershire sauce and catsup may be served on the side.

Tiny Tim Turnovers. Roll pie pastry 1/8 inch thick and cut into 2-inch squares. Place a teaspoon of well-seasoned chopped liver, well-seasoned ground-ham salad, or curry-seasoned ground-chicken salad in the center of each square. Fold into a triangle and press edges together. Bake in a hot oven for 10 to 12 minutes.

Dips

Anchovy Dip for Shrimp or for Slices of Cooked Lobster Tail. Mix equal parts of mayonnaise-type salad dressing and sour cream. Season with finely chopped parsley, minced onion, lemon juice, tarragon vinegar, and a generous amount of anchovy paste.

California Dip. For onion lovers. Mix 1 package of dry onion soup mix with 1 pint of sour cream.

Deviled Cheese Dip. Mix 2 parts of pimento cheese spread with 1 part of deviled ham. Moisten with salad dressing and flavor with minced parsley, minced onion, and Tabasco.

Devil Sauce for Steamed Clams or Hot Broiled Fish Bits. Use equal parts of melted butter, Worcestershire sauce, and catsup, spiked with mustard and lemon juice.

Dips for Crisp Vegetables. Arrange icy cold radishes, green onions, cauliflower bits, and strips of carrot around a bowl of mayonnaise flavored with catsup and horseradish.

Dutch Cucumber Salad Dip. Add about 1/2 cup of coarsely grated or ground seeded cucuml er (skin and all, if skin is not waxed), finely chopped green onion and 1 tablespoon each of lemon juice and sugar to a 3-ounce package of cream cheese. Salt and pepper to taste. Serve with rye melba toast. A good appetizer with a light drink such as sauterne or vegetable juice cocktail.

Eggplant Pakistan. Pare and thinly slice a small eggplant. Sauté in butter with 1 finely chopped green pepper. Chill and serve with a topping of sour cream or yogurt highly seasoned with chili powder and garlic salt. Serve cold with sesame seed crackers or Indian bread (Pappadums).

Hot Mushroom and Seafood Dip. Mix 1 can of condensed cream of mushroom soup, 2 large packages of cream cheese mashed, 1-1/2 cups of grated sharp cheddar cheese, and 1/4 cup of water. Season with grated onion and Tabasco sauce. This can be done ahead of time. Just before serving, heat the mixture and add flakes or lumps of crabmeat and shrimp, coarsely chopped. Serve in a chafing dish with melba toast rounds or round crackers for dunking.

Lassie Snack. To delight children, mix equal parts of unsulphured molasses and peanut butter and serve as a dip with crisp apple wedges or crackers. Serve with pineapple juice, apple juice, or milk. A straw with a maraschino cherry on the top makes the beverage more interesting.

This is also a healthful snack for the grown-up with a sweet tooth.

Middle East Taste Tempter. Exotic, but easy to make! Mash canned chick-peas (garbanzos) smooth as silk, or put them through a food mill. Season—don't thin—with lemon juice, olive oil or sesame seed oil, salt, and freshly ground pepper. Use garlic salt or some fresh mashed garlic in the dip if desired. Mound on a serving plate. Make a shallow depression in the center by pressing the top with a spoon. Fill with a bit of oil.

Sea Goddess Sauce. A gourmet tartar sauce. Into equal parts of sour cream and mayonnaise, fold minced anchovies or paste, lots of finely chopped chives and parsley, lime juice, and tarragon white wine vinegar. Season to taste with salt and coarsely ground white pepper. Serve with cold shrimp, lobster, crabmeat, steamed scallops, or tuna fish.

Shrimp Cocktail with Red Caviar Sauce. Mix equal parts of mayonnaise and chili sauce. Add minced dill pickle and a jar of red caviar, a good dash of Tabasco, a little salt, and some lemon juice. Serve with cold cooked shrimp. To preserve their firm texture and sweet flavor, never cook shrimp more than 3 minutes.

Sophisticated Raw Vegetable Dip. Flavor sour cream with mustard, mayonnaise, a dash of curry powder, and salt. Serve with green onions, raw cauliflower, fresh raw asparagus tips, and cherry tomatoes.

Variation on vegetable dip: Substitute chopped dill weed for the curry powder and serve with equal parts of cubed avocado and chunks of Alaska king crab or lobster. Garnish with watercress and a twisted slice of lemon.

Sweet-and-Sour Sauce. Combine 3/4 cup of chili sauce, 1 tablespoon of lemon juice, 1/4 cup of red currant jelly, a dash of Angostura bitters, and 1 teaspoon of soy sauce. Delicious as a dip for fried shrimp. Or serve the shrimps with boiled rice and this sauce, and you have a Chinese dinner at home.

𝔉ruit 𝒜ppetizers

Apple Cheese Fingers. As an appetizer, salad, or quick snack, serve crisp apple fingers with a softened sharp cheese spread. The cheese spread may be laced with chili sauce and celery seeds. Or try yellow Delicious apples and fingers of sharp cheddar cheese.

Avocado Pineapple Bobs. Put a cube of avocado and a cube of fresh pineapple on a cocktail pick. Arrange the picks in a shallow dish and cover with fresh garlic French dressing made with lime juice instead of vinegar. A bit drippy but luscious—especially favored by the "vitamin kids."

Bride's Bouquet Fresh Fruit Cup. Place a small lace paper doily and a round of waxed paper inside a large sherbet glass so that the edge of the doily shows above and around the edge of the glass to give a nosegay effect when you serve these colorful fresh fruits: strawberries, seedless grapes, and Mandarin orange sections.

Candy-Minted Fresh Fruit Cup. Crush 1/4 pound of soft after-dinner mints and add to 1 cup of fresh, diced pineapple and the sections from 3 peeled, seedless oranges. Chill overnight and serve garnished with a fresh mint leaf dipped in powdered sugar.

Champagne Fruit Cup for Wedding or New Year's. For a colorful and refreshing fruit cup, use Mandarin orange sections, banana cubes, small green seedless grapes, and halves of ripe strawberries. Fill deep sherbet glasses 2/3 full of ice-cold champagne and float generous spoonfuls of the mixed fruit in the champagne.

Christmas Appetizer. Slices of banana served in chilled cranberry juice cocktail.

Cool Sherbet Starter. Put small scoops of mint, lime, or lemon sherbet in stemmed glasses. Fill glasses with chilled ginger ale and add a squeeze of fresh lemon juice. Garnish with fresh mint leaves.

Fall Fruit Cup. Cantaloupe balls, watermelon cubes, and seedless grapes in orange juice.

Fresh Mint Fruit Cup. Crush fresh mint leaves with a little powdered sugar in a few drops of fruit juice (to release essence from mint) and set aside in refrigerator to steep. Pour the strained essence over fresh fruit cup.

Hawaiian Fruit Cocktail. Cubed watermelon, cubed fresh papaya, canned or fresh pineapple chunks, and thickly sliced bananas. Marinate the fruits in a generous amount of passion fruit juice (available in frozen concentrate form, or use the canned nectar). Chill thoroughly before serving.

Mandarin Grapefruit. Makes a perfect Thanksgiving dinner starter. Prepare half a grapefruit for serving. Drain canned Mandarin orange sections and place a section of orange on the top of each section of the grapefruit.

Melon Balls with Prosciutto. Just before serving, wrap thin slices of prosciutto around ripe melon balls, spear with toothpicks, and serve immediately.

Melon Mélange. Arrange balls of watermelon, honeydew melon, and cantaloupe in sherbet glasses so that their delicate colors are attractively displayed. Top with a teaspoonful of undiluted, still partially frozen lemonade concentrate and garnish with a twist of lemon.

Papaya with Prosciutto or Fresh Figs with Prosciutto. Have prosciutto sliced as thin as tissue paper, allowing 2 or 3 slices for each serving. Peel and quarter papaya and remove all but 3 or 4 of the seeds. Arrange the prosciutto slices on a salad plate so they overlap a bit. Top the slices with either the quarter of peeled papaya or a fresh fig cut from top almost to bottom and spread out petal fashion. Garnish with wedges of lime and pass the black pepper grinder.

Sherry-Broiled Grapefruit. Prepare halves of grapefruit, removing all seeds, the core, and the white membrane between the sections. Put 1 tablespoon of maple syrup in each half. Broil for 15 minutes. Add 2 or 3 teaspoons of sherry to each half just before serving.

Tart Fruit Cup. Serve grapefruit sections, thinly slices unpeeled apple, and cubes of jellied cranberry sauce in sherbet glasses with a mixture of cranberry juice cocktail and grapefruit juice.

Cold Hors d'Oeuvres

All-Gone Cheese Balls. Serve cubes or small balls of sharp cheese, stuck on thin pretzel sticks to be used as edible picks.

Avocado-Filled Eggs. Slice hard-cooked eggs in half lengthwise. Remove the yolks and mash with an equal amount or more of ripe mashed avocado. Moisten with lemon juice, a bit of olive oil, and a generous amount of salt. Pile a heaping portion of the mixture in the hollow of each egg white. Top with a slice of stuffed green olive. Serve on an hors d'oeuvre tray or on a bed of greens for a salad.

Blue Deviled Eggs. Add crumbled blue cheese and mayonnaise to the mashed yolks for deviled eggs. Sprinkle with paprika.

Boiled Shrimp with Dill Sauce. Cook shrimp for 3 minutes in boiling, seasoned water. Drain and chill. Serve with fresh dill sauce made from 2 parts of mayonnaise and 1 part of sour cream, sweetened a bit and seasoned generously with chopped fresh dill and a crushed garlic clove.

California Artichoke and Shrimp Appetizer. Cook whole artichokes. Pull off leaves and use the most attractive ones. Put a dab or rosette of mayonnaise on the broader, tender end of each leaf, and top with 2 or 3 tiny shrimp, cooked in an herb-and-lemon-flavored bouillon. Arrange leaves in wheel fashion so the tapered tips point out. Save the tender artichoke heart for another dish.

Cheese Log. A decorative and delicious addition to the cocktail or buffet table. Combine 3 ounces of blue cheese, a 5-ounce jar of sharp cheddar cheese spread, and two 3-ounce packages of cream cheese with 1 teaspoonful of onion salt (or 1/2 teaspoon of grated onion and 1/2 teaspoon of salt), 3/4 teaspoon of Worcestershire sauce, and 1/4 cup of minced parsley. Turn the mixture out on waxed paper or foil and shape into a log by rolling in the paper. Chill. Just before serving, roll the log in chopped pecans and garnish with pecan halves and sprigs of parsley. Serve at room temperature with a variety of crackers.

Cheese-Nut Stuffed Celery. Celery stuffed with sharp cheese spread, topped with chopped walnuts instead of the usual paprika.

Cheese Pumpkins. Roll soft yellow cheese into good-sized balls, flatten slightly and make vertical ridges with the dull edge of a knife dipped in water. Insert a small piece of green pepper for a stem.

Continental Appetizer. Curls or balls of sweet butter, several little radish roses, and a small crusty salt roll. Or three sardines, a lemon wedge, and a little bouquet of crisp watercress.

Delicious Marinated Mushrooms. Heat 1/2 cup of olive oil, 2 tablespoons of lemon juice, 3 tablespoons of white vinegar, 1 teaspoon of salt and a *bouquet garni* of 6 peppercorns, a few sprigs of parsley, 1 bay leaf, 1 teaspoon of tarragon, and 1/4 teaspoon of thyme. Add 1 pound of small, cleaned mushrooms. Cook slowly for 5 to 10 minutes. Cool in the liquid and refrigerate overnight.

Double-Cross Deviled Eggs. Cut hard-cooked eggs in half crosswise instead of lengthwise. Devil the yolks; garnish with caviar, rolled anchovies, toasted blanched almonds, a strip of pimento, a piece of crisp bacon, a sprig of parsley, or a slice of stuffed green olive.

English Walnuts or Pecans with Blue Cheese. Cream equal parts of cream cheese and blue or Roquefort, cheese. Add sweet or sour cream to soften just a little. Chill. Form cheese mixture into marble-sized balls. Press half a nut on opposite sides of each ball. Squeeze nut halves together slightly so that a thick line of cheese appears between the halves. Keep cool until ready to serve. Crisp celery hearts and these nuts are fine for snacks before dinner.

French Cheese Salad Appetizer Plate. Arrange small cubes of Swiss cheese, diced celery, diced hard-cooked egg, and a small amount of grated or minced onion held together with mayonnaise and lightly flavored with mustard and dill seeds on a fresh leaf of romaine. Top with minced parsley. Garnish with radish roses or slices of radish and scored cucumber slices.

Guacamole Variation. Refreshing as an appetizer or a patio supper salad. Avocado cubes, peeled tomato cubes, lime juice, salt, grated onion, a dash of Tabasco, and a dash of chili sauce. Serve icy cold in a sherbet glass or in a small bowl lined with lettuce.

Herring Waldorf. Mix a jar of herring tidbits in wine sauce with minced sweet red onion and some chopped unpeeled apple. Moisten with sour cream. Serve on lettuce with peeled tomato wedges. Garnish with sliced, scored cucumbers and black olives. Delicious with thin slices of dark rye bread or party rye bread and sweet butter.

High-Protein Stuffed Celery. Chop pimentos very fine and mix with 1/2 pound of dry cottage cheese. Add mayonnaise to taste. Spread on celery, arranging 3 slices of stuffed green olive on top.

Individual French Hors d'Oeuvre Plates. On small plates serve paper-thin sliced raw carrot marinated in French dressing with thyme, a mound of meat or liver or fish pâté, a whole pimento, and an anchovy.

Jellied Crabmeat Cocktail. Prepare gelatine with 1 cup of boiling water and 1 envelope of unflavored gelatine softened in 1/4 cup of lemon juice. Cool. Add 1 cup of Russian dressing and a teaspoon of salt. Fold in 1 cup of crabmeat. Chill in individual molds. Serve each on watercress garnished with several lumps of fresh crabmeat and a wedge of lemon.

Low-Calorie Stuffed Eggs with Cheese. Add 3 tablespoons of cottage cheese to the egg-yolk mixture for deviled eggs. Mound high. Garnish with a strip of pimento laid lengthwise.

Miniature Pâté Maison. Mix liver sausage, liverwurst, or chopped cooked liver with mayonnaise and finely chopped pimento-stuffed green olives. Shape into small balls and roll in chopped chives. Serve on picks, or make the balls a little larger (about egg size) and serve on a plate with crackers and a small cocktail spreader.

Mussels Rémoulade. The rémoulade sauce: To a cup of mayonnaise add 1 teaspoon of minced parsley, 1 tablespoon of mashed anchovies, 1 teaspoon of dry mustard, 1 tablespoon of chopped capers, 1 crushed garlic clove, 2 chopped egg yolks, and 1 teaspoon of chopped chives. Thin to desired consistency with equal parts of lemon juice and white wine.

The mussels: Clean and scrub the shells thoroughly. Cook in a cupful of white wine with 2 chopped green onions for just a few minutes, or until shells open. (Some of this broth can be used to thin the sauce instead of using the lemon juice and white wine.) Cool the mussels in the broth. Drain and toss in the rémoulade sauce. Serve with a few sprigs of watercress and thin slices of toasted French bread.

New Twist for Black Olives. Fill large pitted black olives with finely chopped green onion. Wrap in a flat anchovy and fasten with a pick.

Olive Pâté with Party Rye Slices and Crisp Radish Roses. Make pâté by pureeing a 12-ounce can of chopped black olives and mixing with a stick of soft butter, 1 crushed clove of garlic, freshly ground black pepper, and a few crushed cumin seeds or other herb. Press mixture into a square pan and chill thoroughly. Cut in squares and serve on small plates with several thin slices of party rye bread and two crisp radish roses.

Pimentos and Anchovies. Crisscross whole pimentos and flat anchovies generously over a mound of shredded lettuce. Serve with lime or lemon wedges and freshly ground black pepper. The juice that clings to the anchovies and pimento combines with the lemon or lime juice to make a delicious dressing without your turning a finger or a fork.

Poor Man's Pâté de Fois Gras. Let 1/2 pound of smoked liverwurst and a 3-ounce package of cream cheese stand at room temperature until softened. Cream them together thoroughly until smooth. Add 1 tablespoon of Worcestershire sauce, 1/8 teaspoon of dry mustard, and a dash of Tabasco. Mix in a few wedges of black olives. Pack in a crock. Serve in the crock or unmold and garnish with black olives. Serve with thin slices of party rye bread or rye melba toast. Good with cold beer or with white wine on the rocks.

Porcupine Ball. Form 2 cupfuls of cheese spread into a ball and roll in finely chopped parsley and ground almonds. Store in the refrigerator. Before serving, bring to room temperature and insert small thin pretzel sticks into the ball to make it resemble a porcupine.

Quick Eggs and Herring. Making this delicious snack or luncheon dish used to be major project for the traditional Scandinavian cook. Preparing the herring by soaking and draining took days. But for the modern American cook, it's a breeze.

Buy a jar of herring in sour cream. Chop the herring into bite-size pieces. Add 3 chopped hard-cooked eggs, the sour cream and onion sauce from the jar, an additional cup of sour cream, a little white wine vinegar, and salt and pepper to taste. Serve with small, piping hot boiled potatoes.

Real Caviar Blintzes. Make thin, small, egg-rich pancakes. Season caviar with onion juice and a bit of grated lemon rind. Place 1/2 teaspoon on each pancake and roll. Keep at room temperature. Serve with sour cream seasoned with Tabasco and salt.

Red Caviar. Serve a mound of red caviar on a few sprigs of watercress. Top with a generous spoonful of sour cream. Sprinkle with chopped chives. Top with a smaller spoonful of chilled red caviar. Garnish with a quarter of a lime and a small bread sandwich made of buttered party rye. Pass the pepper grinder.

Red or Black Artichoke Hearts. Serve artichoke hearts in individual bonbon cups topped with sour cream and a generous dab of caviar, black or red, depending on your mood and pocketbook. Or for the "gambling" crowd, some black and some red.

Roquefort Sticks. Form a mixture of Roquefort or blue cheese and cream cheese into small balls. Roll in finely chopped parsley. Use thin celery sticks or crisp shoestring potatoes as edible skewers.

Shrimp Baskets. Spear both ends of a large cooked shrimp or prawn with a pick, pressing the ends together as closely as possible without breaking the shrimp. Fill the basket formed by the shrimp with a thick tartar sauce, thick Green Goddess sauce, or Sea Goddess sauce.

Smoked Danish Sprats. Serve with sweet butter and Rye Krisp; a perfect accompaniment for Danish beer—each makes the other more delicious!

Stuffed Black Olives. Stuff large pitted black olives with a mixture of cream cheese and blue cheese to which you have added chopped pecans. Serve on picks.

Stuffed Radish Roses. Cut red radishes from tip almost to stem to form petals, first cutting out each radish center. Stuff centers with a dab of crabmeat salad or caviar. Cut the radishes ahead of time, but do not fill until just before serving so they will stay crisp.

Three-in-One Eggs. Cut hard-cooked egg into thirds lengthwise. Remove and devil the yolks. Mix canned Smithfield deviled ham with 1/3 of the yolk mixture and fill 1/3 of the wedges. Fill the rest of the wedges with the plain deviled yolk mixture and garnish half with bits of anchovy and half with slices of stuffed green olives.

Tomato First. Peel tomatoes and cut in half. Over each half pour sour-cream sauce, made by adding mustard to sour cream and seasoning with salt and pepper. Garnish with sliced, hard-cooked eggs.

Variety Cocktail Kebabs. Serve frankfurter chunks and cubes of mustard pickle on a pick. Other ideas for picks: ham cubes and a cube of Swiss cheese; a small square of pickled herring and a pickled onion; a cube of sharp cheese, a small stuffed green olive and a cube of salami.

Whipped Cottage Cheese. Add a little cream to the cheese and beat it in an electric blender until fluffy and smooth. Garnish with chopped chives and bits of chopped ripe tomatoes, or serve a mound of the cheese on a thick slice of peeled tomato. Top with chopped chives.

Hot Hors d'Oeuvres

Bacon and Walnut Bundles. Bacon should be partially cooked before combining with the other foods. Wrap large walnut halves in 1/2 or 1/4 of a thin slice of bacon. Broil for a few seconds.

Barbecue Cheese Brochettes. Alternate small squares of sliced white bread and Swiss cheese on small skewers. Dip alternately into egg and milk beaten together and flour. Fry in deep hot oil for just a minute. Serve plain or with a dip of tomato sauce.

Beef Oriental. Marinate thin squares of tender beef in a mixture of soy sauce, ginger, and garlic. Brown quickly in a hot oiled chafing dish. Serve with the heated marinade, adding a pinch of sugar and a squeeze of lemon.

Chinese Appetizers. Wrap a piece of chicken liver and a thick slice of canned water chestnut in a thin slice of partially cooked bacon. Broil until the bacon is crisp. Serve hot with a daiquiri or other rum drink. You may also serve hot egg rolls (the frozen, ready-to-heat-and-eat kind). This dish is called Rumaki on some Polynesian restaurant menus.
  Prepare quick sweet-and-sour sauce by spiking mashed plum or red currant jelly with mustard and grated lemon rind.

Chutney Rarebit. Serve cheese rarebit on buttered toast. Sprinkle with chopped or ground peanuts. Garnish with a generous spoonful of chutney.

Cocktail Shish Kebab. Broil several bite-size pieces of lamb on small skewers. Serve with a sauce made of yogurt or sour cream seasoned with salt, pepper, and herbs. I prefer the Greek lamb herbs; equal parts of dried mint and oregano and a pinch of rosemary. Pita (Bible bread) should be served, to pull the bits of lamb off the skewer after they have been dunked in the sauce.

Creole Rarebit. Make rarebit using tomato juice for part of the required liquid. Add 2 tablespoons each minced green pepper and onion which have been lightly sautéed in 1 tablespoon butter. Serve in a chafing dish with toast triangles for dunking.

Curried Broiled Oysters. Add curry powder, chopped chives, and parsley to whole-egg mayonnaise. Put a spoonful of the mixture and a small piece of thinly sliced, partially cooked bacon on each raw oyster. Broil until oysters are plump and bacon is crisp. Serve with watercress and a wedge of lemon.

Date-Bacon Bundles. Wrap dates in thinly sliced, partially cooked bacon and broil. Large stuffed green olives broiled in bacon are traditional. Some of each could be served on picks for afternoon tea, TV snack, or appetizer tray.

Different Cocktail Meatballs. Make miniature meat balls from equal parts of ground raw veal and ground cooked ham, highly seasoned. Cook in a chafing dish in half butter and half oil.

Flaming Sausages. Put small pork sausages in a chafing dish and cook slowly on one side. Pour off grease. Turn sausages over. Add 1/2 cup of dark brown sugar and 1/2 cup of soy sauce and simmer sausages, cooked side up, in this mixture. Add 1/2 cup of heated light rum and ignite.

Green Pizza. Cover pizza dough with sautéed onion and green pepper slices, crushed oregano, anchovy fillets, and sliced pitted black olives instead of the usual tomato and cheese topping.

Herb Snacks. Simmer 1/4 pound of butter, a spoonful of cognac, and some chopped fresh basil for 10 minutes. Add 1/2 box of Triscuits and stir until brown and crisp. Sprinkle with salt and freshly ground black pepper. Serve in warmed, shallow earthenware dish.

Hot Stuffed Artichoke Bottoms. Fill warmed fresh or canned artichoke bottoms with tiny circles of sliced mushroom stems creamed with sour cream and a *roux* of butter and flour, highly seasoned. Garnish the serving plate with some of the artichoke leaves if you cooked them yourself.

Liver-Stuffed Mushrooms. Stuff mushroom caps with highly seasoned chopped chicken liver. Bake for 15 minutes. Serve hot or cold as an appetizer.

Miniature Crab Cakes Amandine. Dip small crabmeat balls in fine toasted bread crumbs and then in egg. Roll them in finely chopped or coarsely ground almonds before frying in hot oil. Or insert 2 slivers of almond into frozen, prepared miniature crab cakes before heating.

Miniature Meatballs. Make meatballs with Grape Nut Flakes soaked in milk as the binder. Brown and place in a chafing dish. Simmer in a sauce of canned tomato sauce, chopped mushrooms, and 1 teaspoon of sugar.

Nutty Fish Cakes. Dip any bite-size fish cakes in fine toasted bread crumbs and then in egg. Roll them in finely chopped peanuts before frying.

Outdoor Oyster Snack. Drain small canned oysters. Dip them in lemon juice, then in thin fritter batter, and deep fry in hot oil. Serve them hot. They can be cooked in an electric skillet on the patio, to be eaten while the host is presiding over the charcoal grill.

Quick Cocktail Fish Balls. Buy small Swedish fish balls in a jar. Drain, roll in seasoned flour, and brown in equal parts of butter and oil. Serve in a chafing dish with cocktail picks.

Quick Tomato Rarebit. Add 1/2 pound of diced American or sharp cheddar cheese to 1 can of condensed cream of tomato soup. Heat in a chafing dish until smooth. Season with Worcestershire sauce, Tabasco, and salt. Serve in the chafing dish with chunks of toasted French bread for dunking.

Sardines in Blankets. Sprinkle small sardines with lemon juice. Wrap in rich pastry and bake in a hot oven.

Scandinavian Hors d'Oeuvres. Boil small potatoes. While piping hot, roll them in a mixture of fine toasted bread crumbs and crumbled blue cheese. Serve on picks. Sour cream or plain yogurt may be served as a sauce.

Stuffed Mushrooms. Make stuffing of 1 part canned Smithfield deviled ham, 1 part fine toasted bread crumbs (the packaged kind), and minced parsley. Stuff the mushrooms and place them in a shallow buttered baking dish. Just before serving time, bake in a very hot oven for 15 minutes.

Swiss Appetizer for Barbecue. Put a chunk of sharp cheese on a foil plate near the grill so that the outer edge will melt. Provide a cheese knife or spatula so each guest can serve himself by skimming off some of the cheese as it melts. Provide each guest with a small warm plate and an individual butter spreader, and pass crusty warm French bread slices, green onions, and radishes.

Tom Thumb Sausage Buns. Make miniature hot dog buns with prepared mix. Serve hot, cooked cocktail sausages or cocktail weiners in the split, warm buns. Spear with fancy picks and serve with a hot chili sauce.

Two-Tailed Pigs. Serve small broiled pork sausages with a salted blanched almond in both ends of each sausage as an edible garnish.

Tray Garnishes

Appetizer Tray Centerpiece. An upturned bunch of perfect, thoroughly washed and dried red radishes. Rub each radish with vegetable oil to give it a shine. Surround with scored, unpeeled cucumber slices sprinkled with parsley.

Christmas Cucumber Garnish. Slice an unpeeled cucumber partially through and insert red radish slices. Scoop out another cucumber, fill it with mustard and sprinkle with celery seed.

Christmas Hors d'Oeuvre Tray. Vari-colored paper or foil bonbon cups placed close together on a plate are perfect for serving soft hors d'oeuvres or cheese balls. This attractive service is particularly appropriate during the winter holiday season, giving the effect of miniature Christmas tree ornaments.

Cucumber Boat and Pepper Cups. Heap grated carrot in a boat made of a scooped-out, unpeeled cucumber. Make two "sails" of salami on picks. Also serve a crisp green pepper cup filled with mustard and a crisp sweet red pepper cup filled with mayonnaise or other dip.

Dragon Holder for Cocktail Picks. Attach a red apple (with eyes of black olives and tongue of a long, flat sliver of carrot) to a crooked-neck squash with toothpicks. Surround the "dragon" with parsley and insert cocktail picks for spearing surrounding appetizers.

Edible Pickle Sailboats for the Relish Tray. Make a lengthwise incision in small gherkins (sweet pickles). Scoop out a bit of the center and fill with cream cheese. In each insert a small "sail" made from a thick wedge of salami.

Sugarplum Tree for Christmas Hors d'Oeuvre Tray. Cut the top off a pineapple (including an inch or two of the pineapple meat), leaving the spiny leaves intact. Wash thoroughly in salt water, rinse thoroughly, and dry. Press the leaves outward and down to look like branches on a tree. Set upright in center of cocktail tray and press a maraschino cherry on each leaf tip.

Twisted Lemon Slices. Cut a lemon into thin slices. Cut halfway through each slice of lemon toward the center. Then twist the cut ends in opposite directions so the rind forms the shape of an "S."

Soups

Hearty Soups

Cooking Tips: Vegetable Cream Soups in Blender. Steam spinach, broccoli, or other green vegetable in water for 10 minutes. Cool in the broth. Puree with cooking broth in electric blender. Add whole milk or cream for desired color and consistency. Heat and season with sesame sea-salt, a pinch of mace, and a drop of Tabasco sauce.

Garnish for Cream Soups. Top with salted whipped cream, adding minced chives and parsley, chopped pimento, toasted bread crumbs, or grated lemon rind, depending on the flavor desired.

Bedford Chowder. Easy and economical. Sauté a grated onion in 2 tablespoons of bacon drippings, stir in 2 cans of frozen cream of potato soup, 1 package of frozen sea scallops, partly thawed and chopped, 1 can of cream-style corn, 2 cups of milk, and a dash of Tabasco. Heat to just boiling. Pour into soup bowls and sprinkle with rose paprika. Serve with oyster crackers or other seafood biscuit.

Boula. This is similar to Bongo Bongo at Trader Vic's. Mix and heat equal parts of cream of pea soup and genuine turtle soup. Season with Madeira wine. Pour hot soup into individual ovenproof casseroles. Top with stiffly whipped cream and sprinkle with freshly grated Parmesan cheese. Place the casseroles under the broiler to brown the cheese.

Crab Bisque. One of the tantalizing standbys of Lillian Russell's day. Cover 1 cup of lump crabmeat with 1/2 cup of sherry and let stand for an hour. Then blend a can of condensed tomato soup and 1 can of condensed green pea soup with 1 soup can of light cream, 1/4 teaspoon of curry powder, and 1/2 teaspoon of paprika. Heat slowly, but do not boil. Add crabmeat and reheat to boiling point. Serve immediately from an antique soup tureen with a crisp salad and hot breads, followed by a sweet.

Cream of Asparagus Soup. Cook a package of frozen asparagus cuts or a small bunch of fresh asparagus in chicken broth. Puree in blender. Combine with an equal amount of thin cream and 1 beaten egg yolk. Heat, but do *not* boil. Stir constantly.

Cream of Cucumber Soup. Simmer 1 large peeled, seeded, and diced cucumber and several outer leaves of Boston lettuce in a little water until tender. Puree by putting through a food mill or in an electric blender. Add to a can of condensed cream of chicken soup thinned with cream to soup consistency. Season with nutmeg, salt, and white pepper. Sprinkle with minced parsley. Good either hot or cold.

Cream of Tomato Soup with Herbs. Thin canned tomato soup with rich milk. Add 1 teaspoon of sugar, 1/4 teaspoon of salt, 1/4 teaspoon each of crushed oregano and dill, and a dash of mace. Serve topped with a spoon of sour cream sprinkled with chopped chives or minced fresh dill.

Cucumber Soup, Jamaican Style. Cut several peeled cucumbers and 1 onion in quarters. Cook in 1 quart of rich chicken stock. Cool. Puree in electric blender. Add cucumber mixture to cream sauce made from a *roux* of 1 tablespoon butter and 1 teaspoon of flour, 1 cup of light cream and a dash of mace. Serve hot with chopped chives. This method may be used to make other cream soups: broccoli, spinach, squash, or Brussels sprouts.

Curried Lentil Soup. To lentil soup, add mashed pumpkin or squash, 1 peeled and chopped apple, a few raisins, grated coconut, and curry powder to taste. Lemon juice adds zest.

India Chicken Soup. Add 1 teaspoon of curry powder to a can of condensed cream of chicken soup. Then add 1 can of chicken consommé thinned with an equal amount of water. Stir in 1/3 can of heavy cream. Heat. Serve with garnish of slivered toasted almonds. A fresh fruit salad with chutney cream dressing and hot rolls make a complete and tasty lunch.

Leftover Corn Soup. Add corn to canned cream of chicken soup. Heat and serve with chopped chives or minced parsley.

Montego Bay Pumpkin Soup. In a double boiler heat 1 part of pureed fresh or canned pumpkin or frozen pureed squash with 2 parts of condensed chicken broth. Season with onion juice, nutmeg, salt, and freshly ground white pepper. Add 1 cup of light cream and 2 beaten egg yolks. Stir until slightly thickened. Just before serving, add a dash of Madeira wine. Serve hot, garnished with minced parsley and a dash of paprika. Or omit the wine, chill thoroughly, and serve cold, garnished with paprika and chopped chives.

Split Pea Soup with Leftover Smoked Tongue. Add strips or cubes of leftover smoked tongue and a few cooked fresh or frozen peas to split pea soup. Serve hot.

Sweet Potato Soup. Serve with slices of cold turkey for a delicious supper after the Thanksgiving holidays. In just enough water to cover boil turkey carcass with a carrot, an onion, a stalk of celery, and a bunch of parsley. Put leftover sweet potatoes through a ricer. Thin the sweet potato puree with the turkey broth; add cream, a pinch of mace, and a pinch of sweet basil. Season to taste with salt and pepper.

Tuna Chowder. Add 1 can of tuna, diced boiled potatoes, and minced onion sautéed in butter to 2 cans of condensed cream of celery soup. Thin with milk. Heat to the boiling point. Add paprika until light pink. Serve with minced parsley.

Light Soups

Cinnamon Consommé. Use equal parts of condensed turtle soup or genuine clear turtle soup and condensed chicken consomme. Heat to boiling with a stick of cinnamon, several slivers of lemon peel, a cup of rosé wine, freshly ground black pepper, 1 crushed clove of garlic, and 1 tablespoon of sugar. Serve in heated bowls and garnish with chopped hard-cooked eggs.

Clear Soup Spiked with Sherry. Drop in a quartered, cooked artichoke heart for garnish.

Cocktail Soup Tray. To make the transition from cocktails to dinner, serve a tray of assorted soups just before you announce the meal.

Summer soup tray: In old-fashioned glasses, glass coffee cups, copper mugs, or even pretty paper cups, serve ice-cold cucumber soup; consommé laced with sherry on the rocks; cream of tomato soup spiked with chili powder and Tabasco and made thinner than usual with cream. Serve ice cold.

Winter soup tray: Hot consommé or clear turtle soup laced with sherry or lemon juice; hot cream of cucumber or cream of asparagus soup; hot cream of tomato soup thinned with tomato juice, seasoned to taste with a dash of chili powder and Tabasco or a pinch of curry powder.

If you don't serve cocktails, the soup tray is an interesting way to enliven the pre-dinner conversation. Make soups a bit thinner than usual when served this way.

Cold Fresh Tomato Soup with Herbs. Peel tomatoes and puree to soup consistency in electric blender. Add a bit of grated onion or fresh onion juice, freshly ground black pepper, salt, a little sugar, and chopped fresh or crushed dried basil. Chill thoroughly. Serve with a dollop of sour cream and garnish with chopped basil.

Consommé Mandarin. Heat 2 parts of condensed chicken consommé with 1 part of water. Season with equal parts of soy sauce and sugar. Serve hot, garnished with thin slices of avocado and chopped watercress.

Holiday Consommé. Heat consommé and top with finely chopped pimento and minced parsley or serve with finely diced, peeled fresh tomato and chopped chives.

Hungarian Iced-Tomato Soup. Peel and chop 1 pound of tomatoes. Heat (don't boil) with 3 cups of white wine. Strain and season with 1-1/2 teaspoons of salt and about 1 tablespoon of sugar. Must not be too sweet. Chill well and pour into bouillon cups or small glass bowls. Top each with a spoonful of whipped cream.

Hungarian Onion Soup. Boil fine egg noodles and drain. Add the noodles and some crumbled bacon to onion soup. Serve with a dollop of sour cream sprinkled generously with rose paprika.

Lady Curzon Soup. To one can of condensed clear turtle soup or consommé, add a *roux* of 1 tablespoon of butter, 1 tablespoon of flour and 1 teaspoon of curry powder. Bring to a boil. Remove from heat, and stir slowly into 1 beaten egg yolk. Add 1/4 cup of sherry and pour into soup cups. Top with a fluff of unsweetened whipped cream.

New Year's Day Brunch. Lace hot beef broth or consommé with sherry. Serve with well-heated Welsh rarebit on toast, garnished with lettuce and tomato with French dressing.

Meat

Cooking Tip: Try these meat accompaniments.

Baked Ham: Pineapple, plums, or raisin sauce.

Roast Beef: Grated fresh horseradish, horseradish-sour cream sauce, or Yorkshire pudding.

Roast Pork: Applesauce, cinnamon apples, poached apples, or apricots.

Roast Veal: Tomato or mushroom sauce, or anchovies and thin lemon slices.

Roast Mutton: Currant jelly or pickled black walnuts.

Boiled Mutton: Caper sauce.

Roast Lamb: Mint sauce, mint jelly in lemon shells, or ginger pears.

Roast Turkey: Whole or jellied cranberry sauce, or raw cranberry-orange relish.

Boiled Turkey: Oyster sauce.

Venison or Wild Duck: Black currant jelly, baked oranges, or black cherries.

Roast Goose: Applesauce, or stewed prunes and apples.

Beef

ROASTS

Cold Rare Beef Vinaigrette. Marinate cold slices of rare roast beef in a vinaigrette sauce. Serve with sliced, peeled tomatoes, slices of sweet onion, pickled beets, and hard-cooked eggs. Garnish platter with greens. Sprinkle minced parsley and chives over the sliced vegetables and serve the vinaigrette sauce on the side. Toasted garlic rolls or cheese bread and a bottle of good dry wine make this a real feast. Serve coffee and a delicate French pastry for dessert.

Cranberry Pot Roast. After you have browned the roast, add 1 cup of water, 2 cups of fresh cranberries, and some brown sugar. Or use a large can of whole cranberry sauce and a cup of water. Cook as usual and serve garnished with seedless orange slices, baked or boiled yams, and whole green beans.

Filet of Barbecued Beef. For parties, an elegant and dramatic way to serve your meat. Barbecue the whole filet on a grill or spit and place it on a handsome platter or a board, surrounded by "tomato baskets," sprigs of crisp watercress, and a log of blue cheese butter. Carve generous slices, and as you serve the steak, put a generous dab of blue cheese butter on top. Place one tomato basket and a sprig of watercress on each plate beside the steak.

For the tomato basket: hollow out medium-size, firm, peeled tomatoes and fill with small radish roses, tiny onions, tiny sweet pickles, and small black and stuffed green olives.

For the blue cheese butter: blend 1/2 pound of butter and 1/4 pound of blue cheese with 1 tablespoon of finely chopped green onions or chives and a pinch of basil or rosemary—fresh, if available. Place on a sheet of waxed paper, shape into a log, and roll in finely chopped parsley. Wrap in waxed paper. Refrigerate until firm.

Quick Sauerbraten. Spread a sweet-and-sour barbecue sauce over leftover slices of roast beef or pot roast. Heat in the oven. Serve with potato pancakes and a wilted lettuce salad (made with bacon, sugar, and vinegar). Serve apple cobbler for dessert and you have an old-fashioned Dutch dinner with new-fashioned ease.

Versatile Rib Roast. Both economical and elegant if you have your butcher prepare at least a four-rib roast this way. It will make three meals. Have the short ribs cut off for braising for one meal, the top of the rib stripped off for delicious soup meat or a goulash (if the butcher will cut it into cubes), and have the eye of the rib left whole to roast or have it cut into four to eight steaks.

STEAK

Beefsteak Rolls Burgundy. Put highly seasoned bread stuffing on thin slices of round steak 1/4-inch thick. Roll. Tie with string or use a skewer. Brown in butter. To the drippings add a bit of flour, a can of consommé, and an equal amount of Burgundy wine. Simmer, tightly covered, until very tender.

Cubed Steak with Noodles. Put cooked noodles under steak in broiler pan and broil. When nearly done, spread the steak with a mixture of mashed blue cheese, butter, and Worcestershire. The cheese mixture and juices drizzle down through the noodles, making a delicious sauce. When cooking noodles for any beef dish, place a beef bouillon cube in the boiling water before adding the noodles.

Filet Mignon à la Richmond. Broil filet on one side. Turn and partly broil on the other side. Then cover with 1/2 pound of mushrooms, ground in the food chopper and cooked briefly in butter with a dash of lemon juice and some chopped chives or minced green onions. Slide the filet back under the broiler and finish cooking. When done, put a few tablespoons of Madeira wine in the broiler pan with the drippings and pour the resulting sauce over the filet.

Serve with watercress and broiled tomato halves seasoned with salt and pepper. Tomatoes could be put in the broiler when the steak is turned. To be really elegant, top the tomato with an anchovy while broiling, and place a gently poached egg yolk on top of each broiled tomato when done.

Oyster-Stuffed Rib Steaks. Elegant barbecue grill main course. Have the butcher cut a pocket in each thick Delmonico or eye-of-rib steak. Stuff and skewer edges together. Don't put stuffing in steaks until just before you are ready to broil them.

Oyster stuffing: sauté sliced celery and chopped onion in

butter. Drain oysters from an 8-ounce can and grind. Add the liquor and enough white wine to make 1/2 cup of the sautéed celery and onion along with the ground oysters. Add the oyster mixture to 1/2 package of herb-seasoned stuffing mix. Salt to taste.

Quick Swiss Steak. Cut cubed steaks or thin round steaks into individual portions. Use a can of onion soup or a package of dehydrated onion soup as the liquid for simmering the steaks. Just before serving, add a cup of sour cream to the gravy. Heat, but do not boil. Serve at once.

Steak Roquefort. Blend 1/4 pound of Roquefort cheese with 1/4 cup of olive oil and a clove of garlic crushed with 1 tablespoon of brandy. Broil a thick porterhouse or eye-of-rib steak, spread with cheese mixture, and slide under the broiler flame just long enough to melt the cheese.

Stuffed Beefsteak. Stuff rump steak with bread-and-raisin stuffing. Braise with 2 cups of red wine. Serve with crisp potato pancakes and a salad of tomato, onion, and cucumber.

Stuffed Flank Steak. Flank steak rolled up around a rich bread stuffing, baked and then carved like a roast is delicious. Bake in a covered pan, adding a bit of butter melted in boiling water to braise the meat.

True Swiss Steak. Have round steak cut 1-1/2 inches thick. Season with salt and pepper. Pound flour into both sides of the steak. Brown in suet slowly and evenly (rendered beef kidney suet is the best). Cover with onion slices seasoned with salt and freshly ground black pepper. Cover pan and simmer until done (several hours).

Variation: Pound dry mustard into steak with the flour. Cook with dehydrated onion soup and water.

BOILED BEEF

Boiled Beef with Horseradish Sauce. Serve the beef hot or cold with a sauce made of 1 cup of sour cream, 1 teaspoon of horseradish, 1 teaspoon of vinegar, 1 teaspoon of sugar, a dash of Tabasco, and salt and pepper.

Cold Boiled Beef with Anchovy Sauce. A good buffet dinner dish with a hot vegetable casserole, a green salad, and hot cheese bread. Make the sauce the day before by mixing equal parts of olive oil and a good wine vinegar. Season with chopped capers, parsley, green onions, minced green pepper and pimento, a can of chopped anchovies, and chopped tomatoes that have been peeled and seeded. Lightly cover the sliced cold beef with part of the sauce and serve the rest on the side.

Suppen Fleisch (Boiled Brisket of Beef). Simmer fresh (not corned) brisket of beef until very tender. Serve with a sauce made of 1 cup of sour cream mixed with 4 tablespoons of horseradish. For a vegetable, serve mashed potatoes or buttered noodles mixed with poppy or caraway seeds.

Top-of-the-Rib Boiled. If you make a vegetable soup with the top of the rib, serve the resulting boiled beef with a horseradish sauce made by mixing several teaspoons of horseradish with 1/2 cup of sour cream, seasoned with a dash of salt and freshly ground white pepper.

CORNED BEEF

Buffet Corned Beef. Cook corned beef and cool it in the water in which it was cooked. Shape the meat into an oblong, as nearly as possible; wrap in heavy foil, and chill with a weight on top. Slice thin and arrange on a platter, slices overlapping. Serve with mustard and horseradish accompanied by a hot black bean casserole (called turtle beans, sold in Italian or Mexican stores).

Black beans take a little longer to cook than ordinary dried beans. When they are cooked, add 1/2 cup of dark rum, salt to taste, and a dash of red pepper or Tabasco sauce. If broth is thin, thicken with a *roux* of butter and flour. Sprinkle the bean casserole with tiny cubes of ham or crisp crumbled bacon and reheat just before serving. Serve a bowl of sour cream as a sauce for the beans.

Corned Beef Hash Surprise. Hard cook some eggs. Place one in each corned beef patty and mask with hollandaise or a sauce made by lacing sour cream with mustard.

Corned Beef Roll with Cabbage Slaw. Roll biscuit dough into a rectangle. Chop or shred 2 cups of cooked corned beef and spread the meat on the dough. Roll like a jelly roll and press edges together. Bake in a hot oven for about 25 minutes. Slice and serve with any desired sauce or gravy. A well-seasoned, creamy red-cabbage slaw is a good accompaniment for this dish.

STEWED OR BRAISED BEEF

Beef Goulash. Have 2-1/2 pounds of top round of beef cut into 1-inch cubes. Add 2 chopped onions and brown. Season with salt, pepper, a full tablespoon of paprika, and a crushed garlic clove. Cover with boiling water and simmer, covered, for 1-1/2 hours. Then add 2-1/2 pounds of drained and rinsed sauerkraut and simmer for another hour or until both meat and kraut are tender. Thicken the sauce with a *roux* of 1 tablespoon each of butter and flour and cook for another 10 minutes. Stir in 1 cup of sour cream and serve with broad noodles, sprinkled with sliced toasted almonds or poppy seeds. Buttered carrots are a traditional accompaniment.

Beef Shank with Brown Rice. Cover cross-cut slices of beef shank with salted water. Add a whole onion, a carrot, a stalk of celery, and several sprigs of parsley. Bring to a boil, then simmer slowly for 2-1/2 to 3 hours. Add 1 cup of uncooked brown rice and cook for another hour. Season well with salt and freshly ground black pepper.

Elegant Beef Stew Made with Tenderloin of Beef. Cook tenderloin to desired doneness and just before serving add carrots cut in 1-inch thick diagonal slices, small new potatoes, tiny canned stewed onions, and a package of frozen peas. The tiny pearl onions look tempting enough to entice people who don't ordinarily like large boiled onions.

Kansas City Short Ribs. Brush short ribs of beef with mustard, salt, and pepper. Refrigerate for 2 hours. Flour the beef, and brown in fat. Add a little tomato juice, cover, and simmer until tender.

GROUND BEEF

Chili Snacks. Prepare thin cornmeal pancakes and serve with thick, rich chili con carne between and over them.

Main Dish Hamburgers. Cook hamburgers in a skillet. Add a can of cream of mushroom soup to the pan drippings for a delicious gravy. Serve with mashed potatoes and a green salad.

New Mexico Chili Casserole. Fill a casserole with alternate layers of highly seasoned chili con carne and broken corn chips, ending with corn chips. Bake covered for about 30 minutes. Uncover and continue baking for 15 minutes. Sprinkle shredded lettuce, peeled and diced tomatoes, and minced onion on top and serve immediately with hot corn bread. Will remind you of the flavor of the tacos served in California and New Mexico.

Quick Tamale Pie. Cover canned chili con carne with corn muffin batter and bake as an upside-down cake. Serve with a green salad garnished with slices of pimento and black olives.

    If you make your own chilicon carne, try the following flavorings: cumin, coriander, oregano, or a bit of grated unsweetened chocolate in addition to the usual chili powder and red pepper.

Spanish Rice with Meat. Brown ground beef, onion, and chopped green pepper in butter. Add uncooked rice and cover with tomato juice. Season to taste with salt, pepper, paprika, and chili powder. Cover and cook over low heat until rice is tender. Add more tomato juice if rice gets too dry. May be finished in the oven.

Stuffed Hamburgers. Make 2 thin, wide hamburger patties for each serving. Cover one patty with crumbled Roquefort or blue cheese, mixed with a few drops of red wine. Place another patty on top; press the edges together. Brown quickly in a little hot oil. Add a little red wine to the pan drippings and serve over the hamburgers.

Stuffed Meat Loaf. Add salt to ground meat. Prepare a moist, seasoned bread stuffing as for chicken or turkey. Pat the salted meat out on a sheet of waxed paper. Put the dressing on the meat and shape to form a loaf. Lay strips of thick bacon on top and bake for about 50 minutes in a moderate oven.

Stuffed Meat Loaf, Italian Style. Make a stuffing using 2 parts ricotta cheese, 1 part mushrooms, 1 part fresh spinach or drained frozen chopped spinach and salt and pepper. Line bottom and sides of a loaf pan with seasoned ground beef. Fill center of pan with stuffing. Top with a layer of ground beef. Bake. Serve with condensed canned mushroom sauce or a marinara sauce.

Tasty Meat Loaf. Add a package of onion soup mix and a small can of evaporated milk to each pound of ground beef.

DRIED BEEF

Asparagus Shortcake. A one-dish meal. Roll rich biscuit dough into thin 3 x 3-inch squares. Spread the squares with butter. Place half of the squares on a buttered baking sheet, buttered side up. Cover each square with another and bake in a very hot oven for 12 to 15 minutes. Cook asparagus. Place several spears of drained asparagus between buttered layers of each shortcake. Pour creamed chipped beef over the top.

Dried Beef Elegant. Pour boiling water over dried beef and drain. Slice cooked artichoke hearts. Sauté both in butter. Add a few tablespoons of white wine, 1/2 can of cream of celery soup, and an equal amount of sour cream. Serve on hot, buttered toasted English muffins. Sprinkle top with Parmesan cheese and a dash of paprika, if desired.

Dried Beef in Mushroom Sauce over Baked Potato. Pour boiling water over dried beef and drain. (Parboiling dried beef makes it less salty and more tender.) Add the beef to a can of cream of mushroom soup, thinned slightly with milk. Season with white pepper. No salt is necessary as the dried beef is usually salty, and the soup, being only slightly diluted, is also well seasoned. Bake potatoes for an hour, or more if you want them to be soft and mealy. Cut a cross in each potato. Squeeze potato open and serve with the dried beef sauce. Buttered broccoli is a good vegetable to serve with this mild-flavored dish.

Parsley Creamed Chipped Beef. Add a generous amount of minced parsley to creamed dried beef for extra flavor and color.

SAUCES AND GARNISHES

Chili-Glazed Apples. A garnish for pot roast or steak. Bake apples, which have been cored and peeled 2/3 of the way down, in thick

sugar syrup and melted butter in a *covered* baking dish for 1
hour or until tender. Then spoon 1 tablespoon of chili sauce over
each apple and continue to bake uncovered for 10 or 15 minutes.

Chili Rice. If you serve boiled rice with any beef dish, add a generous amount of chili powder and a dash of cayenne or crushed
red hot peppers with the butter. It's the gourmet touch.

English Thyme Dressing. To serve with pot roast. Add ground beef
suet, the juice and chopped rind of 1 lemon, 1 teaspoon of dried
thyme, 1 teaspoon of salt, and a beaten egg to bread crumbs.
Form into balls and bake in a shallow oiled pan in a hot oven for
about 20 minutes or until balls are firm. Serve with slices of pot
roast and the gravy.

Glorious Steak Garnish from Humble Beginnings. Do you know
what to do with the mushroom stems that are left over after
removing the decorative and tender caps? Slice the stems evenly
about 1/4-inch thick. (You will have little rounds that look like
miniature mushroom caps.) Sauté the sliced stems in butter and
season well with salt and pepper. Just before serving, add some
sour cream. Do not boil after the sour cream is added. Serve immediately.

Individual Yorkshire Puddings. Put pan drippings from the roast
and additional oil, if necessary, in hot muffin tins. Bake Yorkshire pudding in the hot greased tins. Minced parsley added to
the batter makes the pudding both attractive and tasty.

Mushrooms or Onions. If you can't make up your mind which you
prefer, try both. Steam large Spanish onions until very tender (1
hour at least). Cover the whole steamed onion with the creamed
mushroom stems described above, and serve with steak or liver.

LEFTOVER BEEF

Glorified Beef Hash. Bake roast beef hash in a shallow casserole,
using sour cream as the binder. Season highly, and cover with
sliced, peeled tomatoes, sprinkled with herbs and minced onion.
When done, remove from the oven, place a dollop of sour cream
on top, and put under the broiler for a few seconds.

Hash-Stuffed Peppers. Stuff parboiled green peppers with beef hash. Cover with chopped onions and canned tomato sauce. Bake for 1-1/2 hours in moderate oven. Or bake hash in scooped-out tomatoes or parboiled or prebaked acorn squash.

Individual Meat Loaves. Bake meat loaf mixture in muffin tins.

Leftover Beef. Heat leftover beef in a sour-cream gravy made with beef consommé or bouillon, and serve with poppy seed noodles.

Meatballs in Cream Gravy. Make meatballs, flatten into small patties, brown, and remove from pan. Add flour and milk to the drippings and cook until of gravy consistency. Return browned meat cakes to cream sauce and simmer for a few minutes. Serve with mashed potatoes and a green vegetable.

Meat Pie. Season 1-1/2 pounds of ground beef and flatten to about 1/2-inch thickness on a greased pie plate, leaving enough extending over the edge for a crust effect. Fill the center with a bread-and-celery dressing and fold the edge of the meat up over the dressing. Lay several strips of thin-sliced uncooked bacon on top and bake in moderate oven for 45 minutes or until meat is cooked and bacon is crisp.

Quick Meat Pie. Place canned beef stew in bottom of a casserole. Add a package of cooked frozen peas. Top with ready-made refrigerator biscuits rolled in bits of crisp bacon and minced parsley. Bake in a hot oven for about 30 minutes.

Swiss Meat Loaf. Add 1-1/2 cups of diced Swiss cheese to your favorite meat loaf mixture before baking.

Tempting Meat Pie Crust. Render suet from quality beef and substitute it for shortening when making crusts. Will accentuate the delicious flavor of your meat pie!

Lamb

ROAST LAMB

Cold Crown Roast of Lamb. An elegant buffet. Fill center with large fresh peach halves marinated in prepared mint sauce and garnished with fresh sprigs of mint. If fresh peaches are not available, buy one of the fancy brands of freestone peach halves—those raggedy ones that are so much like home-canned peaches.

Crown Roast of Lamb with Celery Stuffing. Have the butcher prepare a crown of lamb. Make a bread stuffing with much thin-sliced celery and some browned ground lamb added. Stuff the crown and lay 3 thin slices of raw bacon over the stuffing. Cover the tip of each rib with a cube of salt pork or a piece of raw potato to keep the tips from burning. Place on a rack in an open roasting pan. Roast in a slow oven, without adding water, for 2-1/2 to 3 hours. (The advocates of pink lamb will disagree violently but I feel lamb is always better well done.) To serve, remove salt pork or potato from the rib ends and slip on paper frills. Surround roast with small glazed onions. Serve with a creamed vegetable and warm pear halves filled with mint jelly to which you have added some chopped fresh mint leaves.

Stuffed Leg of Lamb. Have a leg of lamb boned by your butcher so that a large pocket is formed in the middle but a piece of the shank bone is left in to hold the shape of the leg. Stuff with a spicy forcemeat made of ground veal, ground cooked smoked ham, and ground mushrooms, highly seasoned. Roast. Don't chill; serve at room temperature. Garnish with watercress and mint jelly in fluted lemon cups and broiled mushroom caps stuffed with deviled ham. Makes an easily carved buffet piece.

STEWED OR BRAISED LAMB

Braised Lamb Shanks in Orange Juice. Wash and drain lamb shanks. Place close together (important, so they don't dry out) in baking pan. Sprinkle with salt and freshly ground black pepper. Bake, uncovered, in a very hot oven for one hour. Then cover, reduce heat to 325°, and bake for one hour more. Add 1 cup of orange juice and 1/2 cup of water. Re-cover and bake for another 45 minutes, or until tender but not dried out. Sprinkle the top of each serving with crushed mixed "lamb herbs" and minced or ground fresh parsley. Serve with brown rice or Italian yellow rice.

Brown Lamb Stew. Brown chunks of lamb before stewing and add 1 teaspoonful of a commercial gravy while it is stewing. When stew is done, arrange herb-biscuit pinwheels on top and bake for about 20 minutes in a hot oven. Make the pinwheels by rolling biscuit dough into a rectangle, 10 x 14 inches. Sprinkle with melted butter, chopped parsley, crumbled dried mint, and a little powdered cumin. Roll up like a jelly roll and cut in 3/4-inch-thick slices.

Lima Beans and Braised Lamb. Cook lima beans. Brown lamb chops in a Dutch oven with chopped onion. Drain off fat. Pour lima beans and their liquor over the chops. Cover. Reduce heat and cook until the consistency of thick gravy. Serve in flat soup dishes, beans on bottom, chop on top.

Minted Lamb Shanks. Bake lamb shanks in equal parts of red wine and beef bouillon flavored with a bit of crushed garlic, lemon, and dry mustard. When done, skim off fat, brush shanks with red currant jelly, and continue baking for half an hour more. Skim off any remaining fat and stir some finely chopped fresh or dried mint leaves into the sauce. Serve sauce on the side.

Polynesian Lamb Shank Feast. Braise lamb shanks, using unsweetened pineapple juice for part of the braising liquid during the last 45 minutes of cooking. Serve with a mixed grill of pineapple chunks sprinkled with powdered ginger, bananas cut lengthwise, and mushrooms with a coconut bread stuffing, sautéed or broiled. Drizzle some of the pan juices over the fruit and mushrooms before broiling.

GROUND LAMB

Lamb Patties with Grilled Pineapple. Wrap lamb patties with bacon and broil. Serve on sautéed, broiled, or grilled pineapple slices with a sprig of fresh mint.

Near East Mixed Grill. Small lamb patties (about 1-inch in diameter) seasoned with lamb herbs (equal parts oregano and dried mint with just a pinch of rosemary), a pinch of cumin, onion, and parsley, broiled on individual skewers. Marvelous with broiled tomatoes, scalloped eggplant and mushrooms. Serve with tossed green salad to which you add both fresh and dried chopped mint. The addition of luscious brine-cured Greek black olives will make the salad perfect.

LAMB CHOPS

Broiled Lamb Chops with Chutney Sauce. Heat 1 part of red currant jelly, 1/2 part of chopped chutney, 1/2 part of lemon juice, and a dash of salt and pepper. Serve with broiled lamb chops, buttered quick-cooking rice, and minted peas.

Deviled Lamb Chops. Buy rib lamb chops 1-1/4 inches thick and make a slit in the rounded side, cutting to the bone (or better yet, have the butcher cut the slit). Fill this pocket with Smithfield deviled ham, using about 2 teaspoonfuls for each chop. Broil or fry chops as usual. When done, top each with another spoonful of deviled ham and minced parsley.

Lamb Chop Élégant. Sauté slices of canned pineapple in butter and place them on rounds of toast. On top of each put a broiled lamb chop. Cover with piping hot undiluted mushroom soup and top with a large sautéed mushroom cap. Looks pretty and tastes delicious.

Lamb Chop Plate. Serve broiled lamb chops with half a tomato, broiled and buttered, and with steamed whole baby carrots rolled in fresh chopped mint.

One Lamb Chop Élégant. Cut a piece of bread the size of each chop. Brown the bread lightly in butter; brown mushroom caps; then brown the sliced mushroom stems. Add a bit of flour to the sliced, sautéed mushroom stems and cover with cream, then salt and pepper to taste. Cook until mixture thickens. Broil the chops and put 1 chop on each slice of the sautéed bread. Top each chop with a large sautéed mushroom cap and serve with the creamed mushroom stems. Broiled tomatoes and minted, buttered peas complete the plate. Garnish with watercress and lemon if desired. Lamb, veal, or pork chops can be served this way. Looks elegant and one chop serves each person generously.

Savory Broiled Lamb Chops. Before broiling, top each chop with 1 teaspoon of Worcestershire and 1 teaspoon of catsup.

SAUCES AND GARNISHES FOR LAMB

Crème de Menthe Apples with Lamb. Add a generous amount of green crème de menthe to a sugar syrup made of equal parts of sugar and water. Poach whole peeled and cored apples gently until they are tender but not mushy. Cool in the syrup. Drain and serve with any lamb dish. You may boil the syrup down to form a thick glaze for the apples after they are drained.

Onion-Mushroom Sauce for Roast Lamb Shanks or Roast Leg of Lamb. About 45 minutes before roast leg or shanks are done, pour off excess fat; add a can of sliced mushrooms, including the liquid, and 1-1/2 cups of chopped onions to the pan drippings. Continue roasting, stirring the onion-mushroom sauce several times. A little white wine can be added if sauce gets too thick. New potatoes, rolled in minced parsley and butter, and spring peas are delightful with this dish.

Surprise Patty Shells. Bake patty shells of rich pie crust or bake the frozen kind. Also bake pastry rounds to fit top of shells, using the same dough. To serve, fill patty shells with creamed mushrooms or peas and top with the baked pastry lids. Serve with broiled lamb chops and a broiled tomato half.

LEFTOVER LAMB

Cold Lamb Plate. Serve lamb with Cumberland sauce (mustard and red currant jelly mixed together). Garnish with a minted pear filled with drained, crushed pineapple into which you have chopped a bit of preserved ginger. Herbed potato salad with a tart garlicky French dressing goes well with this plate.

Cold Roast Lamb with Curried Cauliflower. Steam a whole head of cauliflower until just tender. Cool and break up into flowerets. Gently fold them into a sauce of 1 cup of mayonnaise or mayonnaise-type salad dressing mixed with a tablespoon of curry powder and an onion finely chopped and sautéed in a little butter. Serve the cauliflower cold with the lamb.

Leftover Lamb Slices. Serve with whole sautéed mushrooms over which you pour some orange juice and sherry to form a sauce when heated. A bit of grated orange rind can be added for additional flavor.

Sliced Lamb in Barbecue Jelly Sauce. Melt some butter; add a generous amount of dry mustard, some salt, pepper, 1 tablespoon of vinegar, and 1/2 cup of currant jelly. Stir thoroughly. Add thin slices of cold lamb and heat well. Serve the sauce over the lamb, on a mound of rice, if desired.

Liver

Baked Orange Slices with Calf Liver. Cut navel oranges in thick slices. Place on a buttered baking tray. Spread with a little honey and pour some garlicky French dressing on top. Bake until the orange slices are soft and tinged with brown. Baste with a bit more French dressing, if necessary. Sprinkle chopped chives or minced green onion on the orange slices and serve with broiled calf liver.

Baked Tomatoes Stuffed with Liver. Moisten chopped or ground liver with a little condensed mushroom soup and some onion juice. Fill center of scooped-out firm tomatoes. Cover with buttered bread crumbs and bake in a moderate oven for about 20 minutes.

Calf Liver Élégant. Dip liver slices in seasoned flour and brown them quickly. Garnish with tiny canned whole onions and sliced seedless oranges heated in the drippings and moistened with sauterne wine.

Calf Liver with Sour Cream Gravy. Sauté onion in butter. Add sour cream, salt, and pepper. Warm, but do not boil. Dip liver in flour and brown quickly. Remove browned liver and add the sour-cream mixture to the pan drippings. Stir, but do not boil. Pour the sauce over the browned liver and serve at once with hashed browned potatoes and a crisp green salad of watercress, grapefruit, and avocado.

Cold Meat Plate. Liver pâté, tongue, chopped spinach and hard-boiled egg salad, and sliced beefsteak tomatoes. Serve with Russian rye bread or pumpernickel and a green pepper circle filled with mustard.

Liver in Mushroom Wine Sauce. Brown thin slices of beef liver in butter. Sprinkle with chopped parsley and add a small can of sliced mushrooms, liquid and all, the juice of 1 lemon, and about 1/4 cup of white table wine. Cook for a few minutes more. Season with salt and pepper and serve immediately.

Quick Liver and Onions. When liver is browned, add some water and a package of onion soup mix.

Pork

PORK CHOPS

Baked Pork Chops in Fruit Sauce. Bake chops in equal parts of sweet cider and unsweetened pineapple juice.

Pork Chops and Sweet Potato Casserole. Cut cooked and peeled yams or sweet potatoes in thick slices. Brown 4 pork chops on both sides and season. Arrange potato slices in a greased square or oblong pan. Cover with brown sugar, grated orange rind, and 1/4 cup each of orange juice and water. Put browned chops on top and bake in moderate oven for 1-1/2 hours.

Pork Chops with Glazed Orange and Apple Slices. Warm slices of unpeeled seedless oranges and slices of unpeeled apple in equal parts of butter and corn syrup. When tender, serve a slice of orange on top of each apple slice, with baked or fried pork chops.

Stuffed Baked Pork Chops. These are delicious with finely chopped cooked prunes and finely chopped cooked apples added to the bread stuffing.

GROUND PORK

Baked Swedish Meatballs. Make balls of equal parts of highly seasoned ground beef, ground pork, and grated raw potatoes. Brown. Add a little water. Cover and bake for an hour in a moderate oven. Thicken the gravy, if desired.

Norwegian Stew. Cook cabbage, string beans, meatballs, and a few caraway seeds together after meatballs are browned. Thicken sauce before serving.

ROAST PORK

Prune-and-Apple-Stuffed Pork Loin. This is a Scandinavian dish. Have the bone separated from the loin but kept attached at bottom. Fill the resulting pocket with soaked, pitted prunes and quarters of apple in equal amounts. Tie together. Roast and serve with caraway cabbage (shredded cabbage seasoned with caraway seeds) and mashed potatoes.

Quick Gravy for Pork Roast. Remove the roast from oven when done and drain off most of the fat from the pan. Add a can of cream of celery soup to the pan drippings and heat. Add a little milk or water, if necessary, to obtain the right consistency.

PORK SAUSAGE

Baked Apples with Sausage. Try baking apples sweetened with brown sugar and stuffed with sausage meat. After 1/2 hour of cooking, pour a can of tiny whole cooked onions around the apples and bake together for another full hour or until apples are tender and sausage is brown.

Kraut and Polish Sausage. Bake garlic or Polish sausage with sauerkraut, caraway seeds, and whole apples on top of the sauerkraut (core the apples and peel halfway down). Before baking, fill the center of each apple with 1/2 teaspoon brown sugar, some dry mustard, and a little of the sausage.

Kraut and Sausage, Vermont Style. Cook thick apple slices in maple syrup for about 5 minutes. Cook sausage, drain, and dip in bottled brown sauce. Arrange layers of undrained, canned sauerkraut, sausage, and apple slices in a greased, shallow baking pan. Top with any leftover maple syrup. Bake in a moderate oven for about 1-1/2 hours.

Meat and Potato Pantry Dinner. Wrap each link of canned Vienna sausage in half a strip of thin bacon. Fasten with a toothpick or put several on a skewer. Broil. Drain and dice canned cooked potatoes or dice leftover boiled potatoes. Place potatoes in top of double boiler with milk and cut-up processed cheese. Heat. Serve the creamy potatoes with the broiled sausages.

Sausage and Sweet Potato Pie. Fill a casserole half full of mashed sweet potatoes. Sprinkle with brown sugar. Top with partially cooked pork sausage meat. Bake until the sausage is done.

Sausage Baked in Bananas. Partially cook small link sausages. Slit unpeeled bananas lengthwise, being careful not to cut through under skin. Place a sausage in the slit. Bake in hot oven for 15 minutes.

Sausage Cakes for Brunch. Finely mince a pound of sausage meat. Add 2 cups of cooked rice and an egg. Mix well. Form into flat cakes and fry in a small amount of oil. Don't hurry them and don't turn too often.

Sausage with Fried Bananas. Cook sausage thoroughly. Remove from pan. Peel and split firm but ripe bananas in half lengthwise. Roll banana halves in flour and brown in the same pan the sausages were cooked in, for about 2 minutes on each side. Serve the fried bananas with the sausages.

SPARERIBS

Baked Sauerkraut. Drain canned sauerkraut and bake it for about 2 hours with some oil or your choice of meat (spareribs, lean short ribs, pork chops, or frankfurters). Add sour cream at the last minute. Serve with tiny white canned potatoes.

Scandinavian Fruit-Stuffed Spareribs. Place a side of small lean spareribs on a rack in a roasting pan. Sprinkle with a teaspoon of salt. Arrange sliced apples and raisins over the meat to within about an inch of the edge of it. Place second side of ribs over the top and fasten with small metal skewers. Sprinkle with another teaspoon of salt and some cracked pepper. Bake in moderate oven for at least 2 hours, basting occasionally with a mixture of apple and lemon juice. Ribs can be parboiled before preparing this dish, if desired.

SAUCES AND GARNISHES FOR PORK

Frosted Applesauce. Mix 2 cups of applesauce, 1 cup of drained crushed pineapple, and 1 teaspoon of minced preserved ginger, if desired. Put in ice tray and freeze for several hours, stirring occasionally. Serve as a sherbet with a roast pork dinner.

Raw Cranberry Relish for Pork or Veal. Grind 2 cups of fresh cranberries. Combine with 1/2 cup of honey and 1-1/2 teaspoons of prepared horseradish. Mix well and chill.

LEFTOVER PORK

Meat-Stuffed Potato Roll. Place highly seasoned leftover mashed potatoes mixed with beaten egg in bottom of greased glass meat loaf pan and push some up around the sides of the pan (at least 1-inch thick). Fill center with ground leftover pork, or ground lunch meat mixed with finely minced onion, celery, parsley, and a dash of mustard. Cover top with at least an inch-thick layer of the mashed potato mixture. Bake in a hot oven until potato cover is brown and crispy. Turn out of the pan and cut into thick slices to serve. A creamed vegetable and watercress on the plate with a slice of this roll makes a gourmet meal out of leftovers.

Pork-and-Apple Pie. Made with leftover pork. Line pie plate with pie crust. Fill with alternate layers of sliced apples and a little brown sugar (not too much) and cooked leftover pork mixed with lots of sautéed onions. Moisten with a little gravy or water (about 2 tablespoons). Cover with top pie crust. Prick top of crust and bake in very hot oven. Serve hot or cold.

Ham

Asparagus Ham Rolls. Lay several cooked asparagus spears on each slice of boiled ham; roll and fasten with toothpicks. Place in shallow pan and brush with butter. Broil. Serve with a mustard-sour cream sauce.

Cold Ham Plate. On individual plates arrange sliced baked ham, Swiss cheese, and a tomato stuffed with well-seasoned mashed avocado. Serve with a sauce made of sour cream laced with a dash of mustard.

Ham and Spanish Rice Casserole. Cover a casserole of Spanish rice with slices of baked or boiled ham. Top generously with coarsely grated sharp cheese. Bake in moderate oven until cheese bubbles.

Ham Baked with Brown Sugar and Madeira Wine. Serve with a salad of Boston lettuce, black olives, and crab legs which have been marinated in oil and wine vinegar, well seasoned with salt and pepper. For a buffet party, the ham can be attractively garnished, and the salad can be served in a large bowl, the lettuce on the bottom and the crab legs and olives arranged in a symmetrical pattern on top.

Ham Sandwich Roll. Roll out a rectangle of biscuit dough. Spread quickly with cooked ground ham mixed with a bit of catsup; roll and fasten with toothpicks. Bake in a very hot oven for about 20 minutes. Slice and serve with a green pea sauce, made from condensed pea soup into which you have stirred a few chopped pimento bits and a few leftover cooked peas.

Veal

VEAL CHOPS OR CUTLETS

Delicate Breaded Veal Cutlet. Dip paper-thin slices of veal in a mixture of toasted bread crumbs, flour, grated Parmesan cheese, salt, and pepper. Fry in 1/2-inch-deep hot oil. Serve garnished with thin slices of lemon, a dash of paprika, capers, and sliced black olives.

Veal Collops. Use small lean pieces of veal about the size of a hickory nut. Sprinkle with pepper, salt, and a dash of mace. Dip in egg, roll in cracker crumbs and fry. Serve with black olive sauce on the side.

Veal Scaloppine. Sauté thin, pounded slices of veal in olive oil with quarters of both red and green sweet peppers. Sprinkle with plenty of salt. (Olive oil in a recipe always makes extra salt a must to bring out the true flavor.) Just before serving add some red wine. If the skin has loosened on the peppers, peel it off. Serve with macaroni or noodles and an Italian salad.

Veal Scaloppine with Viennese Noodles. Cook and drain wide noodles. Brown the cooked noodles lightly in a skillet with melted butter, chopped pecans, and poppy seeds. Serve with veal scaloppine.

Veal Steak or Venison Steak, Norwegian Style. With a delicious brown sauce. Pan fry thin steaks in hot oil. Season with salt and pepper to taste and remove to a warm platter. Turn heat down under the pan. Add 1/2 pint of sour cream in which you have mixed 1/2 cup of slivered Gjetost (Norwegian goat cheese, dark in color but sweet and delicious). Heat slowly until cheese melts. Return the meat to the sauce pan and simmer for just a few minutes at a very low temperature. Serve with raw cranberry-orange relish or canned lingonberries.

Veal with Black Olives. For a breading that will not fall apart, try this thin batter: sift together 1 cup of flour, 1 teaspoon of baking powder, and 1/2 teaspoon of salt. Beat 1 egg with 3/4 cup of milk. Mix with the dry ingredients. Dip cutlets in the batter and fry in oil or fat heated to 375°. Garnish the golden-brown breaded veal cutlets with thin slices of lemon, capers, and pitted black olives.

ROAST VEAL

Cold Roast Veal or Roast Pork Plate. Serve cold veal or pork, sliced, with chilled cinnamon poached apples and whipped cream, cole slaw, and giant stuffed green olives.

Madeira Sauce for Roast Veal. Melt 2 tablespoons of butter, stir in 2 tablespoons of flour, add 1 tablespoon of chopped mushrooms or chopped mushroom stems. Cook for a minute or two and stir in 1/4 cup of white wine, then 1/2 cup of Madeira wine, and 1/4 cup of sour cream.

Roast Leg of Veal with Chestnuts in Cream. Drain a can of cooked chestnuts. Add a generous amount of butter and cream and heat in the oven for 10 minutes. Before serving, add a jigger of brandy. Season with a pinch of salt, if desired. Brussels sprouts with seasoned bread crumbs make a good accompaniment.

Roast Veal. Serve roast veal with creamed Forkhook lima beans and a garnish of broiled fresh pear halves, topped with mashed sweet potatoes or yams flavored with grated orange rind.

Roast Veal Seasoning. Mix a little mace with soft butter and spread on veal before roasting.

Roast Veal with Prunes and Bacon. Have the butcher bone a 4-pound round of veal. Stuff the space with bread dressing. Sprinkle the veal with salt and pepper and coat with flour. Bake until meat is tender. Baste every 15 minutes with 1/4 cup of butter melted in 1 cup of boiling water. Just before serving, broil pitted, uncooked prunes, wrapped in partially cooked thin-sliced bacon. Serve the bacon-wrapped prunes as a garnish with the veal.

Veal Pot Roast. Use veal rump roast or leg of veal. Add some white wine and a bay leaf for the last half hour of cooking. Thicken sauce with a *roux* of flour, butter, and sour cream. Serve with paper-thin slices of lemon sprinkled with paprika.

Poultry and Game

Game

Braised Pheasant. Cut pheasant in pieces. Flour and brown as you would fried chicken. Add a dash of good red wine. Cover and simmer until done. Stir red currant jelly into the gravy. Serve with mashed potatoes and steamed shredded and buttered cabbage.

Braised Quail. Flour and sauté whole quail in butter. Place in a casserole. Pour more melted butter over the quail. Add a cup of chicken broth and a few spoonfuls of white wine to casserole. Cover and bake in quick oven. To serve, blaze with warmed cognac and add a few seedless grapes to the sauce. Serve in a toasted giant-sized buttered bread croustade, or on a bed of steamed wild rice.

Currant Sauce for Venison Steak. Mix currant jelly, orange juice, and a bit of lemon juice with the pan drippings.

Leg of Venison, Norwegian Style. Soak venison overnight in vinegar and water. Lard with fresh pork suet. Brown in butter. Pour boiling milk over the venison, almost covering the meat. Simmer slowly until tender. For sauce, make a *roux* of flour and butter. Mix in the liquid from the cooked venison. Add some lingonberry jelly, some shredded Norwegian goat cheese (Gjetost), and some sour cream. Serve with French-cut string beans.

Pheasant. Serve pheasant with brown rice to which a few chopped toasted pecans have been added just before serving.

Roasted Rock Cornish Game Hen. The easiest and most elegant fowl for roasting and serving. Wash birds with salt water. Drain and dry thoroughly. Stuff lightly with a stuffing made from toasted bread crumbs and the ground giblets sautéed in butter with some minced parsley and green onions or chives. Season stuffing with salt and pepper—no heavy spices whatsoever. Put a tablespoon or two of stuffing in each bird. You need not sew them, just press wings and legs to the body. Spread softened butter over the birds. Season with salt and pepper. Place in roasting pan, breast side up, and cook in very hot oven (425°-450°) for 1 hour and 15 minutes. After 1/2 hour pour some sherry over the birds and baste with the butter which has melted down. Baste again at the end of 1 hour. Serve with steamed wild rice with some of the sherry sauce poured over it. A mound of mashed yellow squash with some bright green cooked peas and some creamed French-cut string beans are interesting vegetables to complete the plate. Garnish with watercress and a brandied apricot.

Venison Dinner. Serve a strong vegetable like creamed onions or mashed turnips, also whole fried hominy and black currant jelly.

Venison Steak, Norwegian Style. See recipe for veal steak, Norwegian style.

Wild Rice Stuffing. Try using half natural brown rice and half wild rice for your poultry or game stuffing. Slivered toasted almonds and tiny whole mushrooms added to the stuffing makes it even more delicious.

Duck

Duck Salad Garni. Mix equal parts of diced duck and celery together with mayonnaise to which you have added a bit of left-over duck gravy or juice (not the fat). Place the salad in the

center of a round platter. Surround it with small mounds of duck
liver pâté(made from duck liver and extra chicken livers) alter-
nating with small bunches of watercress and slices of preserved
orange, topped with a Mandarin orange section. You can buy
whole preserved oranges, or make your own by slicing a navel
orange and poaching it in sugar syrup.

Duck Roasted and Garnished with Glazed Fruit. Cut thick slices of
unpeeled apple, thin slices of unpeeled seedless oranges and
lemons. Dip slices of fruit and pitted prunes in brown sugar, and
sauté in butter. Serve a stack of 2 apple slices, 1 orange slice, 1
lemon slice, and a prune for each portion.

Orange Mint Stuffing for Duck. Add the following to dry bread
stuffing: 1/4 cup of washed and drained seedless raisins, 1 tablespoon of grated orange rind, 1/2 cup of diced seedless orange
sections, 1 tablespoon of crumbled dry mint leaves, and 1/4 cup
of orange juice.

Roast Duck with Liver and Tarragon Stuffing. Add 1 cup of
chopped sautéed chicken livers and the duck liver, and 1 teaspoon of dried tarragon (or 2 teaspoons of fresh) to dry bread
stuffing. Moisten with white wine and stuff the duck.

Roast Young Duckling with Fruited Rum Sauce. Roast duck. Remove from roasting pan and cut in halves or quarters with
poultry shears. Pour off most of the fat. Add 1 can condensed
chicken consommé, 2 teaspoons of tomato paste, a jar of strained
apricots (baby food), and the juice of an orange. Scrape the pan
and simmer. Thicken with flour mixed with water. Season with
salt and freshly ground black pepper. Serve the pieces of duck
on individual oval-shaped hazelnut meringues. Top with a
glazed, spiced peach half or apricot half and the sauce. Pour 1/4
cup of flaming rum over all just before serving.
    To make the meringue, add ground hazelnuts and grated
orange rind to meringue mix and bake. To make the glazed peach
or apricot, drain canned spiced peaches or spiced apricots. Cook
the syrup down. Place the peaches or apricots in a baking dish.
Drizzle with some of the reduced syrup and sprinkle with sugar.
Bake until brown and sprinkle with sliced almonds, blanched
and toasted.

Frosted Applesauce Garnish. To gild the duckling, mix 2 cups of applesauce, 1 cup of drained crushed pineapple (coarse), and 1

teaspoon of finely chopped or ground preserved ginger. Put in
ice tray. Stir occasionally. Serve a bit soft.

White Seedless Grapes. Add grapes to shredded lettuce, tossed with
a garlicky French dressing. Try with duck or game dinner.

Turkey

Circles of Gold Garnish for Turkey. Sprinkle pineapple slices with a
mixture of light-brown sugar and finely grated lemon rind. Sauté
in butter. Place a pitted, stewed prune in the center of each warm
pineapple slice, and serve with a spoonful of red currant jelly
masking the prune.

Cold Turkey Plate. Serve sliced turkey with sweet-potato salad,
made with diced cooked sweet potatoes, drained pineapple
chunks, and pecan halves mixed with salad dressing. Garnish
with watercress and slices of jellied cranberry sauce.

Turkey and Sliced Water Chestnuts in Cream Sauce. Serve with
cooked rice instead of the usual à la king.

Turkey Diable. Dip thick slices of cold breast of turkey in a mixture
of oil, dry mustard, and freshly ground black pepper. Dip in fine
dry bread crumbs. Broil or grill until brown on both sides. At the
same time, broil or grill drained pineapple slices which have been
dipped in oil. Serve the turkey slices and pineapple slices on a
plate slightly overlapping. Prepare a sauce of 1 can of condensed
chicken consomme boiled down to 1/2 cup. Mix the consommé
with 1/2 cup of tarragon vinegar boiled down separately to 1/2
its volume: stir into the hot mixture, 1 tablespoon of mustard
and 2 tablespoons of butter. Serve with hot shoestring potatoes,
watercress, and raw cranberry-orange relish.

Turkey Salad Amandine. Add chopped toasted almonds and fluffy
cooked rice to turkey salad. Serve with a slice of jellied cranberry
sauce topping a slice of pineapple.

Ways with Cranberry Sauce. Cook fresh cranberries in orange juice
and sugar instead of water and, when cool, add ground blanched
almonds; spike whole canned cranberry sauce with horseradish

to serve with pork or boiled beef; marbleize canned whole or jellied cranberry sauce with sour cream to serve with cold turkey or chicken plate; mix 1/2 cup of mincemeat thoroughly with 1 can of whole cranberry sauce. Chill and serve with turkey.

Chicken

BAKED, BRAISED, OR STEWED CHICKEN

Braised Fryer Chicken. Season and flour halves of fryer chickens. Brown in electric skillet or large roasting pan in equal parts of butter and oil until golden brown. Add 1/2 cup of water. Cover and bake for 1-1/2 hours. Remove cover. Add green olives, capers or mushrooms, cooked artichoke hearts, and a bit of white wine. Serve on a mound of rice laced with cashew nuts, minced parsley, and mace.

Mexican Chicken. Cook chicken fricassee with tomato juice instead of water. Add stuffed green olives (half whole and half minced), and pitted black olives (half whole and half minced). Serve on a bed of rice.

Poor Man's Dumplings. Make cornmeal dumplings, using stock from the meat or chicken soup instead of milk for the liquid in the batter. Season with freshly ground black pepper. Drop the dumpling batter by spoonfuls into the boiling broth. Cover the pan. Steam until done, about 15 minutes. Don't peek.

Roast Chicken Gravy. After removing the cooked bird from the oven and pouring excess fat from the roasting pan, add a can of condensed cream of chicken soup and a little milk to the pan drippings.

FRIED CHICKEN

Chicken Delmonico. Brown seasoned and floured chicken lightly in equal parts of butter and oil. Add about 1/2 cup of water, cover and steam for 1-1/2 hours. Remove cover. Place the chicken on a warm platter. Add coarsely sliced, large, fresh mushrooms and cooked artichoke hearts to the pan juices and cook for about 5 minutes only. Add 1/2 cup of good white wine just before serving. Pour the sauce over the chicken.

Chicken Normandy. Brown floured and seasoned split frying chickens in equal parts of butter and oil. Pour in some cognac, allow to warm, then light it, shaking pan gently until the flame dies. Add thyme and 1/2 cup of white wine. Cover and cook for 1-1/2 hours. Uncover and add heavy cream to the drippings to make a thin sauce. Serve sauce over the chicken on a bed of mashed potatoes.

Chicken with Capers. Brown floured and seasoned pieces of chicken in equal parts of butter and oil. When brown, add 1/2 cup of water. Cover and braise for 1-1/2 hours. Remove cover. Add 1/2 cup each of halved stuffed green olives and pitted black olives and 1/4 cup of large capers with some juice. Serve with steamed wild rice or steamed cracked wheat.

Deviled Chicken. Bone chicken breasts, then soak in salt water, and rinse, drain, and dry. Salt and pepper the boned breasts inside and out before cooking. For a delicate stuffing, mix bread crumbs, finely chopped parsley, butter, freshly ground black pepper, and a dash of Tabasco. Dip the stuffed breasts in flour and brown in butter. Bake in covered casserole with rosé wine for 1-1/2 hours. Uncover to brown, if necessary.

Elegant and Easy Sauce. With fried chicken, serve a cream sauce made by heating a can of condensed cream of celery soup thinned with heavy cream and seasoned with a good pinch of dill or sweet basil.

Fried Chicken. Serve with red currant jelly and bread sauce (bread stuffing baked in a buttered casserole for about 30 minutes in a moderate oven).

Herbed Peaches with Fried Chicken. Heat peach halves in butter. Sprinkle with dill, thyme, or rosemary.

LEFTOVER CHICKEN

Almond-Rice Casserole. Put chopped leftover chicken and cooked rice in a buttered casserole. Mix 1 can of condensed cream of mushroom soup and 1 can of condensed cream of chicken soup, and pour over the chicken and rice. Scatter whole blanched almonds over the top and bake in a moderate oven for 35 to 40 minutes. Place under broiler for a few minutes if almonds need further toasting.

Avocado Regal. Remove seeds and halve and peel avocados. Dip them in lime juice and salt. Keep at room temperature. Fill with piping hot chicken à la king. Garnish with a cube of jellied cranberry sauce or a spoonful of whole cranberry sauce.

Baked Chicken Mousse. Half fill a square or oblong baking dish with well-seasoned, ground chicken moistened with condensed cream of mushroom soup, a bit of scraped or minced onion, and minced parsley. Cover with an unsweetened custard sauce (2 tablespoons of flour and 2 beaten egg yolks to 2 cups of milk). Sprinkle Parmesan cheese on top. Bake in moderate oven until custard is set. Let stand a few minutes. Cut in squares and serve.

Chicken Omelet. Just before folding the omelet, fill with a mixture of ground cooked chicken and chopped black olives moistened with a can of condensed cream of mushroom soup spiked with a bit of mustard.

Cold Chicken Élégant. Place several thin slices of white meat of chicken on a bed of finely shredded or chopped greens. Marinate asparagus tips in a tart French dressing. Place 4 or 5 cold marinated asparagus tips on top of the chicken slices. Mask with an herbed mayonnaise (minced parsley, chives, basil, dill, and/or tarragon). Garnish with strips of pimento and mammoth black olives.

Creamed Chicken with Toast Circles. Cut rings from toasted bread slices with a doughnut cutter. Butter, sprinkle with grated Parmesan cheese, and place on top of creamed chicken.

Elegant Next-Day Fried Chicken. Reheat fried chicken breasts in cream in double boiler. Remove breasts when hot. Add the mashed yolks of several hard-boiled eggs. Season with salt, pepper, and paprika. Stir and cook a bit. Arrange the breasts on toast and pour the sauce over them. Serve with baked orange slices and buttered peas or green lima beans.

Fluffy Chicken Loaf. Mix 1 can of sliced mushrooms with 1 part soft bread crumbs, 1 part rice, and 2 parts cooked, diced chicken. Season with 1/4 cup of chopped pimento, and salt and pepper to taste. Moisten with a mixture of chicken broth and beaten egg. Bake until firm (about 1 hour). Garnish with strips of pimento and serve with mushroom sauce made by adding minced parsley and a squeeze of lemon juice to a can of heated, condensed cream of mushroom soup.

Great Brunch. Golden brown chicken hash with small browned sausages pressed into the top. Serve with a green salad and a fruit dessert.

Jellied Chicken Mousse. Make with ground instead of chopped chicken if you want to be sure it holds together.

Quick Chicken Curry. Heat 1 can of condensed cream of chicken soup with the same amount of light cream. Season with curry powder, paprika, fresh-pressed garlic, a dash of sugar, and some grated or flaked coconut. Add bite-size chunks of chicken. Serve garnished with diced, peeled tomatoes; steamed seedless white raisins; coconut; chopped green onions; thinly sliced cucumber and radishes; or chutney.

CHICKEN LIVERS

Chicken Liver Kebabs, Chinese Style. Wrap chicken liver and a slice of water chestnut in a half slice of partially cooked bacon. Spear with metal skewers and charcoal broil, turning now and then. Serve with sauce of mashed red currant jelly spiked with mustard and grated lemon rind.

Chicken Livers Paprika. Sauté floured chicken livers with 2 sliced onions. Sprinkle thickly with paprika, salt, freshly ground black pepper, and a pinch of thyme. When livers and onions are done, add sour cream and a slightly beaten egg yolk to make a sauce. Serve on a bed of broad noodles or on toast.

Fish and Shellfish

Fish

CANNED FISH

Anchovy Lasagne. In a rectangular baking-serving dish, spread a layer of marinara sauce (a meatless tomato and garlic sauce); a layer of well-drained, cooked lasagne; a layer of drained, canned flat anchovy fillets; a layer of ricotta cheese; and a layer of thin-sliced mozzarella cheese. Repeat. Top with marinara sauce, then with grated Parmesan or Romano cheese, and finally with a sprinkling of olive oil. This may be done in advance. Just before serving, bake at 375° until the top is lightly browned and bubbly.

Cold Salmon Platter. Serve cold, cooked salmon with a sauce made of 1/2 pint of slightly sweetened and salted whipped cream to which you slowly add 2 tablespoons of vinegar and finely chopped cucumber. (Peel and seed the cucumber and drain off as much juice as possible.) A dash of cayenne pepper improves the dish.

Crisp Tuna Pancakes. A treat for the children. Add chunk-style tuna to raw potato pancake batter. Fry until crispy brown and serve with whole cranberry sauce or sour cream.

Easy Tuna Fish. Mix 2 cups of cooked rice with 1 can of condensed cream of mushroom soup, and a can of tuna fish. Top with grated cheese. Bake until cheese bubbles. Serve with a tossed green salad. No frills, but good.

Fiesta Pancakes. A pantry-shelf dish for unexpected company. Make a sauce of tuna fish (or minced, hot cooked sausages), chopped onion, green pepper, garlic, oregano, salt, lots of chili powder, a can of condensed tomato soup, sliced black olives, and a bit of water, if necessary. Serve over cornmeal pancakes.

Fish Cakes with a Flair. Combine your favorite fish-cake mixture with a can of lobster or crabmeat, diced fine. Add the yolk of an egg. Season with lemon juice. Shape, roll in toasted bread crumbs, and fry. Serve with hot spoon bread or corn bread and lots of coffee. Ideal for a Sunday brunch.

Fish on Herbed Biscuits. Serve creamed fish on biscuits made with finely minced parsley and celery seed added to the dough. Split the biscuits. Toast and serve hot with the creamed fish poured over top.

Herring in Sour Cream Served with Crisp Potato Pancakes. Serve a salad and fresh fruit for dessert. Hot boiled potatoes make a fine meal with the herring if you don't have time for pancakes. Add salt, paprika, and butter. A watercress and tomato salad is a good accompaniment.

Pint-Sized Tuna Pizzas. The kids will love them. Mix tuna fish, a small can of tomato sauce, oregano, salt and pepper, and a bit of olive oil. Split English muffins and spread tuna mixture over each half; sprinkle with grated Parmesan cheese and top each pizza with a slice of American cheese or with coarsely grated mozzarella cheese. Broil 6 to 8 inches from heat, or bake 20 minutes at 375°.

Salmon Croquettes in Green Sauce. Blend 1 cup of condensed cream of asparagus soup with 1/3 cup of cream and heat thoroughly.

Add 2 tablespoons of minced parsley, 1 tablespoon of minced chives, and serve over salmon croquettes.

Salmon Dumplings. Roll biscuit dough about 1/4-inch thick and cut into 4-inch squares. Fill with a mixture of salmon, coarsely chopped mushrooms, lemon juice, and minced parsley. Bring corners of dough up around salmon filling. Bake on greased baking sheet for about 20 minutes in a hot oven. Serve with cheese sauce generously laced with fresh lemon juice.

Sassy Sardine Supper. Arrange whole sardines on buttered toast. Cover with a hot cream sauce (or condensed cream of celery soup) to which you have added buttered bread crumbs and chopped hard-cooked egg. Garnish with a slice of hard-cooked egg and 1 sardine.

Tuna Waffles. Mix 1 can of condensed cream of celery soup with 1/4 cup of milk. Add 1 can of tuna fish. Heat and serve over buttered hot waffles.

FISH FILETS

Baked Filets with Almond Sauce. Place fresh or thawed frozen filets on an oiled baking dish. Cover with chopped green onions and a sauce made by cooking a few slivered almonds in butter until lightly browned, then adding 1 tablespoon of boiling water, 2 tablespoons of lemon juice, and 1 chicken bouillon cube. Bake for about 20 minutes in moderate oven.

Baked Fish with Sour Cream. Filets of halibut, sole, or other white fish can be prepared this way. Lightly sauté onion and green pepper rings in butter in a flat baking dish. Put well-seasoned fish filets in the same dish and cover with the sautéed onions and pepper. Bake in a moderate oven. Ten minutes before the fish is done, cover with sour cream and sprinkle with salt and pepper. Serve immediately with small, parslied, boiled potatoes.

Baked Sole and Shrimp. Arrange filets of sole in individual buttered baking dishes. Sprinkle a few tiny cooked shrimp over the sole. Mix equal parts of catsup and dry white wine. Pour the sauce over the fish and lay a thin slice of lemon on each filet. Bake for about 30 minutes. Serve with artichoke hearts and green peas.

Baked Stuffed Halibut Steak. Put one large halibut steak in an oiled baking pan. Sprinkle with salt and pepper and spread lemon bread stuffing thickly on the fish. Cover with another halibut steak. Fasten with toothpicks or skewers and spread with soft butter. Bake in a moderate oven for about 45 minutes. Serve with a sauce made by mixing 1 tablespoon of horseradish with 1 can of condensed tomato soup. Pour the sauce over the fish. Sprinkle with chopped chives and minced parsley.

For the lemon bread stuffing, make your usual bread stuffing, omitting strong herbs and adding, instead, 1 tablespoon of lemon juice and about 2 teaspoons of finely grated lemon rind.

Broiled Salmon or Fresh Mackerel with Anchovy Sauce. Make sauce by mixing 1 tablespoon of anchovy paste, 1 tablespoon of lemon juice, and a dash of Tabasco with 1/4 pound of melted butter. Heat and pour over broiled fish.

Filets of Fish with Anchovy Sauce. Sauté floured fish filets (sole, haddock, or perch) in butter. Remove to warm serving plate. Place an anchovy on each filet. Add the anchovy oil, butter, and lemon juice to the pan in which the fish was browned. Blend well and heat to boiling point. Pour sauce over the fish.

Fish Sticks in Blankets. Roll biscuit dough out to form 4-inch circles. Wrap each frozen fish stick in dough. Bake on a cookie sheet in a hot oven until browned. Serve with tomato sauce.

Fish with Avocado. Delicately browned pieces of filet of sole served with balls or cubes of avocado are delicious. Roll the pieces of avocado in lemon or lime juice, allowing about 1/2 an avocado for each serving. Any sauce may be used with the fish and the avocado. Garnish with wedges of lime.

Halibut Florentine. Bake or poach halibut filets and place them in individual baking dishes. Make creamed, chopped spinach, adding egg yolk and grated onion. Cover each filet with creamed spinach, at least 1/2-inch thick. Sprinkle with grated Parmesan cheese and broil or bake until bubbly.

Quick Version of Royal Halibut Pie. Bake egg-size pieces of halibut (about 2 pounds in all) in white wine until done. Line 2-quart casserole with a rich, light pie crust and bake the crust. Drain the cooked halibut and put in the baked crust. Add to the wine sauce in which the halibut was baked 1 dozen oysters and 1 dozen mushrooms, both broiled, and enough fine bread crumbs to make a medium batter. Beat 2 eggs into the mixture and cook over low heat for a few minutes until set. Pour the mixture over the halibut pieces in the baked pastry. Cover with more of the same rich pastry, unbaked. Bake in very hot oven until brown, about 20 minutes. Serve hot or cold. Good as a snack with ale. Reputedly a favorite dinner dish at Buckingham Palace.

Savory Stuffed Haddock. Make savory stuffing by mixing equal parts of chopped hard-boiled eggs and soft bread crumbs, seasoned with chopped filets of anchovy, mustard, and finely minced parsley. Spread the stuffing between 2 slices of haddock. Secure with toothpicks or skewers and bake on an oiled baking pan in a moderate oven for 45 minutes. Serve with lemon and butter sauce, flecked with chopped chives and sprinkled with paprika.

Sherry-Baked Fish. Place floured and seasoned fish filets in a flat baking pan or casserole generously oiled. Top each filet with a thin slice of onion, minced parsley, and a few celery seeds. Dot with butter. Pour about 1/2 cup of sherry around the fish and bake. When fish is baked, remove it to a hot platter. Stir another 1/2 cup of sherry into the pan and bring to a boil on top of the stove. Beat a cup of light cream and 2 egg yolks and stir into the sauce. Heat, stirring constantly. Don't boil. Pour sauce over fish and sprinkle with minced parsley.

Swedish Fish Sauce. For poached or steamed fish. Make a *roux* of 2 tablespoons each of butter, chopped onions, and flour. Add 1 cup of fish stock, 1/4 cup of white vinegar, 1/2 teaspoon of salt, and 1 teaspoon of sugar. Simmer for 5 minutes and add 1 cup of sour cream and the following seasonings: minced parsley, minced dill or dill weed, a pinch of thyme, and freshly ground white pepper. Reheat, but do not boil. Serve with small, boiled new potatoes.

WHOLE FISH

Baked Stuffed Rainbow Trout. The stuffing is delicate and delicious. Lightly brown chopped parsley, chopped green onion, and chives in about 2 tablespoons of butter. Sprinkle with 2 tablespoons of flour and blend. Use just enough milk to make a thick paste and add anchovy paste or several mashed anchovies. Add a few soft bread crumbs. Stuff the trout and season with salt and pepper. Wrap in well-oiled brown paper and broil under low flame, turning frequently, or bake in very hot oven for 30 minutes. Remove paper when trout is cooked. Garnish with lemon and parsley and serve with crisp cucumbers in sour cream and with crisp shoestring potatoes.

Fish-Head Stew. For this stew, fish bones are a must. You may use fish heads or not, but they supply added flavor. This is a Caribbean dish, but it is also popular in all countries where fishing is a way of life.

Cook fish, bones, and heads in a pot of water with a piece of lemon, 1 bay leaf, a few black peppercorns, and a dash of cayenne. When fish is done, remove from the bones and strain the broth. To the broth add various vegetables in this order: a handful of chick-peas (garbanzos), a few each of navy beans and dried lima beans, coarsely diced potatoes, a diced yellow turnip, and 2 finely diced onions. Simmer until these vegetables are done. Then add the greens: finely chopped celery, cabbage, chopped summer squash, corn, green peas, and a few leaves of escarole or watercress (any fresh vegetable is good). Do not overcook the greens; they should be crisp like Chinese vegetables. Lay the fish on top of the green vegetables while they are cooking.

To serve: Pour the broth into cups and drink like clam broth, flavoring it with a jigger of rum, if desired. Stir the stew and serve in bowls, with the vegetables. Garlic bread is good with this. For dessert: Serve broiled Jamaican bananas or plantain to carry out the Caribbean theme. Play Calypso records for an added touch of authenticity.

Gourmet Griddle Cakes from Leftover Whitefish. Combine equal parts of flaked cooked whitefish and a rich, highly seasoned cream sauce. Bake thin griddle cakes and spread with the sauce. Roll up and place in buttered baking dish. Sprinkle with grated cheese and bake in moderate oven until cheese browns and bubbles. Serve with extra cream sauce. It's really worth cooking the whitefish especially for this dish. Or use tuna fish. Calories are ignored, of course.

New Orleans Baked Fish with Oyster Stuffing. Select any fish suitable for stuffing and baking. For the stuffing, grind oysters, add cracker crumbs, considerable melted butter, parsley, salt, pepper, a little white wine, some of the oyster liquor, and a bit of gumbo filé powder (pulverized leaves of sassafras). Baste the fish with a mixture of oyster liquor and butter. Bake for 45 minutes to 1 hour, depending on size of the fish.

Steamed Fish. You can steam a whole fish easily in the oven by placing the fish on a rack in the roasting pan, adding hot water to bottom of the pan, but not allowing the hot water to touch the fish. Cover the pan and steam, using moderate heat. While steaming the fish, cook some broad noodles. Drain, and mix with plenty of melted butter and shredded sharp cheese. Put the noodle mixture in a shallow baking dish, with the steamed fish on top. Cover with Sauce Mornay (cream sauce with added egg yolks, Parmesan cheese, a dash of red pepper), and brown under the broiler. This dish can also be made in individual servings by poaching small filets of fish and following the above directions.

SAUCES AND GARNISHES FOR FISH

Almond and Olive Sauce. Make a medium-rich cream sauce. Just before serving add 3/4 cup of sliced, stuffed green olives and 1/2 cup of slivered toasted almonds. Serve over poached or steamed fish.

Apple Tartar Sauce. Enhance ready-made tartar sauce by adding a finely chopped apple, sour cream, and lemon juice. Or try a sauce made from 1/2 cup of sour cream, 1 teaspoon of mustard, salt, and pepper. This is delicious on cold meats and cooked vegetables, too.

Cooked Watercress with Fish. For a change, try serving chopped cooked watercress as a vegetable with fish. Use 2 bunches for 4 people. Chop the watercress coarsely and steam for a few minutes without water, adding butter, and a spoonful of heavy or sour cream. Serve with lemon wedges.

Emerald Salad Relish with Fish. Prepare lime gelatine with 1 tablespoon of vinegar substituted for that amount of water. Add a good dash of salt. Cool. When slightly thickened, add a bit of grated onion, 2 tablespoons of horseradish, and two cups of drained, chopped cucumbers.

Stuffed Salad with Fish Dinner. As a salad with an elegant broiled fish such as trout or pompano, try tiny tomatoes, peeled and stuffed with julienne of cucumbers, peeled, partially seeded, and cut into thin strips, in sour cream dressing. Serve on a bed of watercress or in crisp lettuce cups.

Tasty Cheese Sauce for Fish Sticks. Melt equal parts of prepared cheese mixture and condensed cream of mushroom soup. Add sherry, a bit of saffron, and salt and pepper. Good also on tuna-rice croquettes or vegetable croquettes.

Walnut Sauce for Poached Fish. Poach a whole fish (shad, sea bass, whitefish, or lake trout). Grind 1/2 pound of walnuts (English or black). Mix the ground walnuts with 2 tablespoons of flour and enough water to make a smooth paste. Add 1 crushed clove of garlic, 1 teaspoon of sugar, and freshly ground black pepper. Add enough fish broth to make into sauce consistency and cook until smooth and creamy, adding more fish stock, if necessary. Pour the sauce over the poached fish. Garnish with glazed, diagonally cut, thick carrot slices; watercress, and horseradish served in lemon cups.

Shellfish

CANNED AND FROZEN SHELLFISH

Clam Fritters. To one cup of prepared fritter batter, add 2 cups of canned minced clams and 2 tablespoons each of minced parsley and chives. Fry in deep fat. Drain and serve with tartar or tomato sauce.

Clams and Eggplant. Mix stewed chunks of eggplant, canned minced clams, minced onion, parsley, and a bit of crushed garlic. Moisten with a rich cream sauce and put in a buttered casserole. Top with soft, buttered bread crumbs and bake until thoroughly heated. Don't overbake or it will turn watery.

Crabmeat-Stuffed Potatoes. For a main luncheon dish, bake large potatoes for at least an hour. Cut in half and scoop out the mealy potatoes. Mash with butter, cream, salt, and a dash of Tabasco. Fold in a bit of grated onion, 1 can of crabmeat, and some cream cheese. Stuff potato shells with mixture, and bake in hot oven until heated through, about 20 minutes.

Crab Montebello. This can also be made with tuna fish. What makes this dish distinctive is the little macaroni squares the crab mixture is served on. Boil 1/2 pound of macaroni until tender. Drain, and mix the cooked macaroni and 1/2 pound of grated American cheese in the top of a double boiler, stirring constantly until the cheese melts. Pour into a flat, oiled pan. Press down. Chill until firm. Cut into squares, dip in cracker crumbs, and fry in hot oil (375°) until brown. Stir the crab into a thick tomato sauce and serve piping hot on the macaroni squares.

Curried Eggs and Oysters. Melt 2 tablespoons of butter with 2 tablespoons of flour and 1 teaspoon of curry powder. Stir until smooth and bubbly. Add canned condensed oyster stew and cook over low heat, stirring until blended and thickened. Add 6 sliced hard-cooked eggs. Serve on fluffy rice.

King Crabmeat on Toast. Mix 1 can of condensed cream of celery soup, one 6-ounce package defrosted king crabmeat, and 1 cup of cooked peas. Heat and serve on toast.

Quick Shrimp Creole. Mix cooked shrimp with 1 can of condensed cream of mushroom soup, 1/2 teaspoon of Worcestershire sauce, 1/2 teaspoon of creole gumbo filé powder (pulverized leaves of sassafras), 1 small can of tomato sauce, 1/2 of a green pepper and a small onion, chopped and sautéed in butter. Heat and serve on a bed of rice.

Shrimp and Rice. Put canned shrimp in the bottom of a buttered two-quart casserole. Cover with cooked rice and top with well-seasoned white sauce to which you have added capers and a dash of Tabasco. Add a thick layer of buttered, soft bread crumbs. Press crumbs down into sauce. Bake uncovered in moderate oven for about 1/2 hour.

Spaghetti with Clam Sauce. Serve with anchovy tossed salad, a loaf of hot garlic bread, and white wine. For dessert, arrange a bowl of fruit, cheese, and unshelled nuts as a centerpiece.

FRESH SHELLFISH

Avocado and Crabmeat. Stretch creamed crabmeat and make it even more delicious by adding cubes of avocado. Serve in patty shells or in a casserole, with a topping of buttered bread crumbs.

Avocado and Crabmeat Mornay. Fill peeled halves of avocado with crabmeat held together with a thick, rich cream sauce or mayonnaise. Cover with grated Parmesan cheese. Bake for 15 minutes in a hot oven until bubbly. Sprinkle with paprika and minced chives.

Baked Oysters on the Half Shell. Cover each oyster with a tablespoon of relish spread combined with tartar sauce. Sprinkle with grated cheese. Bake for 7 minutes in a hot oven or broil until sauce bubbles and cheese melts. Serve with quarters of lemon.

Broiled Lobster. To broil a lobster the easy way, parboil for 5 or 10 minutes immediately before broiling. As soon as the lobster is cool enough to handle, split it down the back. Throw away the stomach and intestines. Remove the coral and green liver and set aside. Rub the exposed meat with melted butter. With shell side up, broil for 10 or 12 minutes; then turn and broil for 5 to 7 minutes. Serve with a sauce of melted butter, lemon juice, a dash of Tabasco, the chopped coral and liver, and a little salt.

Broiled Oyster Plate. Pie plates of foil, half filled with rock salt (or with crumpled aluminum foil if you can't get rock salt) make perfect baking and serving plates for broiled oysters or clams on the half shell.

Cold Lobster Plate. Cooking Tip. Put plenty of salt in the water in which you boil lobster. Serve a pickled, spiced pear as a garnish and put tartar sauce in scalloped lemon shells. Lemon shells can be made easily from halves of lemons after juice is squeezed out. Remove the pulp and cut even points around the tops with kitchen scissors.

Crab Custard in Casserole. Add grated onion, seasoning, and a sprinkling of cracker crumbs to crabmeat. Fold the mixture into an unsweetened egg custard mixture and bake in individual casseroles in a pan of hot water. Serve with a thin cream sauce made with a small can of tiny mushrooms, including the liquid, and 1/2 teaspoon of Worcestershire sauce. Lace generously with sherry.

Creamed Crabmeat and Avocado. Into a medium white sauce flavored with anchovy paste and dry mustard, stir equal parts of lump crabmeat and diced avocado that has been dipped in lemon juice. Heat and serve immediately in patty shells or on toast.

Sprinkle with chopped parsley and garnish each serving with a thin slice of lemon, cut and twisted.

Creamed Oyster Rolls. Prepare creamed oysters. Scoop out the centers of Vienna rolls and brush the edges generously with butter. Toast under the broiler and serve hot, filled with the oysters. Garnish with paprika, watercress, and sliced tomatoes. Any creamed fish can be served this way.

Delicate Fried Oysters. Dip oysters in lemon juice, then in very fine toasted bread crumbs, and then in egg which has been slightly beaten with a little of the oyster liquor and a touch of grated lemon rind. Roll in crumbs again. Fry in deep fat or oil.

New England Kitchen Clambake. Place thoroughly scrubbed clams in their shells in the bottom of a large kettle. Cover with a layer of foil. Place pieces of fish on the foil and cover with foil. Add several mild sausages and another layer of foil. Some preboiled onions and carrots next, then foil and peeled white potatoes, with foil on top. Pour 2 cups of water into kettle and cover tightly. Put a brick on top of pan to hold lid tight, if necessary. After about 1 hour, when potatoes are tender, all is done. Serve the broth first. Then the clams with loads of melted butter for dunking, and last the sausages and vegetables.

Oyster Fritters. Using biscuit mix, substitute the liquor from the oysters (boil and skim the liquor first) for 1/2 of the required liquid, to make a fairly stiff batter. Put oysters in the batter and drop one oyster at a time, with a bit of the batter, into hot fat and fry until brown. Drain and serve immediately.

Oysters in the Pan. Leave each oyster on deep half of shell and place them on rock salt preheated in a large pan. Sprinkle with lemon juice and cover with the following: 1 cup of mayonnaise mixed with 1/2 cup of soft butter, 1/2 cup of cracker crumbs, finely chopped parsley, chives, and grated onion, a pinch of curry powder, and salt and pepper. Place a small piece of partially cooked, thinly sliced bacon on top and put in a hot oven until oysters are plump and bacon is crisp. Serve in the pan in which they were cooked, garnished with sprigs of parsley and lemon wedges.

Oysters Maryland. Drain oysters and dip in catsup and then in fine, dry bread crumbs. Place in buttered shallow baking dish. Sprinkle with minced, raw, thin-sliced bacon. Bake in hot oven for about 6 minutes or until bacon is crisp. Serve immediately with lemon wedges, dipping one side of each wedge in paprika.

Scalloped Oysters. Add a little finely grated lemon rind and use toasted fine bread crumbs instead of the usual crackers for a delicate and delicious buffet or side dish.

Scalloped Sea Scallops. Place a layer of sea scallops in buttered individual casseroles or scallop shells. Cover with a sauce made by adding 2 tablespoons each of heavy cream, white wine, and lemon juice to a can of condensed cream of chicken soup. Season with a bit of onion juice, 1/2 teaspoon of finely chopped fresh rosemary or a pinch of crushed dried rosemary, salt, and freshly ground black pepper. This can be done ahead of time. Just before baking, top with buttered soft bread crumbs. Bake in a very hot oven for 15 minutes. Broil a few seconds for additional browning of crumbs, if necessary. Garnish with artichoke hearts marinated in a lemon and oil French dressing.

Scallops Variety. Scallops can be served almost any way that shrimp can (they are less expensive and really delicious): boiled and served with a creamy green mayonnaise or rémoulade sauce; boiled with herbs in court bouillon, and served with a hot tomato cocktail sauce; or made into a Jambalaya or a curry.

Shrimp Cooking Tip. Don't overcook shrimp—3 minutes at most.

Shrimp in Blankets. Soak shrimp in milk seasoned with salt and pepper. Wrap in thinly sliced, partially cooked bacon. Broil on both sides until bacon is crisp. Serve with creamed potatoes and a green salad.

Sweet-and-Sour Shrimp. For a change from hot horseradish sauce: mix 3/4 cup of chili sauce, 1 tablespoon of lemon juice, 1/4 cup of red currant jelly, melted, and a dash of Angostura bitters. Delicious hot as a luncheon dish or cold as an appetizer.

Eggs

Baked Eggs in Mashed Potato Nests. Crumble crisp bacon into mashed potatoes and stir in an egg and salt and pepper. Put mounds of the potato mixture on a cookie tray. Indent top with a spoon and break an egg in the hollow. Bake in a moderate oven until the eggs are set, about 15 minutes. Easy but impressive.

Cheese Pudding. To a custard of 2 eggs, 1 egg yolk, and 2 cups of milk, add 4 slices of bread, cubed, 1/2 pound of cubed sharp cheese, and salt and pepper to taste. Pour into individual casseroles and sprinkle with paprika. Bake and serve hot.

Cherry Omelet. A plain omelet served with sour cream and whole cherry preserves is delectable.

Curried Eggs and Sautéed Raisins. Sauté soft, seeded muscat raisins in butter until plump. Drain on a paper towel and sprinkle lightly with coarse salt. Serve warm as an accompaniment to curried eggs. The raisins by themselves are also good as a snack.

Glazed Apple Omelet. Serve omelet with glazed apple slices. Melt equal parts of butter and brown sugar in a skillet and add thinly sliced, unpared apples. Sprinkle with salt and cinnamon and cook for 10 to 15 minutes, stirring gently until the apples are tender and glazed.

Mushroom Scrambled Eggs. Blend 1 can of condensed mushroom soup with 8 beaten eggs. Scramble and serve with fried apple slices. Toasted English muffins complete the menu. Plenty of hot coffee, of course. Serves six. For a fancy, but easy, Sunday brunch.

New Year's Brunch. Top shirred eggs with diced smoked turkey or smoked ham warmed in a bit of butter. Serve with buttered toast triangles, spiced red currant jelly, and cream cheese.

Sautéed Chicken Livers with Hard-Cooked Eggs. Serve sautéed chicken livers on toast, covered with a white sauce into which you have folded sliced hard-cooked eggs and finely minced green onion or chopped chives.

Scrambled Eggs with Julienne Tongue. Cut tongue in fine strips. Brown in butter and sprinkle with port wine. Serve with scrambled eggs.

Shirred Eggs with Cheese Sauce. Make sharp cheese sauce with mustard and a dash of Tabasco sauce (or use frozen Welsh Rarebit). Put 1/2 cup in the bottom of each individual baking dish. Break 2 eggs on top and pour a tablespoon of cream or milk over the eggs. Bake in moderate oven until set, about 12 minutes.

Shirred Eggs with Ham and Bananas. Sauté in butter fingers of cooked ham or smoked turkey and bananas split lengthwise and dusted lightly with brown sugar. Serve with shirred eggs or an omelet.

Smokehouse Eggs. Mix together and fry diced, cooked smoked ham and diced raw bacon. Add equal parts of chopped watercress and chopped lettuce. Scramble eggs. Stir the hot meat and greens into the eggs just before they are done.

Sunday Morning Omelet. Mix crabmeat or any cooked white fish, flaked, with a few chives, salt, pepper, and lemon juice. Fold the fish mixture into the omelet. Serve with delicate mashed potato cakes and a scooped-out half lemon filled with hot (both spicy and temperaturewise) tomato cocktail sauce or with warm tartar sauce.

Sunny Side Up. Sauté a chopped onion in butter with a dash of Worcestershire sauce. Add corned beef cut in 4 thick slices. Slightly indent the center of each slice with a spoon. Put an egg in each indentation and sprinkle with salt and pepper. Cover the skillet and cook slowly until eggs are set. Serve the nests with the butter-onion sauce spooned over the eggs.

Swedish Eggs. Dip shelled, whole, hard-cooked eggs in slightly beaten egg white. Cover with raw sausage meat. Dip in egg white again and roll in bréad crumbs. Fry in deep hot oil until brown. Cut into halves lengthwise. Serve hot with creamed green tomatoes.

Watercress Scrambled Eggs. Add buttered croutons and coarsely chopped watercress to scrambled eggs at the last minute. Serve with a generous bunch of watercress and peeled, sliced tomato.

Vegetables and Grains

Note: For best flavor, steam or stir-fry vegetables. (See Cook's Dictionary.)

ARTICHOKES

Artichoke Hearts with Bread Sauce. Cook artichoke hearts until tender but not soft. Make a highly seasoned stuffing of fine toasted bread crumbs, grated Parmesan cheese, mashed garlic, and minced parsley, held together with olive oil and a beaten egg. Heap some of the filling on each artichoke heart. Place the stuffed hearts in an oiled casserole and bake until the top is golden and the hearts are heated through.

Fried Artichoke Hearts. Dip frozen artichoke hearts, just slightly thawed, into well-beaten egg, then in a mixture of equal parts of flour and crumbs. Fry slowly in 1/4 inch of oil until crisp and browned on both sides, about 10 or 15 minutes. Sprinkle with paprika and serve with len on wedges.

ASPARAGUS

Asparagus Chinese Style. Cut tender part of fresh asparagus spears in thin diagonal slices. Sauté in hot oil for 2 minutes only. Pour over the still-crisp cooked slices a sauce made of chicken broth slightly thickened with cornstarch and flavored with soy sauce, mashed garlic, salt, and pepper to taste. Cook for 1 minute longer. Serve at once. This is an interesting vegetable to serve with broiled or fried chicken pieces or boiled beef cubes. Thin slices of zucchini squash can also be cooked this way.

Asparagus or Broccoli Parmesan. Sprinkle salt, olive oil, mashed garlic, freshly ground pepper, and freshly grated Parmesan cheese over steamed asparagus or broccoli.

Asparagus Polonaise. Serve hot asparagus sprinkled with buttered crumbs, chopped hard-boiled egg, and minced parsley.

Asparagus Royal. Cook asparagus spears. Serve with a rich cream sauce (see below), using 1/4 cup of sherry for part of the liquid. Stir in a little Parmesan cheese. Spoon sauce on each serving of drained asparagus and sprinkle with slivered toasted almonds.

Easy Sauce for Asparagus. Dilute 1 can of condensed cream of chicken soup with 1/3 cup of rich cream and the yolk of one egg. Heat and pour over the asparagus. Garnish with pimento slivers.

Quick Hollandaise. Cook 3/4 cup of mayonnaise and 1/4 cup of thin cream in the top of a double boiler for 5 minutes. Add a dash of salt and 1 tablespoon of lemon juice.

BEANS

Apples and Beans Belmont. Cook fresh or frozen cut green beans in a small amount of salted water. Five minutes before they are done, add an equal amount of sliced cooking apples and a table-spoon of sugar. Cover and cook for 5 minutes. Just before serving, add 2 tablespoons each of butter and cream.

Canned Whole Green Beans. Sauté minced green onions in butter. Add a bit of flour and dry mustard, then the bean liquid. Add the beans and chopped black or green olives.

Chili Green Beans. Add chili powder and crumbled bacon to steamed green beans.

Cut Green Beans Pimento. Fold chopped pimento into cream sauce for cooked green beans.

Delicate Cheese Lima Beans. Cook Fordhook lima beans. Drain, if necessary. Add 1/2 teaspoon of minced onion, 1/4 cup of grated American cheese, 1 tablespoon of butter, and 1/2 cup of light cream. Toss lightly with fork over low heat until cheese melts. Season to taste with salt and pepper.

Dill Green Beans. Add 2 chopped, peeled fresh tomatoes and a teaspoon of dill seeds to cooked French-style green beans. Season with butter, salt, and freshly ground pepper.

Green Beans and Bacon Dumplings. Cook cut green beans in more water than usual. Make baking powder dumplings with crumbled cooked bacon and minced parsley and drop in the boiling broth. Cover and cook for 15 minutes. Don't peek. Serve with butter, salt, and freshly ground black pepper.

Green Beans Gourmet. Steam cut green beans. Dress with a cup of small cubes of bread browned in butter and garlic. Salt and pepper to taste.

Green Beans in Lemon Rings with Steak. Cut rings of lemon rind about 1/4-inch thick. Boil the lemon rind rings in sugar syrup until tender. Warm whole green beans and lemon rind rings in a mixture of lemon pulp and butter. The sweet lemon flavor is particularly compatible with beefsteak.

Green Beans or Cauliflower with Parmesan Sauce. Add large pieces of black olives, chopped parsley, and grated Parmesan cheese to white sauce or to a can of condensed cream of celery soup. (You may omit the cheese from the sauce.) Pour sauce over the vegetables, sprinkle with cheese and slide under the broiler until the sauce bubbles. The sauce is good on fish or also with chicken on toast.

Green Beans Savory. Steam beans until tender but still crisp. Dress with mayonnaise to which you have added chopped chives, minced parsley, minced pimento, a bit of lemon juice, salt, and freshly ground pepper.

Italian Butter Beans. Cook flat broad green beans until still a bit crisp. Dress with a bit of butter and finely chopped pimento.

Lima Beans with Canadian Bacon. Cook Fordhook lima beans. Sauté 6 to 12 thin slices of Canadian bacon. Flavor a white sauce, or a can of condensed cream of celery soup, with minced onion, a bit of brown sugar, salt, pepper, and 1/4 teaspoon of tumeric. Add cooked beans to the sauce. In a casserole, alternate layers of the creamed beans with bacon slices and top with slices of fresh peeled tomatoes. Bake in hot oven for about 20 minutes.

String Beans New Orleans. Cook frozen French-cut string beans in little or no water until tender but not mushy. Season with olive oil, chopped chives, crushed dried basil or chopped fresh basil, creole gumbo filé powder (pulverized leaves of sassafras), salt, and freshly ground black pepper.

BEETS

Beets à la Russe. Grind pickled beets and mix with sour cream, a dash of cayenne, salt and pepper. Serve hot or cold.

Beets Continental. Use canned baby beets. Add a bit of tarragon-flavored wine vinegar to the beet juice and thicken with a *roux* of butter and flour. Heat the beets in this sauce, with a teaspoon of caraway seeds. Serve with a generous dab of sour cream.

Flemish Beets. Put canned Harvard beets through food chopper. Heat and add sour cream and a pinch of dill.

Frenchman's Beets. Place thinly sliced beets in heavy pan. Sauté the beets and a few sliced green onions in butter. Add a bit of sugar and salt. Dampen several large lettuce leaves with water and lay over the beets and onions. Cover lightly, bring to a boil and then lower heat and simmer for 1/2 hour. To serve, shred crisp lettuce head and toss with the beets. Serve with a dab of sauce made by adding finely grated orange rind to sour cream.

Marmalade Beets. Add 1/3 cup of orange marmalade, a lump of butter, lemon juice, and a dash of ground ginger to a can of tiny whole beets. Thicken juice with a little cornstarch, if desired.

BROCCOLI

Broccoli Baroque. Serve cooked broccoli with melted butter and crumbled Roquefort or blue cheese.

Chopped Broccoli or Spinach Brittany. Cook chopped broccoli or spinach until barely tender. Drain well and turn into a buttered casserole. Cover with a can of condensed mushroom soup, spiked with sherry and nutmeg, and mixed with the yolk of an egg. Top with fresh, soft, buttered bread crumbs. Bake in a moderate oven for about 1/2 hour until crumbs are brown and top is "set." Remove from the oven and let stand a few minutes.

BRUSSELS SPROUTS

Brussels Sprouts in Celery Sauce. Place cooked sprouts in buttered casserole. Top with a can of condensed cream of celery soup, and sprinkle with grated cheese. Bake until cheese melts and casserole is heated through.

Brussels Sprouts with Chestnuts. Combine 2 parts of cooked Brussels sprouts with 1 part of cooked whole chestnuts. Mix in rich cream sauce and pour into buttered casserole. Top with crumbs and heat thoroughly. Serve very hot with roast lamb and a ginger-pear salad.

Mock Artichoke Hearts. Cook Brussels sprouts in very little water with a bay leaf. Marinate in 2 parts of olive oil, 1 part of lemon juice, crushed garlic, freshly ground black pepper, and salt.

Shredded Brussels Sprouts with Bacon Dressing. Shred Brussels sprouts. Fry 6 slices of lean bacon. Chop fine. Add 1/4 cup of water and 1/4 cup of vinegar, salt, pepper, and sugar to taste. (Chopped green onion may be added if desired.) Pour hot dressing over the Brussels sprouts and serve.

CABBAGE

Cabbage Cooked in Orange Juice. Shred cabbage. Add orange juice, salt, pepper, sugar, and a bit of lemon juice. Cook in butter in a covered skillet. A good accompaniment for duck or game.

Cranberry Cabbage. Steam finely shredded cabbage with a can of whole cranberry sauce and 1/4 cup of butter.

Curried Cabbage. Cook shredded cabbage in a small smount of half milk and half consommé. Flavor with curry powder and salt to taste.

Danish Trick for Cabbage. Rapidly boil 3 cups of finely shredded cabbage for 7 minutes in very little salted water. Drain. Add 1/2 cup of sour cream, 1/2 teaspoon of caraway seeds and reheat briefly.

Shredded Red Cabbage. Sweet and sour. Steam with raisins, serve piping hot apples and onion sautéed in butter, sweeten with light brown sugar.

Steamed, Finely Shredded Cabbage. Cook in 1/2 cup butter, using no water. Add salt and pepper to taste and drizzle over it a few tablespoons of rich cream. Don't overcook.

Sweet-and-Sour Red Cabbage. Steam finely shredded red cabbage with raisins in red wine and 1/4 cup of butter. Sweeten to taste with sugar or honey. This is delicious served with game or pot roast.

CANNED VEGETABLES

Canned Vegetable Plate. Drain green asparagus spears, heat in butter and garnish with strips of pimento; heat whole baby carrots in lemon juice and honey; warm artichoke hearts in butter and sprinkle with crumbs and cheese; sprinkle a whole peeled canned tomato with sugar and crushed oregano and heat in butter. Spoon the resulting juice on top. Garnish with parsley and tomato wedges.

CARROTS

Mashed Carrots. Serve a mound of buttered mashed carrots and a spoonful of cooked peas with chicken dinner. Chicken gravy over this dish makes even the children love vegetables. Or, make a depression in the top of the mound of mashed carrots and fill with green peas; flavor with honey, lemon, and butter.

CAULIFLOWER

Cauliflower with Anchovy Butter. For a whole head, mix 1/4 pound of sweet butter and 1/2 teaspoon of anchovy paste. Garnish with rolled anchovies.

Cold Jeweled Cauliflower Plate. Cook one perfect whole white cauliflower with as little water as possible. Cool. Then drain and chill. Place on a bed of crisp watercress and cover cauliflower thickly and completely with mayonnaise studded with capers and halves of black olives. Surround with fresh-cooked shrimp, hard-boiled egg quarters, and peeled tomato quarters.

Colorful Vegetable Trick. Add a little finely chopped pimento to melted butter and pour over cauliflower. Another interesting way to serve cauliflower is to sauté coarse bread crumbs in butter until crisp and brown. Add finely grated lemon rind to the crumbs and sprinkle them generously over buttered or creamed cauliflower just before serving.

CELERY

Chopped Pascal Celery and Diced Peeled Cucumber. Remove cucumber seeds and chop both vegetables. Cook in water with salt and 1 teaspoon of sugar until tender but a bit crispy. Mix with rich cream sauce and serve with toast points. Good with fish or chicken.

Creamed Celery and Almonds. Mix steamed pascal celery with a can of condensed cream of celery soup to which an egg yolk has been added. Put in casserole. Top with buttered crumbs and slivered toasted almonds. Heat through.

Whole Celery Hearts. Cook small whole celery hearts in chicken consommé and serve topped with sliced black olives and minced parsley.

CHESTNUTS AND WATER CHESTNUTS

Chestnuts in Cream. Put 2 pounds of chestnuts in casserole. Cover with 3 cups of rich cream and 4 tablespoons of butter. Bake in a moderate oven for 45 minutes. Ten minutes before serving, pour a large jigger of cognac or brandy over the chestnuts. Salt and pepper to taste.

Dutch Fried Chestnuts. Sauté slightly cooked, peeled chestnuts in butter with a pinch of salt and a teaspoon of sugar. Serve with cooked creamed cabbage.

CORN

Corn Élégant. Only fresh, partially cooked corn on the cob should be used for this dish. Cut 3 cups of the cooked corn off the cob using a serrated knife with a sawing motion. Blend a large package of cream cheese, 3 tablespoons of butter, 1/4 cup of corn milk, and a scant teaspoon of garlic salt. Add the corn. Stir over low heat until cheese melts and forms a smooth sauce.

Corn-Stuffed Peppers. Add whole-kernel corn to stuffing for peppers.

Just Like Fresh Corn off the Cob. Melt 2 tablespoons of butter in a saucepan. Add one package of frozen corn kernels, 2 tablespoons of water, 3/4 teaspoon of salt, and a dash of pepper. Cover and cook over medium heat for 10 minutes, stirring once.

Whole-Kernel Corn. Spike with celery seeds and crumbled bacon.

CUCUMBERS (See Celery, Mushrooms)

EGGPLANT

Baked Eggplant. Brown 1/2-inch-thick slices of eggplant in oil and place in a casserole with a can of tomato sauce and a can of pitted black olives. Sprinkle with grated Parmesan cheese and bake in hot oven until cheese melts. May be put under broiler for a few seconds to brown the cheese.

Baked Eggplant Halves. Wash and dry eggplant and cut in half lengthwise. Crisscross the top with gashes 1/2-inch deep. Sauté halves of eggplant in olive oil, cut side down, for about 10 minutes. Set them upright in a baking dish. Make a paste of mashed anchovies, garlic, bread crumbs, beef bouillon or stock, and minced parsley. Spread over the cut side of the eggplant, dot with butter and bake in hot oven for about 30 minutes.

Double Eggplant. Place a slice of cheese between 2 slices of eggplant, which have been dipped in egg and bread crumbs and fried. Heat in moderate oven to melt cheese. Spike sauce with lemon juice.

Eggplant Benedict. A main-course vegetable or a center of interest for a vegetable plate. Dip 1/2-inch-thick slices of eggplant in flour. Brown in oil. Serve with a poached egg on each slice. Top with hollandaise sauce.

Eggplant Italian Style. Sauté 1/2-inch-thick peeled eggplant slices in olive oil until tender. Salt and pepper well while cooking. Serve immediately, topped with parsley and grated Parmesan cheese.

Eggplant Louisiana. This casserole is made of coarsely chopped, parboiled eggplant, sliced onions, peeled and chopped fresh tomatoes, canned shrimp, and toasted bread crumbs, all seasoned with salt and white pepper and creole gumbo filé powder (pulverized leaves of sassafras). Bake for 1/2 hour in covered dish. Uncover. Garnish with whole shrimp and peeled tomato quarters dipped in melted butter; place on top of the casserole and cook uncovered for another 5 minutes.

Eggplant Pizza. Dip 1/2-inch-thick slices of eggplant in seasoned flour and brown in oil. Place on shallow baking pan or cookie tray. Cover with pizza topping, broil and serve. Good hot or cold.

Eggplant Rarebit. Top a thick slice of floured and fried eggplant with a thick slice of peeled fresh tomato, well salted and peppered. Top with a sharp Welsh rarebit or cheese sauce and broil until bubbly.

HOMINY

Golden Canned Hominy. Add to cooked green beans or green lima beans.

Hominy with Maple Syrup. Heat canned whole or ground hominy. Drain. Sprinkle with salt, pepper, and butter and maple syrup.

LENTILS

Stewed Lentils. Soak overnight, one part lentils in 2 parts water, salted to taste. Then cook slowly for about 3 hours until soft and dry. Add lemon juice, melted butter, minced onion, and chopped parsley.

Zippy Lentils. Season leftover stewed lentils with tomato paste or sauce and chili powder or curry powder, adding some raisins and chopped apple before reheating. Serve the Mexican-flavored lentils with hot corn bread. Serve the curried lentils with sesame crackers or pita (Bible bread).

MUSHROOMS

Creole Cucumbers. Stew slices of unpeeled cucumber in well-seasoned canned tomatoes and add sautéed mushrooms. Stewed canned tomatoes, flavored with onion, are perfect for this.

Elegant Vegetable for Steak. Serve canned pitted black olives and canned button mushrooms in a sauce of condensed cream of mushroom soup. Garnish with chopped parsley.

Main Luncheon Dish. Add sherry to creamed mushrooms to put over boiled wild rice. Top with minced parsley and serve with a tossed green field salad and fresh warm French bread. Lemon ice with crème de menthe makes a fine dessert.

Mushroom Fritters. Mix sliced cooked mushrooms with fritter batter to which you add a dash of nutmeg, a dash of cayenne, and minced parsley. Fry in hot oil.

Mushrooms Deluxe. Cook tiny white mushrooms in butter; add a bit of lemon juice, salt, and pepper. Arrange in heated rich pastry shells. Top with a dab of sour cream at room temperature.

Mushrooms with Noodles. Toss cooked thin noodles with lightly sautéed fresh mushrooms, salt, butter, and sherry wine.

Paprika Mushrooms. Sauté whole mushrooms in butter with chopped onion. Season with salt and a tablespoon of rose paprika. Toss well and fry until light brown. Sprinkle with 1 tablespoon of flour. Mix thoroughly and add a cup of sour cream. Serve over boiled rice.

ONIONS

Broiled Onions. Roll drained small canned onions in butter on a pie tin, then roll in a mixture of dry bread crumbs and grated Parmesan cheese. Place under broiler for about 7 minutes. Serve with steak or hamburgers.

Glazed Onions. Boil 3 pounds of small white onions in salted water until tender. Drain. Heat 1/4 cup of butter and 3 tablespoons of sugar in heavy skillet. Add onions and shake gently to coat. Cook slowly until onions are golden. A good dish for a buffet or as a side dish at a large dinner party.

Onions and Apples Valley Forge. Parboil onions and cut in 1/2-inch-thick circles. Slice unpeeled, cored apples in 1/2-inch-thick circles. Fry the onion and apple slices in bacon drippings or butter. Drain. Serve with crisp bacon or veal chops.

Onions in Bread Sauce. Cook several pounds of small white onions or use 2 cans of small cooked onions. Heat a quart of milk with a whole onion stuck with cloves. Add salt, pepper, and 2 cups of fine stale bread crumbs. Cook uncovered in top of double boiler for 30 minutes, stirring occasionally. Remove the onion. Add 2 tablespoons of butter and the drained, boiled onions. Turn into a buttered casserole. Top with a cup of bread crumbs which have been sautéed in butter. Sprinkle with paprika. Run under the broiler or bake in a very hot oven until the top is crisp. This dish may be made ahead of time and heated in casserole just before serving.

Stuffed Spanish Onions. Parboil large sweet onions and remove part of the center. Place in a buttered baking dish. Fill and surround with condensed cream of mushroom soup. Bake until very tender but still firm enough to hold their shape. Fill centers with small whole cooked mushrooms and spoon some of the mushroom sauce from the baking pan on top. Serve with turkey or roast pork.

PARSNIPS

Colcannon. Cook potatoes and parsnips together and mash with milk and butter. Add onion and steamed shredded cabbage, salt and pepper to taste.

Parsnip Fritters. Mash parsnips and bind together with a few tablespoons of flour and egg and milk. Season with salt, pepper, and a dash of nutmeg or mace. Makes soft batter, which is dropped by spoonfuls into hot oil.

Molasses-Glazed Parsnips. Heat molasses and a little butter in heavy skillet. Drop in thick pieces or slices of cold cooked parsnips. Cook until brown and glazed. Serve hot.

PEAS

Baked Split Peas and Canadian Bacon. Wash and soak 1-1/2 cups of split peas in cold water overnight. Drain. Lightly brown 6 slices of Canadian bacon in a skillet. Add the drained peas, 1-1/2 cups of water, 1 teaspoon of salt, and some freshly ground black pepper. Pour into a bean pot or casserole and bake in a slow oven for about 4 hours.

Curried Peas. Cook frozen peas in very little water. Drain and mix with a can of condensed green pea soup and a teaspoon of curry powder. Don't overcook. The peas must be green, green, green. Delicious with roast lamb or lamb chops.

French Petit Pois. Sauté several sliced green onions in a little olive oil. Add cooked tiny peas, some chopped head lettuce, a pinch of thyme, and salt and pepper.

Holiday Peas. Mix a can of condensed cream of chicken soup with a can of sliced mushrooms and a small jar of pimentos, chopped. Add frozen peas which have been cooked in boiling water until just thawed. Turn into a covered casserole. Heat in moderate oven just before serving.

Norwegian Vegetable Dish. Young tender new peas, cooked in their pods, served with sausages.

Peas and Avocado. Just before removing fresh or frozen buttered green peas from stove add diced avocado and a pinch of sugar.

Peas and Dumplings. Put frozen or fresh peas in generous amount of chicken broth. When broth comes to boil, drop in baking powder dumplings. Cover and cook for 15 minutes without removing the cover.

Peas and Squash. Cook sliced yellow summer squash and green peas separately, combine to serve. Season with butter, salt, and freshly ground pepper.

Peas in Tart Shells. Bake pie pastry in little tartlet pans. Fill the pastry cups with creamed peas. Serve with lamb chops.

Peas with Green Onions. Soak 1 teaspoon of cumin seeds in 1/4 cup of water. Wilt a bunch of chopped green onions (tough leaves removed) in butter. Add the cumin seeds, water, and 2 pounds of fresh shelled peas. Cover and cook slowly until almost done, then add 1/2 cup of heavy sweet cream. Cook quickly until cream is absorbed. Salt to taste.

PEPPERS

Green Pepper Boats. Cut sweet green peppers in half lengthwise. Remove seeds. Put in boiling water and parboil for 5 minutes. Drain well. Fill with your favorite stuffing and bake. Garnish with strips of pimento.

Pantry-Shelf Macaroni. Cook macaroni in boiling water to which you have added a bouillon cube. Drain and mix with cooked bacon bits, sautéed chopped green pepper and onion, and some small stuffed green olive slices.

Scalloped Onions and Green Peppers. Delicious with ham or chicken. Bake or sauté green peppers and remove skins. Cut in eighths. Drain canned small onions. Heat peppers and onions together in butter. Add slivered toasted almonds, seasoned bread crumbs, salt and pepper to taste.

POTATOES

Bacon Potatoes. Add crumbled bacon to mashed potato cakes or baked stuffed potatoes.

Baked Potato Anchovy. With a vegetable plate, serve a mealy baked potato (baked for at least 1-1/4 hours), gashed, squeezed, and garnished with a generous chunk of anchovy butter (butter creamed with anchovy paste).

Baked Potato Florentine. Fill scooped-out baked potato shells with nutmeg-flavored creamed spinach. Border each shell with the scooped-out mashed and seasoned potato put through a pastry tube. Heat thoroughly.

Baked Potatoes Roquefort. Add both a chunk of butter and a chunk of Roquefort or blue cheese to hot mealy baked potatoes before serving.

Better than Caviar. Mix a cup of coarsely sliced, pitted black olives with a cup of sour cream, onion salt, and chopped parsley. Cut a cross in top of potatoes that have been baked for at least 1 hour. Squeeze gently until potato pops open. Put a pat of butter in each potato and heap with the olive-cream mixture. Serve with broiled lamb chops and a watercress, pineapple, and grapefruit salad.

Deviled French Fries. Sprinkle French-fried potatoes with a mixture of garlic salt, chili powder, and dry mustard.

Duchess Potatoes Amandine. Add slivered almonds to mashed potato cakes before baking.

Herbed Potatoes. Sprinkle dried thyme and chopped parsley over buttered boiled potatoes and serve with fish or roast lamb.

Mashed Potatoes with Herbs. Add 1 tablespoon each of chopped fresh mint, chives, and minced parsley to hot mashed potatoes. Serve a mound or scoop of potatoes with a small chunk of butter. Good with roast lamb.

Miniature Potato Kugels. Mix leftover mashed potatoes with egg and cheese and put in well-oiled muffin tins. Bake in moderate oven until brown. Turn out and serve. Or, pack finely grated, seasoned raw potato and a bit of grated onion in oiled muffin tins and bake in very hot oven for about 1/2 hour.

Mystery Mashed Potatoes. Grated onion and just a whisper of mace added to mashed potatoes make them extra delicious.

Pennsylvania Dutch Potato Stuffing. Stir generous amount of sautéed chopped onions, celery, and crisp bread croutons into mashed potatoes. Thin with egg and milk. Bake in a casserole.

Perfect Hashed Browns. Quick, foolproof, and delicious hashed brown potatoes. Grate cold boiled potatoes on coarse grater. Cover bottom of a large skillet or griddle with oil. When oil is hot, place generous mounds of the grated potato in the pan, sprinkle with salt and pepper and press down with spatula. Brown thoroughly on one side and flip over like a pancake. When other side is brown, serve immediately. Mounds can be made ahead, flattened, and frozen between waxed paper.

Piquant Creamed Potatoes. Add chopped dried beef to creamed potatoes.

Polonaise Potatoes. Drain tiny canned boiled potatoes. Sauté in melted butter and roll in crisp toasted bread crumbs before serving piping hot.

Potato Nests. To a cup of mashed potatoes add 1 well-beaten egg, 1/4 cup of cream, salt and pepper. Spoon onto baking sheet, hollowing out center to form nests. Bake until lightly browned. Serve filled with poached eggs, creamed mushrooms, creamed chicken or creamed fish.

Potato Turnover Topping for Casserole Dishes. On waxed paper, roll out pie crust to make a 12-inch circle. Spread half of the crust (to within 1/2 inch of outer edge) with a thick layer of highly seasoned leftover mashed potatoes, minced parsley, grated onion, paprika, and butter. Fold over the other side of crust to form a giant turnover. Place on baking sheet; peel off the waxed paper. Cut into 6 pie-shaped wedges; prick the top of each wedge with a fork. Bake in very hot oven for 20 to 25 minutes or until pastry is brown. Arrange the potato turnovers on top of a casserole meal, or serve instead of potatoes with any meal.

Potato-Walnut Croquettes. Add ground English walnuts, bread crumbs, milk, eggs, and a bit of onion salt to leftover mashed potatoes. Roll in fine crumbs and egg, and brown in a little butter.

Rich Creamed Potatoes. Add boiled potatoes or leftover potatoes to canned condensed cream of chicken soup.

Real Pennsylvania Dutch Potatoes Made in Electric Skillet. Slice raw peeled potatoes on coarse, wide blade of grater and fry in oil in electric skillet at 360°. Cook for about 30 minutes; turn just once. Don't stir. Put cover on pan for part of the time. Season well with salt and coarsely ground black pepper while frying. Perfect accompaniment for steak. Also wonderful for brunch or a he-man breakfast.

Rosie O'Grady Potatoes. Pile fluffy mashed potatoes in a buttered casserole. Cover very generously with coarsely grated sharp cheese. Bake uncovered in moderate oven for 15 minutes.

Thanksgiving Day Two-Toned Potato Casserole. On one side of a buttered casserole place mashed white potatoes; on the other side, mashed sweet potatoes. Dot with butter. Cover and heat. Sprinkle minced parsley on the mashed potatoes and grated orange rind on the sweets. Makes a pretty buffet vegetable dish.

Tiny Canned Potatoes. Cream drained canned small potatoes with a can of condensed cream of chicken soup and sprinkle with minced parsley or finely chopped pimento.

Small New Potatoes. Partially scraped, cooked in very little water. Serve with chopped chives, crushed thyme, and sour cream.

Vegetable Cutlets. Hubab from India. Mix ground or finely chopped green chili peppers, ginger, and fried onion with potatoes, peas, and cauliflower, which were boiled together and mashed. Add a bit of flour, if necessary. Fry cakes in hot oil. Serve immediately.

Whipped Potatoes, Pimento. Add a small jar of pimento pieces to hot mashed potatoes toward the end of the whipping.

RICE AND WILD RICE

Brown Rice with Pine Nuts. Sauté pine nuts (pignolia nuts) in butter until golden brown. Mix with cooked brown rice. Season to taste with salt and freshly ground black pepper.

Chicken Flavor. Use chicken bouillon instead of water to cook wild rice to be served with fowl or used for stuffing the bird. Also cook noodles this way for serving with poultry.

Quick Almond Rice. Mix a can each of condensed cream of mushroom soup and condensed cream of chicken soup. Pour over a casserole of quick-cooking rice mixed with slivered toasted almonds. Sprinkle more almond slivers on top. Bake for 35 to 40 minutes in moderate oven. Good served with a vegetable plate or with a chicken dinner.

Quick Fried Rice. Rinse and drain cooked fresh or leftover cooked rice. Heat oil in heavy skillet. Add chopped green onions, coarsely ground barbecued pork or shrimp, and the rice. Heat thoroughly, stirring constantly. Season with soy sauce and salt.

Rice with Croutons. Serve as a side dish with any casserole. Add a cupful of very small croutons, which have been sautéed in butter and toasted in the oven, to well-buttered cooked rice just before serving. Toss gently with two forks.

SALSIFY

Mock Oysters. To two cups of mashed cooked salsify, add 1 beaten egg, salt, paprika, and a little butter. Shape into small oval croquettes. Roll in dry bread crumbs. Place on buttered baking pan or tray. Bake until brown. Serve like fried oysters.

SAUERKRAUT

Boiled Sauerkraut. Add caraway seeds and, when almost done, add a finely grated raw potato or baking powder dumplings.

Philadelphia Sherry Sauerkraut. Bake sauerkraut for 3 hours with lean beef short ribs, 2 pounds smoked sausage, and thick slices of cored, but unpeeled, cooking apples. Sprinkle with 1/2 cup of sherry 15 minutes before done.

Vegetarian Baked Sauerkraut. Combine one can of sauerkraut, 1/4 cup of melted butter or oil, 1/4 cup of water, 3 quartered and cored apples, a small sliced onion, 1 tablespoon of brown sugar, 1/2 teaspoon of salt, and 1/2 teaspoon of caraway seeds. Bake in uncovered 1-1/2-quart casserole in moderate oven for 1-1/2 hours. Serves 6.

SPINACH

Blue Cheese Spinach Casserole. Hard cook several eggs. Make creamed spinach. Fold in 1/4 cup of coarsely crumbled blue or Roquefort cheese. Place alternate layers of the spinach mixture and sliced hard-cooked eggs in a buttered casserole. Top with toasted crumbs and a few more crumbles of blue cheese. This may be done the day before. Cover casserole. Bake for 20 minutes. Take cover off for the last 5 minutes to brown the cheese and crumbs, or slide under broiler for a minute.

Piquant Spinach. Add crumbled bacon and horseradish to buttered chopped, cooked spinach.

Spinach à la Hamburg. Serve cooked, chopped spinach with cheese sauce and croutons.

Viennese Spinach. Cook 1 package of frozen chopped spinach without added water. While the spinach is cooking, prepare a sauce by melting 2 tablespoons of butter and blending it with 2 tablespoons of flour, and 1/2 teaspoon of salt. Add 1/2 cup of sour cream. Cook until sauce is very thick, almost a paste. Add the cooked spinach and mix well.

Other Ways with Frozen Chopped Spinach. Cook and dress with chopped hard-boiled egg and minced onion; nutmeg-flavored cream sauce; a little horseradish sour cream; or crumbled bacon, warm lemon juice, and honey.

SQUASH

American Indian Dinner. Soak 1/2 cup of finely diced well-cooked salt pork overnight. Drain. Cook the diced pork until tender in 6 cups of fresh water with 1 cup of fresh lima beans and 1 cup of string beans cut in 1/2-inch lengths. Then add 1 cup of diced squash or pumpkin and, just before serving, add 2 cups fresh-cooked corn cut off the cob. Serve with Indian bread (corn bread) and sassafras tea sweetened with maple syrup. A good dish for the children, particularly Boy Scouts, with a story to go with it.

Baked Vermont Acorn Squash. Cut squashes in half and remove seeds. Butter cut sides. Place on an oiled baking tray and fill with equal parts of pure maple syrup and heavy cream. Bake until tender. If the liquid boils away, add more. Takes 1-1/2 hours usually, but well worth it.

Creole Baked Summer Squash. Make a stuffing of ground oysters, chopped spinach, crumbled cooked bacon, and toasted bread crumbs. Season with salt, freshly ground black pepper, and creole gumbo filé powder (pulverized leaves of sassafras). Mound the stuffing on halves of parboiled summer squash. Bake.

Fruit-Baked Squash. Fill baked acorn squash halves with plump grapefruit sections, sprinkle with light brown sugar, and broil to heat grapefruit and melt sugar. Serve with baked ham or fried chicken.

Meal in a Squash Shell. Mash and season baked acorn squash. Add leftover lima beans, corn, crumbled cooked bacon, cooked sausage or hamburger. Pile back in shell, sprinkle with grated cheese and bake until slightly browned.

Sausage-Stuffed Squash. Bake acorn squash until tender. Cut in half, remove seeds and loosen pulp but leave in the shell. Flavor sweetened applesauce or poached apples with cinnamon. Brown small balls of hickory-smoked sausage or small sausage links. Pile applesauce in the squash shells and top with the sausage balls or links. Bake until sausage is thoroughly cooked.

Summer Squash Circles. Pare squash and cut in 1/2-inch slices. Roll in cornmeal. Sprinkle with salt and pepper. Fry in oil. Serve piping hot.

SWEET POTATOES AND YAMS

Applesauce Nut Sauce for Sweet Potatoes. Place cooked halved yams or sweet potatoes in a buttered casserole. Sweeten applesauce with dark-brown sugar; add a bit of lemon juice, and a pinch of mace. Cover the potatoes with the applesauce mixture. Sprinkle generously with broken English walnuts. Dot with butter and bake in moderate oven for 35 to 40 minutes.

Festive Sweet Potatoes. Place slices of pineapple on a buttered cookie tray. Heap mashed sweet potatoes on pineapple. Top with a maraschino cherry dipped in pineapple juice. Broil 4 inches below heat for 5 minutes. Remove from pan with spatula.

Glazed Mashed Yams. In a mound of mashed yams, place 1/4 of a peeled banana. Drizzle top of banana with melted apricot jam, no water added. Bake on oiled cookie sheet.

Island Vegetable Bake. Interesting casserole for an outdoor buffet. Cut cooked yams and raw bananas in half lengthwise and arrange in a flat baking dish. Sauce: Mix 3/4 cup of frozen tangerine juice (prepared according to package directions), one grated onion, 1/4 cup of brown sugar, 1 teaspoon of salt, 1/4 teaspoon of nutmeg or mace, 2 tablespoons of butter. Pour sauce over yams and bananas and bake in moderate oven.

Orange-Candied Sweet Potatoes. Make syrup of 1 cup of light-brown sugar, 1/2 cup of orange juice, 2 tablespoons of water, and a dash of salt. Add cooked, peeled sweet potatoes and simmer or bake for 20 minutes, turning often.

Quick Yam Soufflé. To a casserole of mashed yams mixed with orange juice and butter, add a meringue made of 2 egg whites stiffly beaten with 4 tablespoons of sugar and grated orange rind.

Spiced Holiday Sweets. Arrange thickly sliced cooked sweet potatoes or yams in a buttered casserole. In a saucepan, cover equal parts of very thin unpeeled lemon slices and very thin onion slices with equal parts lemon juice and water. Sweeten to taste with molasses and brown sugar. (I prefer more brown sugar than molasses.) Add a dash of Worcestershire sauce, a pinch of powdered allspice and of cinnamon, a bay leaf and a few raisins. Thicken the sauce with cornstarch. Add butter, salt and pepper to taste and pour over the potato slices. Bake in a moderately hot oven until heated through.

Sweet Potato and Banana Casserole. In buttered casserole put alternate layers of cooked sweet potato slices, raw banana slices (both about 1/4-inch thick), and gingersnap crumbs. Dot generously with butter and pour 1 cup of boiling water on top. Bake covered for 30 minutes in a moderate oven. Remove cover and brown top before serving. Flaming rum may be poured over top to brown.

Sweet Potato Gems. Top individual mounds of mashed sweet potatoes with a canned pineapple chunk which has been coated with brown sugar.

Yam and Vegetable Platter. Peel boiled or baked yams and arrange on plate with cooked cauliflower and French-cut string beans. Serve with hot old-fashioned boiled dressing flavored with mustard.

Yam Casserole. Mash cooked yams with butter and orange juice. Bake in a shallow casserole or pile in orange shells and top with brown sugar, grated orange rind, and chopped walnuts. A must with the holiday turkey. (Can be prepared ahead of time.)

Yams Baked in Orange. Cut the tops off 6 navel oranges and scrape out pulp. Poach the shells in sugar syrup for about 5 minutes and drain. Fill with mashed yams whipped with butter, a little sugar, orange juice, and a bit of grated orange rind. Bake on a greased cookie sheet until lightly browned on top.

TOMATOES

Baked Tomatoes Supreme. Cut tomatoes in half. Grind (don't chop) fresh mushrooms, stems and all. Sauté the ground mushrooms in a little butter with a pinch of oregano and minced parsley. Add a dash of Worcestershire sauce and a few toasted dry bread crumbs. Pile on the tomato halves and bake in a moderate oven for 15 minutes, or until tomatoes are heated through. Serve on rounds of toast. Place 2 anchovies crisscross over each tomato. Garnish with watercress and a lemon wedge.

Broiled Tomatoes Rockefeller. Steam chopped spinach. Drain well. Mix with a few toasted bread crumbs, grated Parmesan cheese, garlic salt, and butter. Pile on tomato halves, sprinkle with more grated Parmesan cheese, and bake for 15 to 20 minutes, or until tomato is heated through and top is brown. May be run under broiler for a minute or two, if necessary.

Castilian Tomatoes. Cut large tomatoes in half and place in shallow baking pan. Sprinkle with salt, freshly ground black pepper, and crushed basil. Pile slices of green olives and slivers of ham on top of the tomatoes. Broil until ham is a bit crispy and tomatoes are well heated but hold their shape.

Fried Green Tomatoes. Slice thick, season with salt, pepper, and minced fresh basil. Dip in beaten egg and cracker crumbs and fry in equal parts of butter and oil.

Hot Raw Tomatoes, Chinese Style. Peel solid ripe tomatoes and cut in eighths. Bake an equal number of whole, thick-fleshed sweet green peppers in a hot oven for about 20 minutes to blister skin. Peel the peppers and cut in eighths. Make a sweet-and-sour sauce by thickening 1 cup of chicken stock, 1/2 cup of white vinegar, and 1/2 cup of honey with 4 teaspoons cornstarch. Season with 1 teaspoon of salt. Cook the peeled pepper pieces in the hot sweet-and-sour sauce for 1 minute. Add the peeled tomato pieces.

Pennsylvania Dutch Tomato Cakes. Season 2 cups of chopped canned whole tomatoes or fresh peeled tomatoes with 1/4 teaspoon of sugar, 1/4 teaspoon of salt, 2 tablespoons of chili sauce, and a dash of pepper. Work 1 tablespoon of butter into 1/2 cup of flour mixed with 1/2 teaspoon of baking powder. Or use prepared biscuit mix. Stir the crumbly mixture into the tomato mixture to make a stiff batter. Fry like pancakes. Serve with brown flour gravy. Excellent with sausages, kidneys, sweetbreads, or liver.

Tomato Frappé. Freeze fresh tomato juice and onion juice. Serve a scoop of the frappé in a sherbet glass with a bit of curry mayonnaise in center. For the mayonnaise, add a teaspoon of curry powder to 1/2 cup of mayonnaise. Makes a cool first course.

Summer Broiled Tomatoes. Slice tomatoes. Top generously with light brown sugar mixed with minced green pepper and onion. Pour a little cream over the top and broil until top carmelizes somewhat.

TURNIPS

Peas in Turnip Nests. Serve green peas in buttered, mashed turnip nests.

Poached Turnips. Cut thick slices of turnip. Poach in chicken broth, then thicken the broth with egg yolk.

Turnip Greens Piquant. Cook 4 slices of bacon until crisp. Drain. Sauté a chopped onion in the bacon drippings and add 1/4 cup of vinegar, 1 teaspoon of dry mustard, 1 tablespoon of sugar. Pour the hot sauce over cooked, chopped turnip greens.

Turnip Treat. Even children will eat turnips when they are steamed and mashed with an equal amount of mashed potatoes.

WILD GREENS

Weeds to Eat. Use Sorrel (field grass) to make cream of sorrel soup. Serve purslane with crisp and thinly sliced radishes and garlicky French dressing. Make a salad with young plantain and a curry French dressing, or cut the leaves—young milkweed stocks (when they are only 5 or 6 inches tall)—and cook as asparagus; drain and serve on hot toast with butter, cream sauce or mock hollandaise. Chop and steam young pigweed leaves and season with butter. Prepare a salad with marsh marigold, chopped, steamed, molded and chilled, and serve with horseradish cream cheese balls and tart French dressing.

ZUCCHINI

Baked Zucchini. Bake thick slices of unpeeled zucchini in canned tomato sauce with a pinch of basil, a bay leaf, a little olive oil, and salt and pepper.

Zucchini Pancakes. Mix paper-thin slices of unpeeled zucchini with equal parts Matzo meal or wheat germ and a slightly beaten egg mixed with 2 tablespoons of water. Season with salt and pepper. Drop by spoonfuls onto an oiled electric skillet set at 380° or a medium hot frying pan.

Salads

Chicken Salads

Apricot Chicken Salad. Add quartered ripe apricots to chicken salad. Garnish with fresh apricot halves filled with cream cheese thinned with horseradish.

Chicken and Cucumber Salad. Mix one part of chopped chicken with 1/2 part of diced cucumber, chopped walnut meats, and cooked small peas combined with French dressing. Garnish with pimento and chopped olives.

Chicken Bengal. Enhance chicken salad by adding a few tablespoons of chopped chutney and some curry powder (about 1 teaspoon to 2 cups of salad). Serve with additional chutney and that intriguing Indian bread, Puris, which is delicious when crisped and browned by frying. Offer bowls of peanuts, shredded coconut, and plumped raisins for those who want interesting flavors and textures.

Chicken Liver Salad. Cut peeled tomato petal fashion. Fill with chopped chicken liver pâté. Garnish with 2 thin slices of cooked bacon. Serve on a bed of endive with Russian dressing.

Chicken Mardi Gras. For a buffet supper or as the center of a cold luncheon plate. Pan fry whole breasts of frying chicken until so tender that meat falls off the bones, about 1-1/2 hours. Cool in the broth. Remove bones and skin and pat the breasts dry. Press breasts into shape and coat the rounded side thickly with the following: 2 parts of mashed cream cheese, 1 part of salad dressing or mayonnaise, fresh onion juice, grated lemon peel, and a dash of salt. Place each breast on a large slice of canned pineapple. Stud the chicken with toasted, blanched almonds and sliced, pitted black olives. Raw cranberry relish in a crystal dish beside a tray of these chicken breasts on the buffet is colorful and makes a perfect accompaniment.

Chicken and Rice Salad. Use 1 part of cooked chicken and 2 parts of cooked rice to make chicken salad. Garnish with cucumber slices and peeled, sliced tomato.

Chicken Salad Hawaii. Add pineapple chunks, slivered blanched almonds, and a dash of fresh onion juice to an all-white-meat chicken salad.

Club Chicken Salad. Add crumbled crisp bacon to chicken salad and serve on a thick slice of peeled tomato.

Cranberry Chicken Salad. Toss cubes of jellied cranberry sauce gently into a salad of shredded lettuce, chopped celery, and chicken. Serve with thin mayonnaise or boiled dressing poured over the tossed salad.

Exotic Chicken Salad. Combine 2 parts of diced chicken and 1 part each of sliced celery, water chestnuts, seedless grapes, and slivered almonds with salad dressing seasoned with a bit of curry powder and soy sauce. Serve mounds of the salad on Boston lettuce surrounded by drained canned whole lichee nuts.

Salad Bowl with Chicken. Add 1 cup of chopped chicken, slices of hard-cooked eggs, thin strips of green pepper, and quarters of peeled ripe tomato to a bowl of greens. Toss with French dressing seasoned with a teaspoon of curry powder.

Sherried Chicken Salad. Make a dressing of highly seasoned sour cream and sherry wine.

Sophisticated Luncheon Salad. Toss Boston lettuce, the tender inside leaves of French endive, and iceberg lettuce with slivers of chicken breast and sliced pitted black olives. Serve with the chutney version of French dressing. Low calorie but tantalizing.

𝒇ish Salads

Artichoke and Crabmeat Salad. Fill artichoke hearts with fresh lump crabmeat. Serve with Russian dressing. Garnish with pimento and sliced black olives. Try this with a cold turkey buffet or serve hot well-seasoned buttered noodles mixed with grated orange rind, orange juice, and ground walnuts.

Avocado Deluxe. Fill peeled avocado halves with lump crabmeat and sprinkle with fresh lime juice. Cover with finely chopped hard-boiled egg mixed with minced parsley. Serve on lettuce leaves with chunks of fresh or canned pineapple and a garlic-cream dressing on the side.

Cold Salmon Parisienne. Serve cold boiled salmon or large pieces of canned salmon with sauce made of salad dressing generously spiked with horseradish, mustard, lemon juice, and a dash of Tabasco.

Cucumber Dressing for Cold Salmon or Tuna Fish Salad. Add finely chopped and well-drained cucumber, lemon juice, salt, and paprika to stiffly whipped cream.

Epicurean Macaroni Salad. Cook and cool macaroni shells. Add minced parsley, chopped anchovies, freshly ground black pepper, and salt to taste. Toss in mayonnaise or salad dressing spiked with mustard.

Dinner Salad. Mix equal parts of large pieces of canned salmon, cooked green peas and cooked macaroni. Toss with a dressing made of mayonnaise, grated onion, and mustard. Chill thorough-

ly and serve on crisp greens with a garnish of hard-cooked egg
and lemon wedges.

Green Goddess Salad. Mix mashed avocado, sour cream, and mayonnaise in equal parts. Spike with a lot of grated onion, and
season well. Add some minced parsley and chives, if you like.
Arrange a variety of crisp greens in bowl. Top with baby California shrimp or Maryland lump crabmeat. Add Goddess dressing and you are in for a rich taste treat.

Italian Barbecue Salad Bowl. Mix equal parts of cooked shell macaroni, drained cooked garbanzos (chick-peas), and flaked tuna
fish. Season with capers, steamed white raisins, chopped dill
pickle, green onions, minced parsley, and crushed garlic. Dress
with mayonnaise thinned with red wine, to which you have
added sugar, chili powder, oregano, salt, and pepper. Heap in a
salad bowl lined with crisp greens. Garnish with stuffed green
olives and capers.

Low-Calorie Luncheon Salad. Combine equal parts of grapefruit sections and freshly cooked and peeled shrimp. Add 1/3 cup of
diced cucumber, 3/4 cup of finely diced celery, and a tangy
garlic French dressing. Serve on coarsely shredded lettuce accompanied by cheese-flavored crackers.

Mimosa Salad. Shred solid head lettuce on an old-fashioned slaw
cutter. Toss chopped hard-cooked eggs and minced chives with
the lettuce. Top with freshly cooked shrimp or lump crabmeat.
Serve garlic-sour cream dressing on the side. The salad may be
garnished with pitted black olives and peeled tomato wedges.

Modern Norwegian Herring Salad. Chop boiled potatoes, cooked
beets, and 1 large onion and place in a bowl. Finely chop 1 jar of
pickled herring and pour over vegetables. Set in cool place overnight to let flavors intermingle. Serve sour cream-mustard dressing on the side.

Oyster Salad. Cook a quart of oysters for 2 minutes only, in salted
water seasoned with tarragon. Drain. Cut in half with scissors.
Combine 2 cups of mayonnaise with 1 tablespoon of lemon juice,
1 tablespoon of anchovy paste, and 1 tablespoon of grated onion.
Mix half with the oysters. Slice a large bunch of celery very fine
and make a bed of it on a platter. Mound the oysters on top and

cover with the remaining mayonnaise. Garnish with anchovy filets and stuffed green olives.

Salad Supreme. Add drained, crushed pineapple, flaked tuna, and finely minced spinach leaves to the usual salad greens for a tossed salad. Sprinkle with curry powder and toss with a good French dressing.

Salmon Mousse. Garnish with crisp, scored cucumber slices and avocado cream in lemon halves. Avocado cream: blend equal parts of sour cream and mashed avocado. Season with lime juice, salt, and Tabasco.

Seafood Salad Dressing. Add chopped black olives and chopped dill pickle to half-and-half mayonnaise and catsup.

Shrimp-Macaroni Salad. Use cooked elbow macaroni and small whole shrimp in equal parts. Dress with sliced sautéed mushrooms, minced green onion, and a well-seasoned French dressing.

Shrimp Salad Antonia. Add chopped apple to creamy shrimp salad. Garnish with whole shrimp and thin wedges of unpeeled apple.

Sliced Cooked Fish. Use leftovers or fish cooked for this purpose. Arrange any sliced or cubed fish on coarsely chopped watercress with slices of stuffed green olives, minced anchovies, capers, the oil from anchovies, and quarters of lime. This makes a tasty treat, served with sesame-seed crackers and chilled white wine.

Tuna Avocado. Fill peeled halves of avocado with tuna fish salad. Top with chopped egg yolk. Garnish with watercress and crisp, unpeeled apple slice.

Tuna Fish Salad. Try adding chopped salted peanuts and lemon juice to tuna fish salad for added texture and flavor.

Frozen Salads

Frozen Pistachio Cheese Salad. Mix equal parts of Roquefort or blue cheese and cream cheese. Add a bit of lemon juice and salt and tint a pale green. Fold into whipped cream and add chopped pistachio nuts. Place in an attractive mold and freeze. Turn out on a round platter over a bed of watercress. Surround with fresh or canned pear halves, each containing a spoonful of mint jelly. This is an elegant buffet salad with any cold meat.

Frozen Tomato Crème. Soften 2 teaspoons of unflavored gelatine in 2 tablespoons of water and dissolve over hot water. Add 2 cans of condensed cream of tomato soup. Chill until partially set and fold in 1/2 cup of heavy cream, whipped. Freeze for 3 hours. Cut in cubes and serve on lettuce with stuffed green olives and small cream-cheese balls rolled in chopped nuts.

Old-Fashioned Frozen Salad. Add 1 teaspoon of salt and 4 tablespoons of mayonnaise to 1 large package of cream cheese. Mix with 4 tablespoons of crushed pineapple, 1/2 cup of chopped maraschino cherries, 1/2 cup of chopped pecans, and 3 mashed ripe bananas. Fold into 1 cup of heavy cream, whipped. Freeze in tray lined with waxed paper for several hours (not too hard). Slice and serve on Boston lettuce or leaf lettuce.

𝔉ruit Salads

Apple Slaw. No nuts, just Waldorf salad, made with coarsely shredded apples, grapes, and chopped celery. And a dressing of softened cream cheese thinned with unsweetened pineapple juice.

Avocado and Grapefruit Sections. Sprinkle with coconut, flavor with grenadine and orange peel, and serve on watercress or shredded head lettuce.

Avocado Cocktail Salad for Bridge Luncheon. Slice off both ends of small, well-formed, ripe avocados. Force the seed through the bottom hole and peel the avocado. You now have an avocado crown. Dip it in lemon or lime juice. Stand it upright on a leaf of lettuce and fill and surround it with a combination of diced vegetables, melon, fruits, chicken salad, or seafood salad. Serve an appropriate dressing on the side.

Avocado Cubes and Fresh Pineapple Chunks. Toss with romaine or Bibb lettuce, and serve with plain or garlic French dressing.

Make a garlic dressing with lime and lemon juice instead of vinegar for this delicate and flavorful salad.

Banana Luncheon Salad. Use equal parts of thickly sliced bananas and seeded Malaga grape halves. Add a generous portion of chopped fresh dates and broken pecans or walnuts. Serve in a lettuce cup with French dressing. For the children or the bridge club, a healthful and delicious treat.

Black Bing Cherry Salad. Not sweet and more elegant than a Waldorf salad. Remove pits from 2 cups of fresh black Bing cherries (large size). Add 1 cup of broken English walnuts, 1 cup of chopped celery, and moisten with cream-style salad dressing or mayonnaise. Serve in a lettuce heart.

Breakfast Salad. Arrange sliced, pared, and cored apple alternately with banana, sliced diagonally, on a bed of cereal flakes. Place a few chopped dates in center. Sprinkle a few seeded raisins over all. Serve with cream and honey or maple syrup.

Canned Pear Halves. Serve pear halves flat side down and pour whipped cream cheese or smooth whipped cottage cheese over them. Top with a dab of grape jelly and serve on watercress.

Cardamom Dressing for Fruit Salad. Add 1/8 teaspoon of powdered cardamom, 1 tablespoon of sugar, and 1 tablespoon of ground pecans to 1 cup of salad dressing thinned with lemon juice.

Children's Salad. Surround grated sweet apple, topped with red raspberries or blueberries, with halves of plums or apricots. Top with whipped cream sweetened with a bit of maple syrup.

Christmas Banana Salad. Cut banana lengthwise and place on a lettuce leaf. Mask with a thick dressing made of 3 parts of cream cheese and 2 parts of jellied cranberry sauce. Sprinkle with chopped pistachios.

Christmas Cranberry Salad from the Pantry Shelf. Place a slice of drained canned pineapple on watercress, top with a slice of jellied cranberry sauce, and sprinkle on a few chopped pistachio nuts.

Christmas Fruit Salad. Arrange a small nest of drained crushed pineapple on a lettuce leaf. Fill the nest with grapes, halved and seeded. Garnish with mayonnaise and slices of green and red cherries.

Christmas Grapefruit Salad. Arrange grapefruit sections alternately with pitted Bing cherries stuffed with blanched almonds. Serve with French dressing.

Christmas Wreath or Luncheon Salad. Using 1-1/2 slices of canned pineapple for each salad, form a large pineapple ring on a bed of crisp lettuce. Moisten a mixture of miniature marshmallows, diced canned peaches, and diced bananas with salad dressing and place in a mound in the center of the ring. Slice seedless grapes in half and place around the pineapple ring. Complete the wreath with a maraschino cherry bow. Cut the cherry almost in half, turn and cut almost in half the other way. Spread the sections out to form a bow.

Chutney Cream Dressing for Fruit Salad. Add finely chopped chutney and a few drops of lime juice to sour cream.

Cinnamon Apple Salad. Delicious with roast veal or pork. Poach small apples in syrup made from melted red-hot cinnamon candies. Turn over once during cooking; don't overcook. When cool, stuff the centers of the apples with cream-cheese balls rolled in ground salted nuts. Serve on a nest of crisp greens.

Elegant Pear Salad. Drain canned pears thoroughly. Fill each pear half with ripe Camembert cheese and mask with mayonnaise which has been mixed with slightly salted whipped cream. Sprinkle the top with chopped pistachios. Serve as a separate course after the meat and no dessert will be necessary. This is a quick and tempting salad for a special occasion.

Elegant Tossed Fruit Salad. Toss lettuce and endive with fresh pineapple cubes, strawberries, and bananas slices. Lime-honey French dressing accents the fresh fruit flavors.

Exotic Tossed Fruit Salad. Toss Boston or Bibb lettuce and watercress with fresh peach wedges, cantaloupe and honeydew balls, and orange sections. Use lime-juice French dressing with a few celery seeds added.

Five-Cup Fruit Salad. Mix the following together and let stand in refrigerator for several hours before serving: 1 cup of seedless oranges and 1 cup of fresh pineapple, both cut in chunks; 1 cup of canned shredded coconut, 1 cup of marshmallows cut in 1/4-inch pieces, and 1 cup of sour cream.

Flecks of Gold Salad. Steam dried apricots, then cut into thin strips with scissors. Add apricot slivers and some broken nut meats to cream-style cottage cheese. Serve on leaf of lettuce with drained Mandarin orange sections or fresh orange slices.

Fresh Fruit Salad with Coconut Dressing. Arrange peeled halves of fresh pears, bananas, sliced apples, sliced oranges, and pitted fresh dates. Top with a generous portion of coconut dressing made by folding a tablespoon of grated orange rind and 1/4 cup of shredded coconut into a cup of mayonnaise and adding 1/2 cup of whipped heavy cream.

Fresh Pear Waldorf Salad. Use chopped fresh pears instead of apples in Waldorf salad. Serve with Camembert or Brie and toasted crackers.

Fresh Ripe Pears in Eighths. Arrange on endive or watercress a fresh pear cut in eighths, seeded and halved Tokay or Malaga grapes, and tiny cream-cheese balls. Sprinkle generously with honey French dressing to make a refreshing and light fall dinner salad. (There is a wheel-shaped steel cutter that does a perfect job of cutting 8 equal sections of fruit.)

Fruited Melon Salad. Peel honeydew melon or cantaloupe. Place a thick slice on a lettuce leaf. Fill with thick (diagonal) slices of banana, apricot halves, and two strawberries or cherries.

Fruit-Nut Salad. Make balls of cream cheese mixed with ground dates, figs, blanched almonds, lemon juice, and salt. Place 4 balls and 1 or 2 whole radishes on a leaf of lettuce. Serve with a mustard dressing, made by adding 1 teaspoon of mustard to 1/2 cup of sour cream.

Fruit Salad Grenadine. Add grated orange and lemon rind and 1/4 cup of grenadine to a cup of French dressing. Serve on salad of grapefruit and orange sections and wedges of red Delicious apple.

Fruit Salad to Go with Duck. Combine segments or slices of seedless oranges (white membranes removed) with canned Bing cherries and marinate in French dressing. Toss the marinated fruit with crisp romaine or other lettuce and serve at once.

Fruit Salad with Boiled Dressing. Combine equal parts of Malaga grapes, pineapple pieces, sliced apples, and broken English walnuts with 1/2 part of seeded raisins and 1 large orange, cut up fine. Serve with Magic Lime Mayonnaise in lettuce cups. (Page 107.)

Ginger-Nut Dressing for Tropical Fruit Salad or Chicken Salad Hawaii. Add 2 tablespoons of finely chopped candied ginger, 1/4 cup of ground walnuts, and 1 teaspoon of honey to 1 cup sour cream.

Golden Pear Salad. Stuff a fresh (or canned) pear half with equal parts of finely grated carrot and cheddar cheese mixed with French dressing. Serve on leaf of lettuce or on shredded head lettuce.

Grape-Cluster Salad. In individual nests of head lettuce or romaine, place a spoonful of mayonnaise combined with chopped nuts. On top, place half a canned pear, thickly frosted with softened cream cheese. Arrange whole seedless green grapes or halved and seeded red grapes close together on the cream cheese so the finished pear will look like a miniature bunch of grapes. Insert a sprig of mint for the stem. A large plate containing these clusters in their individual lettuce cups makes a most appetizing salad for a buffet.

Grapefruit Sections. Marinate halves of Malaga grapes and halves of fresh walnuts in French dressing and serve on romaine. Refreshing with a rich dinner.

Holiday Fruit Salad No. 1. Arrange a slice of canned pineapple, peeled avocado rings, sliced banana, and halves of English walnuts on a lettuce leaf with tart French dressing.

Holiday Fruit Salad No. 2. Shred crisp head lettuce. Arrange in wreaths with tiny scoops of canned jellied cranberry sauce. Fill the center of wreath with a salad of fruits in season. For dressing, add 1/4 teaspoon of mint extract and a bit of orange juice to equal parts of mayonnaise and whipped cream.

Individual Fruit Bowls. Prepare grapefruit sections, spears of fresh pineapple, and quarters of banana (cut slightly on the bias).

Wash, dry, and hull some beautiful, large strawberries. Peel, core, and slice a Delicious apple. Dip the grapefruit in honey and then in freshly grated coconut. Dip the pineapple spears in cake frosting and then in freshly grated coconut. Dip the banana pieces in lemon juice and roll in ground pecans. Arrange the fruits in large brandy snifters or pile on shredded lettuce. No dressing is necessary, but, if served as a salad, a creamy whipped-cream dressing can be passed.

Island Magic Salad. Heap equal parts of papaya, banana, and fresh pineapple chunks in a fresh pineapple shell. Heat together equal parts of rum, corn syrup, and orange juice. Cool and pour over the fruits.

Lassie Fruit Salad Dressing. To 1 cup of salad dressing or mayonnaise add unsulphured molasses and lemon juice to taste. (Usually about 1/2 cup of molasses and 3 tablespoons of lemon juice to each cup of mayonnaise.)

Magic Lime Mayonnaise. Beat the following ingredients together, using a rotary beater: a can of sweetened condensed milk, 1/2 cup each of lime juice and oil, 1 egg yolk, 1/2 teaspoon of salt, a dash of Tabasco, and a teaspoon of dry mustard.

Minted Fresh Fruit Salad. Mix equal parts of orange and grapefruit sections (white membranes removed) with fresh pineapple cubes and miniature marshmallows. Marinate in French dressing flavored with 1/2 teaspoon of mint extract. Serve on leaf lettuce. Garnish with frosted fresh mint leaves. To frost leaves, cook thick sugar and water syrup. Cool till lukewarm. Dip washed and dried mint leaves in the syrup, shake, then dip in granulated sugar. Place on a buttered plate to harden. Don't flatten them out; let them curl a little.

Minted Fruit. Arrange your choice of fresh and canned fruits on lettuce. Serve with a dressing made by mashing 2 tablespoons of mint jelly with 1/4 cup of mayonnaise, folding the mixture into a cup of whipped cream. Makes enough for 6 individual fruit salads.

Papaya or Cantaloupe Salad with Lime. Peel and slice papayas or ripe cantaloupe lengthwise. Serve on a bed of finely sliced romaine, arranging the papaya slices in fan shape and placing a thin slice of lime, cut to center and twisted into "S" shape, at the bottom of each "fan." Serve with French dressing to which you have added some lime juice, chopped chives, and freshly ground white pepper.

Pear Miscellany Salad. Place half of a canned or fresh ripe pear on lettuce leaf. Fill center with frosted blueberries (made by stirring blueberries into slightly beaten egg white, shaking them in granulated sugar, and drying them on waxed paper). Place a spiced crabapple at the stem end of the pear.

Peeled Avocado Halves. Serve these on a bed of shredded lettuce with a lemon French dressing to which you add a bit of sugar, some sliced pickled onions, and a few Mandarin orange sections.

Prune-Apple Salad. Mix equal parts of uncooked, slivered dried prunes, finely chopped celery, and chopped apples. Moisten with creamy salad dressing, seasoned with a pinch of salt. Serve on lettuce leaf.

Quartette Fruit Bowl. Line large individual fruit bowls with romaine. Mark 4 sections in the bowl with half slices of fresh or canned pineapple, rounded side down. Arrange a different sliced or diced fresh fruit in each section. Fill the center with mayonnaise which has been folded into sweetened whipped cream.

Royal Carrot Salad. Mix equal parts of finely grated carrots and finely diced unpeeled apples with some minced celery, crushed pineapple, softened seedless raisins, and 1 sliced banana. Toss with a cream-cheese dressing and serve on a bed of romaine.

Stuffed-Apricot Dinner Salad. Stuff spiced, peeled apricot halves with cream cheese, thinned with orange juice and grated orange rind. Serve on bed of watercress.

Stuffed-Pineapple Salad. Quarter fresh pineapples, including green top. Scoop out the fruit and fill the shells with equal parts of mashed avocado and cottage cheese seasoned with plain or onion salt, chopped fresh chives and freshly ground black pepper. Garnish with cubes of the pineapple that was cut out of the shells.

Sunshine Health Salad. Place a slice of fresh pineapple on a bed of shredded head lettuce. Fill the center with freshly grated apple and top with ground almonds.

Tart Fruit Salad. Use grapefruit, pineapple, and watercress. For dressing combine 1/3 cup of sugar, 1 teaspoon of dry mustard, 1 teaspoon of salt, 1/2 teaspoon of scraped onion, and two tablespoons of vinegar. Blend well in mixer and gradually add 1 cup of oil, alternately, with 3 more tablespoons of vinegar. Then add 1 teaspoon of celery seeds. Delicious with a fish dinner.

Tokay Salad. Mix diced unpeeled apples and halved, seeded Tokay grapes. Moisten with mild salad dressing. Arrange in individual lettuce cups and cover each portion thickly with coarsely grated sharp cheese.

Tossed Fruit Salad. Use lettuce and chicory with cubes of unpeeled apple and diced celery. Add chopped pecans before tossing the salad in mayonnaise thinned with grapefruit juice. Tossed fruit salads are most refreshing for dinner in medium portions, and they make a satisfying, low-calorie lunch when served in king-size portions.

Tropical Salad. Use slices of pineapple and circles of avocado, marinated in garlic French dressing. Serve on watercress or romaine and sprinkle with freshly grated coconut.

Waldorf Slaw. Add finely chopped apples, minced celery hearts, broken walnut meats, and a little celery seed to creamed cole slaw.

White Christmas Salad. Mix equal parts of pitted oxheart cherries, cut marshmallows, and pecans with whipped cream. Serve in a mound on Boston lettuce.

Winter Fruit Salad. Combine grapefruit and orange sections (white membranes removed), seedless grapes, thick slices of banana and avocado, and a few bits of maraschino cherries. Blend gently with a boiled fruit salad dressing folded into whipped cream.

Jellied Salads

JELLIED CHEESE SALAD

Molded Blue Cheese Salad. Serves 8. Dissolve 1 package of lemon gelatine in 1 cup of boiling water. Beat in 1 cup of sour cream

and 1/2 cup of crumbled blue cheese. Chill until firm. Serve on a
bed of watercress.

JELLIED CHICKEN SALADS

Jellied Chicken-Cranberry Salad. Melt 1/2 teaspoon of unflavored
gelatine in 1 can of whole cranberry sauce, warmed. Set aside to
cool. Make jellied chicken salad, mincing or grinding the chick-
en. Put a layer of the chicken jelly in the bottom of a loaf pan.
When partially set, put the cooled cranberry sauce on top. When
that is set, pour the rest of the jellied chicken on top. Chill, then
slice thickly and serve on a bed of greens. Crisp hot rolls and
dessert make this a grand luncheon.

Jellied Ground-Chicken Loaf. Add 1 package of unflavored gelatine
to 3 cups of chicken consommé. Season well with salt and freshly ground white pepper. Add 1 tablespoon of lemon juice. Fold
in 2 cups of ground chicken, 1/3 cup of chopped black olives,
1/3 cup of ground blanched almonds, 1/4 cup each of chopped
celery leaves and minced parsley. Chill in loaf pan and slice to
serve.

Jellied Raw Cranberry Salad. Add 1 tablespoon of softened and
melted unflavored gelatine to 2 cups of raw cranberry relish.

JELLIED FRUIT SALADS

Avocado Ring. Dissolve 1 package of lime gelatine in 1 cup of boiling water. When it begins to set, whip and add 1-1/2 cups of
mashed avocado, 3 tablespoons of lemon juice, 1/2 cup of
mayonnaise-type salad dressing, and 1/2 cup of heavy cream,
whipped. Garnish with frosted green seedless grapes.

Chutney Aspic for Curry or Roast Lamb Dinner. Prepare 2 packages
of lime gelatine, substituting unsweetened pineapple and orange
juice for part of the liquid. Add two drained, 9-ounce cans of
crushed pineapple and 1 cup of chopped chutney. For dressing
thin mayonnaise with fruit juice spiked with finely grated orange
rind. Interesting for a buffet.

Easy Serve Jellied Salad. Break up lemon-flavored gelatine by turning a spoon through it several times. Place the broken gelatine on

a bed of greens and cover with seedless green grapes and a dab of mayonnaise.

Fruited Ginger Ale Mold. Prepare lime gelatine, using ginger ale for half of the required liquid. Add a drop of mint extract, canned pineapple chunks, and canned Mandarin oranges. Make a quick sour-cream dressing by mixing 3 tablespoons of frozen orange-pineapple juice concentrate and 1 teaspoon of finely grated orange rind into 1/2 cup of sour cream.

Fruit Salad in Mint Gelatine. Make lime gelatine, adding 1/2 teaspoon of pure peppermint extract. Add a large jar or can of fruits for salad (not diced fruit). Serve on a round platter with greens. Good with lamb.

Jellied Mandarin Orange Salad. Make lemon-flavored gelatine, substituting frozen orange juice concentrate for half of the liquid. When partially thickened, fold in drained Mandarin orange sections and chill until firm. Serve with banana mayonnaise made by adding mashed banana and drained crushed pineapple to mayonnaise and then folding in whipped cream.

Jellied Peanut Prune Salad. Stuff large prunes with orange marmalade and peanut butter. Arrange prunes in orange-flavored gelatine. When set, cut in squares, a prune in each square. Serve on lettuce with mayonnaise.

Jellied Waldorf Salad. Prepare 1 cup of lemon gelatine. When it begins to thicken, add 1 cup of finely diced ripe apples, 3/4 cup of finely minced celery, and 1/2 cup of finely chopped walnuts, paprika, salt and white pepper. When firm, serve on lettuce with whipped-cream mayonnaise.

Loganberry Jelly. Dissolve an envelope of plain gelatine in 1/4 cup of cold loganberry juice (available in cans or bottles). Mix with 1-3/4 cups of hot loganberry juice. Pour into individual molds and chill until set. Serve on a bed of watercress and garnish with a few fresh berries of any kind.

Molded Grapefruit Salad. Make lemon gelatine, using the juice from canned grapefruit sections as part of the liquid. When partially set, add 1 cup of finely diced unpared apple, the grapefruit sections, and a few broken walnut meats. Serve with mayonnaise, thinned with a small amount of the grapefruit juice.

Raspberry Ring with Cottage Cheese. Prepare two packages of strawberry gelatine with 2 cups of boiling water, 1-3/4 cups of cold water, and a package of frozen red raspberries. Pour into individual ring molds. To serve, fill the center with cottage cheese. Garnish with drained pineapple chunks.

Thanksgiving Buffet Salad. Pour cranberry jelly or jellied raw cranberry relish in a high ring mold. Fill the center with celery hearts or curls and ripe olives. Chill and unmold.

Walnut Dressing for Jellied Fruit Salad. Thin mayonnaise slightly with pineapple juice. Fold in whipped cream and chopped walnuts.

JELLIED MEAT SALADS

Jellied Corned Beef Salad. Add finely minced celery, chopped hard-cooked eggs, finely chopped cucumber, onion, and ground corned beef to lemon gelatine mix. (Use 1 tablespoon vinegar in the liquid.) Chill and serve with green pepper rings and cucumber.

Jellied Ham Salad. Melt two cans of tomato aspic. Cool. Add 1-1/4 cups of boiled, ground ham and 1 teaspoon of mustard. Chill and serve as a main course on a bed of greens, garnished with deviled eggs and stuffed green olives.

New Orleans Ham Mold. Heat a can of condensed chicken gumbo soup. Gradually add a 3-ounce package of cream cheese until blended. Add 2 teaspoons (1 envelope) of unflavored gelatine softened in 2 tablespoons of cold water. When mixture begins to thicken add 1 cup of ground ham and 4 tablespoons of mayonnaise-type salad dressing. Pour into mold and chill overnight. This is even more elegant with ground smoked turkey.

JELLIED VEGETABLE SALADS

Borscht Jellied Salad. Make lemon gelatine using equal parts of canned consommé, water, and beef juice for the liquid. Add 1 tablespoon of vinegar, a dash of salt and freshly ground black pepper. When partially set, fold in drained julienne-style beets, finely shredded cabbage, and a bit of grated onion. Serve with sour cream.

Christmas Aspic. Chill tomato aspic in star molds. Serve on salad plates with a tip of endive leaf and a strip of pimento extending from each point of the star. Put a dab of mayonnaise in the center of the star.

Holiday Salad. Chill a can of tomato aspic and serve with avocado slices and a Roquefort-sour cream dressing.

Jellied Asparagus Salad. Use canned asparagus cuts or cook frozen asparagus cuts. Make lemon gelatine, using 1 cup of boiling water and 1/2 cup of the asparagus juice. When it begins to set, add 1-1/2 cups of coarsely chopped asparagus, some minced celery, and ground green pepper. Good with a fish dinner.

Jellied Potato Salad. Make lemon gelatine with 1-1/4 cups of water and 3 tablespoons of vinegar or lemon juice. Marinate 4 or 5 sliced, boiled potatoes in highly seasoned French dressing. Mix with chopped celery, green peppers, and grated onion. Pour 2/3 cup of the gelatine in the bottom of a mold and arrange cucumber and radish slices in it in attractive fashion. Beat the remaining gelatine mixture until foamy and add marinated potato salad, including 1/2 cup of the marinade. Spoon the mixture over the decorated gelatine and chill until firm. Unmold on a bed of salad greens, garnish with hard-boiled eggs, and serve with mayonnaise.

Jellied Spiced-Beet Salad. Prepare gelatine by using 1 cup of boiling water, 1/2 cup of pickled-beet juice, 1/2 teaspoon of salt, 2 tablespoons of horseradish, 1/4 cup of cold water, 2 tablespoons of sugar, 1/2 teaspoon of onion juice. Fold in 2 cups of finely diced, drained, pickled beets. Chill. When firm, cut into small cubes. Serve several cubes on lettuce leaves and garnish with tiny whole pickled beets and mayonnaise.

Pineapple-Beet Relish Salad. Prepare one layer of lemon gelatine with drained crushed pineapple, and another layer of raspberry-flavored gelatine, using pickled beet juice as half of the required liquid. Fold in ground pickled beets, minced onion and celery, and a tablespoon of horseradish. Serve a slice of the jellied salad on lettuce or watercress, with mayonnaise.

Vegetable-Mint Jelly Salad. Prepare lime gelatine, adding 1/2 teaspoon of peppermint extract. When partially set, add 1 cup of finely minced celery, 1 cup of cooked frozen peas, and a few tablespoons of diced pimento. Serve with minted mayonnaise. Fine with lamb.

Zippy Buffet Salad. Prepare lime gelatine adding 2 teaspoons horseradish, 1/4 teaspoon of salt, 1/2 teaspoon of Worcestershire, and a couple of dashes of Tabasco. When gelatine is partially set, beat to a froth, pour into individual molds or a fancy small mold and chill. Garnish cold meat platter with watercress, molds of this salad, and sliced tomatoes or small whole peeled tomatoes.

Meat Salads

Avocado Duchess. Halve small avocados and scoop out pulp. Save the shells. Mix the pulp with cream cheese, lime juice, salt, and onion salt to taste. Stir in a generous amount of crumbled bacon. Fill the shells with this mixture, garnish with strips of pimento.

Boeuf Marinade. Marinate paper-thin slivers of lean, cooked roast beef for 24 hours in a sauce made of one part of red wine vinegar and 2 parts of pure olive oil, seasoned with garlic, mustard, basil, salt, and freshly ground pepper. To serve, sprinkle with minced parsley and chives (or minced green onion). Serve with a bowl of crisp relishes. Cold lamb is fine this way, using rosemary instead of basil.

Cold Meat Plate. Goose-liver pâté, tongue, chopped spinach and hard-boiled egg salad, sliced beefsteak tomatoes. Serve with Russian rye bread or pumpernickel and a green pepper circle filled with mustard.

Corned Beef Salad Meal. Put shredded head lettuce on dinner place. Arrange slices of corned beef, onion rings, slices of hard-cooked eggs (1 egg to a plate), slices of peeled tomatoes, and slices of boiled potatoes (which have been marinated with minced parsley in a highly seasoned French dressing). Pour over it a sauce made of equal parts of mayonnaise and sour cream seasoned with mustard, garlic salt, pepper, Worcestershire sauce, and lemon juice.

Double Devil Salad. Add a good portion of canned deviled ham and horseradish to French dressing and serve over a tossed green salad. Toss dressing thoroughly with greens. Top salad with julienne sharp cheese over one half and julienne boiled ham over the other half.

Dutch Lunch Plate for Patio. Use giant-size chop plate or hors d'oeuvre tray. Arrange a large mold of potato salad in the center of a generous amount of leaf lettuce. Surround with cole slaw and sliced liverwurst. Make an outer circle of thick slices of dill pickle, sliced tomato, and tiny sweet pickles alternated with bon-bon cups of mustard. Serve with slices of buttered dark rye bread. Guests may help themselves from the large salad platter, or you may serve them.

Grape and Sweetbread Salad. Combine 2 parts diced, cooked sweetbreads with 1 part seedless grapes, some diced celery, and slivered blanched almonds. Mix lightly with a cup of mayonnaise, which has been combined with 3/4 cup of heavy cream whipped and slightly salted. Serve in lettuce cups garnished with a tiny bunch of frosted, seedless grapes.

He-Man's Plate. Use thoroughly chilled oval serving platters or individual steak platters. Arrange crisp leaves of romaine to form about 8 or 9 cups on the plate. Fill end cups with spears of baked ham; two side cups with spears of sharp cheese; another two cups with asparagus spears vinaigrette; two cups with cooked peas, chilled and marinated in vinaigrette. Place a few crisp radishes and olives in a lettuce cup in the center and place 2 halves of deviled egg on each side of the center cup. Serve with hot garlic bread, cut on the diagonal. Serve mustard-sour cream dressing separately.

Hot Macaroni Salad. To cooked macaroni, add pickle relish, chopped crisp bacon, minced onion, green pepper, and celery. Toss in dressing made of equal parts mayonnaise and chili sauce, spiked with dry mustard and a bit of Worcestershire. Heat in double boiler.

Meal-in-a-Dish Potato. Mix 6 medium-size cooked potatoes, 3 boiled eggs, 1 medium-size cucumber chopped, 1 small jar dried beef cut fine, and 1 small onion chopped fine. Cover with a spicy boiled dressing.

Picnic Cole Slaw. Add 1 cup each of chopped cold tongue and ham, 1 green and 1 red pepper, ground, and 2 ground green onions to one head of shredded cabbage. Moisten with a cup of mayonnaise which has been folded into a stiffly beaten egg white and sweetened with 1 tablespoon of sugar.

Sun Deck Fruit Platter. Using large platter or hors d'oeuvre tray arrange banana ham rolls (halves of banana dipped in orange juice and rolled up in a thin slice of boiled or baked ham). Put peeled wedges of honeydew melon and cantaloupe alternately on two sides of the platter, deviled eggs on the other two sides of the platter, and mounds of pineapple chunks and strawberries in between. Serve with sesame seed crackers.

Vegetable Salads and Dressings

Cooking Tips: Peeling Tomatoes. To peel easily, spear with a big cooking fork and hold over a flame for a few seconds, turning constantly, then peel immediately. This is much quicker than the usual dipping in boiling water.

Perfect Salads: The greens must always be served crisp and dry. Wash thoroughly in cold water several hours before serving. Drain them and then dry by placing in a clean muslin bag, pillow slip, or plastic bag. Keep the bag of damp greens in the refrigerator until serving time.

Ideal Accompaniment: Sesame Wedges, listed alphabetically in the Vegetable Salads section.

Unusual Dressing: Sour Cream-Garlic Dressing, also listed alphabetically in this section.

Apple Relish. Mix equal parts of finely chopped, unpared apples, finely grated cabbage and minced celery. Dress with chopped green pepper, chopped pimento, and a sauce of equal parts sugar and lemon juice spiked with ginger, dry mustard, salt, and white pepper.

Asparagus Salad. Cut romaine in fine shreds and on it arrange eight asparagus tips. Serve with a dressing of mayonnaise, generously laced with lemon juice and horseradish. Garnish with Greek black olives and sweet red pepper rings or pimento rings.

Asparagus Slaw. Toss finely shredded cabbage and diced tender asparagus tips with a dressing of half sour cream and half mayonnaise. Sprinkle with finely minced parsley.

Avocado Anchovy Salad. Combine 1/2 pint of sour cream and three 1-ounce packages of cream cheese with a squeeze of lemon or lime juice. Add cubes of avocado and bits of anchovies. Serve on watercress. Elegant.

Avocado-Artichoke Salad. Marinate cooked artichoke hearts and avocado rings in French dressing. Combine with Romaine lettuce. Garnish with a slice of peeled lime.

Avocado-Asparagus Luncheon Plate. Arrange watercress on the side of a plate. Arrange a peeled half of avocado, 4 or 5 asparagus spears, and several slices of tomato beside it. Fill the avocado half with Russian dressing spiked with horseradish, fresh or jarred.

Avocado-Cucumber Tossed Salad. Toss romaine, minced celery, cucumber, peeled and diced, avocado diced in 1/2-inch cubes, and grated Parmesan cheese with garlic French dressing made with oil and equal parts of lemon juice and red wine vinegar.

Avocado Slaw. Add a mashed ripe avocado, a little lemon juice, crumbled blue cheese, and a generous spike of herb seasoning mix to your creamed cole slaw. Serve for lunch in peeled whole tomato cut in quarters to form a flower.

Bacon and Egg Salad. Add 4 sliced, hard-cooked eggs and 4 slices of crisp crumbled bacon to salad greens. Toss with garlic French dressing. Garnish with green onions, radishes, celery sticks, and peeled tomato wedges.

Barbecue Slaw. Toss finely shredded cabbage, finely minced onion, and lots of crumbled bacon, with salad dressing thinned with a little lemon juice and spiked with freshly ground black pepper.

Beet Salad. To a head of shredded cabbage add 1/3 part of finely grated beets and some chopped onion. Toss with dressing made of 1/2 cup of sour cream mixed with 1 tablespoon each of lemon juice and sugar. Season with salt and pepper.

Beet-Nut Salad. Mix 1 can of drained, julienne beets with 1 can of drained, crushed pineapple. Add 1/2 cup of crushed walnut meats and 2 tablespoons each of lemon juice and sugar. Serve on shredded lettuce. Top with salad dressing. Fine with roast chicken dinner.

Black Diamond Salad. Toss shredded head lettuce, thinly sliced green onions, Mandarin orange sections, small pitted ripe olives, and small flowerets of parboiled cauliflower with tarragon-flavored French dressing.

Black Olive and Apple Salad. Toss chunks of black olives and diced unpeeled red apple with a dressing of half mayonnaise and half French.

Black Olive Relish Salad. Delicious with meat. Mix 1 can of sliced or chopped ripe olives with 1/2 cup of mayonnaise, 2 tablespoons of chili sauce, 1 chopped pimento, and 1/4 cup of chopped celery. Serve on lettuce.

Brussels Sprouts Salad. Add minced parsley and hard-boiled egg to Russian dressing. Pour over cooked, drained, and cooled Brussels sprouts. Serve on a bed of romaine and garnish with black olives and pimento.

Buffet Bean Salad. Use 2 parts of cooked whole green beans to 1 part of cooked lima beans. Cool and drain thoroughly. Mix with two thinly sliced green onions, some thinly sliced celery hearts, and a generous portion of pimento strips. Toss gently with Italian dressing and chill overnight. Turn once or twice in the marinade. Serve in lettuce cups. Garnish with stars cut out of whole pimentos.

Buffet Salad. Chilled canned tomato aspic sliced 1/2-inch thick, garnished with watercress and quartered deviled eggs makes an attractive and tasty buffet salad to serve with chicken à la king.

Canned Tomato Aspic. Serve slices of canned tomato aspic with tiny balls of sharp cheese on endive or watercress for a quick and eye-appealing salad.

Cantonese Chef's Salad. To a can of drained Chinese vegetables, add minced green onions, ground green pepper, thinly sliced radishes, and chopped black olives (about 1/4 cup each). Marinate in highly seasoned French dressing (on the tart side). Serve in peeled tomatoes cut in petal shape.

Carrot and Nut Balls. Prepare equal parts of finely grated carrots and ground almonds moistened with mayonnaise. Form into balls. Serve on crisp lettuce leaves with black olives.

Carrot and Peanut Salad. Finely grate carrots and hold together with equal parts of salad dressing and peanut butter. Top with ground raisins and halves of peanuts.

Carrot Salad. To finely grated carrots add finely chopped celery and softened seeded raisins. For dressing, soften cream cheese to desired consistency with canned pineapple juice or orange juice.

Cauliflower Slaw. Same as cole slaw but use finely shredded raw cauliflower with sour-cream dressing, seasoned with caraway seeds, minced green onion, and minced celery leaves.

Charlotte's Confetti Potato Salad. To potato salad add green pepper, pimento, celery, green olives, parsley, and green onion, all finely minced. Also, thinly sliced radishes, 2 tablespoons of sweet pickle relish or minced sweet pickle and finely crumbled crisp bacon.

Cheese and Black Olive Salad. Blend 2 cups of dry cottage cheese with 1 cup of chopped black olives and 2 tablespoons of horseradish. Bind the mixture with French dressing and shape in a long roll. Chill. Slice and serve on watercress with whole black olives.

Cheese Nut Salad. Put a mound of well-seasoned cottage cheese on a lettuce leaf. Make a hollow in the center and fill it with cubes of jellied cranberry sauce. Garnish with halves of walnuts or pecans.

Cheese Salad. Mix equal parts of slightly cooked and drained frozen peas, diced celery, and cubed mild yellow cheese. Toss with Thousand Island dressing and bite-size pieces of lettuce. Serve on a lettuce leaf and top with wedges of peeled tomato.

Chutney Cole Slaw. Add 2 tablespoons of chopped chutney to each 2 cups of old-fashioned sour-cream cole slaw.

Club Cole Slaw. Add 1 each of red and green sweet pepper, ground, and 1 cup of drained pineapple tidbits to 1 head of finely grated cabbage. Sprinkle with 1/4 cup of sugar and 1 teaspoon of salt. Let stand in refrigerator for half an hour or more. Mix 1 cup of mayonnaise, 2 tablespoons of lime juice, 1/2 teaspoon of dry mustard, and 1 teaspoon of celery seeds. Add dressing to marinated cabbage.

Cole Slaw. With fish, serve cole slaw to which you add minced parsley and chopped, crisp seeded cucumber.

Colorama. Toss romaine, green pepper rings, pimento strips, finely grated carrot, red radish fans, green and black olives with mayonnaise spiked with horseradish. To make radish fans, slice radish (not all the way through) and drop into cold water so fans can spread.

Combination Fall Vegetable Salad. Place a mound of cottage cheese in the center of a large plate. Surround with mounds of raw beets, raw potato (peeling and all), cucumber, and raw carrots, all grated. Sprinkle seedless raisins and chopped dates over all and serve with a cream-cheese or sour-cream dressing.

Combination Tossed Salad. Combine shredded lettuce and minced parsley with peeled tomato diced, finely slivered green pepper, green onions, celery leaves, watercress—all chopped. Toss with garlic croutons and garnish with sardines, hard-boiled eggs, and black olives. Use a lemon, oil, and fresh tarragon dressing.

Combination Vegetable Potato Salad. Combine equal parts of chopped boiled potatoes, cooked string beans, finely grated carrots, and 1/2 cup of grated raw turnip. Mix with boiled dressing or salad dressing. Garnish with watercress and red radish roses or fans.

Combination Vegetable Salad. Top shredded lettuce, chopped green pepper, green onions, celery, watercress, and parsley with shredded Swiss cheese and chopped hard-boiled eggs. Garnish with sardines and peeled tomato quarters. Use a dressing of olive oil, lemon juice, and tarragon-flavored wine vinegar.

Cooked Spinach Timbale Salad. Mix 2 cups cold, cooked, well-seasoned frozen chopped spinach with four finely chopped hard-cooked eggs and some chopped chives, or finely minced green onion. Press the mixture into timbale molds and chill. Remove from the molds and place on a lettuce leaf garnished with slices of hard-cooked eggs, sliced tomatoes, and pickled beets. Serve with mayonnaise or French dressing.

Cooked Vegetable Buffet Salad. Boil a few large carrots, a head of cauliflower, and a bunch of broccoli in separate kettles of salted water. Separate the cauliflower and broccoli heads into flowerets. Cut carrots into balls or diagonal 1/2-inch thick slices. Marinate vegetables separately overnight in a vinaigrette dressing. To serve, line a bowl or platter with crisp greens and arrange the vegetables with an eye to color and design. Sprinkle with more vinaigrette dressing.

Corn Slaw. Add a can of drained whole-kernel corn and finely diced red apple to cole slaw made with boiled dressing.

Cosmopolitan Salad. Wash, drain, and dry equal parts of romaine and crisp spinach. Sprinkle with chopped anchovies, sesame seeds, some fresh dill and tarragon (or a pinch or two of the dried herbs, if the fresh are not available), and crumbled blue cheese. Toss the salad with French dressing.

Cottage Cheese Stuffed Tomato. Peel a tomato, and cut four ways almost to the bottom. Fill with cottage cheese and sprinkle toasted almonds on top. Serve on shredded lettuce. Healthful and nutritious.

Cranberry Tossed Salad. Add 1 cup of coarsely ground and slightly sweetened fresh cranberries to a tossed green salad. Serve with garlic French dressing spiked with a bit of mustard.

Crisp Dinner Salad No. 1. Place leaves of romaine on salad plate, then two thick slices of peeled beefsteak tomato. Top with shredded endive. Serve with Thousand Island or well-seasoned French dressing.

Crisp Dinner Salad No. 2. Serve half and half coarsely chopped watercress and finely chopped or shredded fresh spinach with a sweet-and-sour dressing. Sprinkle crumbled bits of warm, crisp bacon on top.

Curried Avocado Rings. Peel and halve avocados. Enlarge the seed cavity by scooping out some of the avocado. Brush halves with lemon juice. Make a filling of 2 parts cream cheese and 1 part blue cheese, seasoned with curry powder, salt, Tabasco, grated lime peel and juice. Add 3 tablespoons each of chopped black olives and chopped nut meats. Pack cheese mixture into the avocado halves, press halves together and wrap in foil. Chill. To serve, cut stuffed avocado into 6 slices, crosswise. Place on crisp greens, and garnish with grapefruit sections. Serve with a tart French dressing.

Curried Cooked Vegetable Salad. Try the curry powder version of French dressing on a cooked vegetable salad made by marinating a cup each of sliced, cooked (but not overcooked) carrots, cooked cauliflower flowerets, and a can of sliced broiled mushrooms.

Curried Rice Salad. Toss 2 cups of chilled, cooked rice with shredded green pepper, strips of pimento, plump seedless raisins, chopped parsley, and minced green onion (or chives). Chill thoroughly. Just before serving, toss lightly with garlic French dressing spiked with 1/2 teaspoon curry powder, salt, and freshly ground black pepper.

Daisy Chain Supper Salad. To potato salad, add broken walnut meats, diced pimento, and finely chopped celery. Pack in a loaf pan and unmold in the center of a large platter. Arrange 1-1/2 to 2 pounds of assorted cold cuts on lettuce around the loaf. Frost the top of the loaf with mayonnaise and garnish with cheese flowers and parsley or watercress. To make cheese flowers, cut slices of mild American cheese with large cookie cutter to form the petals. A small ball of sharp cheese in the center completes the flower.

Delectable Cucumbers and Radishes. Toss thin slices of cucumbers and radishes with an equal amount of coarsely chopped head lettuce. Dress with salad dressing thinned with pineapple juice and flavored with a pinch of curry powder—just enough to impart a delicate, mysterious flavor.

Delicate Tossed Salad. Mix 2 parts of shredded lettuce and 1 part of coarsely chopped watercress. Add diced peeled tomato and diced avocado. Toss with garlic dressing made with equal parts of lime juice and olive oil, well seasoned.

Easter Egg Salad. Shape cream cheese into small "eggs." Roll some of them in finely minced chives and some in paprika. Leave some plain. Serve one of each in a nest of chopped watercress and coarsely shredded head lettuce moistened with a sharp French dressing.

Egg and Olive Relish Salad. Top finely shredded lettuce with sliced hard-cooked eggs, sliced black olives, and chopped chives. Use a lemon and oil dressing lightly flavored with onion juice or crushed garlic.

Emerald Cooked Vegetable Salad. While still warm, combine equal parts of cooked green beans cut in 1-inch pieces, Fordhook lima beans, and cooked peas with chopped green onions, minced fresh mint, and a garlicky French dressing. Add 1/2 teaspoon of creole gumbo filé powder (pulverized leaves of sassafras). Chill for several hours, mixing gently 2 or 3 times. Makes a lovely buffet salad with cold lamb, ham, or beef.

Endive Salad, Dutch Style. Wash endive and dry. Mix with boiled dressing and freshly fried squares of bacon. Doubly good if the boiled dressing is heated before pouring over the endive. (This endive is called curley endive or chickory.)

Fall Dinner Salad. A mound of finely grated raw beets served on crisp watercress with garlic dressing is colorful and refreshing.

Fancy Potato Salad. Add chopped green onions, celery, black olives, walnuts, parsley, and pimento to the potatoes before adding dressing.

Field Salad. Mix rugala (a green that is sometimes called lamb's tongue), watercress, Bibb lettuce, and coarsely chopped endive. Serve with a dressing of olive oil and white wine vinegar, highly seasoned with salt, freshly ground pepper, and a little dry mustard.

Finger Salad. Stuff celery with cottage cheese seasoned with caraway seeds. Add carrot sticks, radish roses, and unpeeled cucumber slices to make a tempting low-calorie finger salad. The fancy cucumber slices are a breeze. Just run a dinner fork lengthwise down the cucumber and then slice.

French Dressing, Variations on. To 1 cup of French dressing, add any of the following: 1/2 teaspoon of chili powder and lime juice (Mexican); 1/2 teaspoon of curry powder; 3 tablespoons of

Roquefort or blue cheese; 1 tablespoon of horseradish; 2 table-spoons of chili sauce and 1 tablespoon of honey; 1/2 teaspoon of mustard, 3 tablespoons of chopped stuffed green olives, and 1 teaspoon of chopped parsley; 2 tablespoons of finely chopped chutney and 1 teaspoon of celery seed; 2 tablespoons of mashed cranberry sauce. Try the chili powder and lime juice version with tossed salad of leaf lettuce, escarole, and chicory and cubes of avocado, wedges of tiny peeled tomatoes, and sliced stuffed olives.

Fresh Herb Salad. Use cooked vegetables. Separately marinate po-tatoes, green beans, and beets, all diced, in a spiked dressing. To serve, combine the potatoes and beans with mayonnaise and put them in a salad bowl lined with lettuce or curly endive. Drain the beets and put them on top of the beans and potatoes. Sprinkle with finely chopped hard-boiled egg, chopped chives and fresh dill. Serve with thin rye bread sandwiches of cream cheese and anchovies.

Fruit and Vegetable Plate with Chutney Cream Dressing. Put a gen-erous mound of cottage cheese on crisp lettuce leaves. Arrange pineapple slices, banana chunks, avocado slices, apple wedges, asparagus spears, tomato wedges, and cucumber slices alternate-ly around the cottage cheese. For dressing use sour cream, spiked with finely chopped chutney or mincemeat, mayonnaise, and Tabasco sauce. Also a dash of salt.

Garden Salad. Mix equal parts of finely grated raw carrot, shredded cabbage, and chopped celery. Add some cucumber chopped fine and a few crisp radishes sliced thin. Toss with Russian dressing.

Gazpacho (South American Salad Soup). Mix a can of condensed consommé with 1/4 cup of wine vinegar, 1/3 cup of olive oil, 2 cans of tomato sauce, 1/4 teaspoon of Tabasco. Grind, using coarse blade: 1 clove of garlic, 1 onion, 2 cucumbers, 2 peeled tomatoes, and half a green pepper. Sprinkle salt and freshly ground pepper on the vegetables. Add to the liquid and chill thoroughly. Serve in small bowls with an ice cube in each. Hot garlic bread goes well with this.

Green-and-Gold Salad. Cook peas and carrots, slice stuffed olives, chop green pepper, and score cucumber slices (pare cucumber very thin, score lengthwise with a fork, then slice). Serve with boiled dressing.

Green Bean Salad Bowl. Toss whole cooked green beans and anchovy filets with cut-up crisp greens. Sprinkle with minced onion and celery. Combine sour cream, sugar, salt, coarsely ground pepper, and capers and spoon over salad. Garnish with bundles of whole beans, slices of egg, and anchovy on top.

Green Herb Salad. Use equal parts of leaves of endive and lettuce or rugala. Sprinkle with freshly chopped tarragon, parsley, basil, and dill. Dress with olive oil, white wine vinegar, salt, and freshly ground pepper. This bland salad is delicious with creamed dishes or rich stews.

Green Salad with Herring Dressing. Add chopped fresh dill to crisp greens. Toss with bite-size pieces of herring filets in wine or sour cream.

Guacamole Dinner Salad. Marinate diced, firm, peeled tomatoes with slivered celery and sliced pitted black olives in a well-seasoned garlic French dressing. Marinate an equal amount of avocado cubes in lime juice. To serve, place a spoonful of the avocado cubes in a small lettuce cup and cover with a spoonful of the tomato-olive mixture and some of the marinade.

Head Lettuce Salad. To separate head lettuce for cups, core and run cold water into the opening. Drain thoroughly and serve with Thousand Island dressing made from equal parts of prepared sandwich relish spread and chili sauce. Chopped hard-cooked egg can be added to the dressing or the salad can be garnished with sliced hard-cooked egg.

Health Carrot Slaw. Mix equal parts of finely grated carrots, ground walnuts, and finely diced unpeeled apple. Moisten with boiled dressing or mayonnaise.

Health Salad. Mix together finely grated raw beet and finely grated raw unpeeled potato. Combine finely grated carrot and cabbage. Then cottage cheese and chives. Form these mixtures into attractive mounds and sprinkle chopped parsley, minced celery, and softened raisins over all. Garnish with 4 stuffed dates and a dab of yogurt or sour cream.

Hearts of Palm Salad. Serve romaine lettuce, avocado rings, and hearts of palm with French dressing. Add chopped pimento to the dressing.

He-Man Salad with Steak. Peel and quarter tomatoes with sliced red onions or even a juicy sweet Bermuda onion and marinate in well-seasoned olive oil and vinegar.

Herb Salad. Combine chopped mint, chopped chives, sage, and minced parsley and serve with tender dandelion leaves. Arrange grated beet root in center with a dollop of softened cream cheese and a stuffed olive.

Horseradish Cream Dressing. Mix 1 cup of whipped cream with 1 cup of mayonnaise. Add 1/4 cup of horseradish, 1 tablespoon of sugar, and 1/2 teaspoon of Worcestershire sauce. Good on sliced cucumbers or shredded cabbage.

Hot Lima Bean Salad. If you like hot potato salad made with a vinegar, brown sugar, and mustard dressing poured over the diced potatoes, you'll be pleased with a hot lima bean salad. It is made the same way, except that cooked large dry lima beans are substituted for the potatoes. Serve with grilled frankfurters for a hearty after-the-game supper.

Hot Slaw. Shred cabbage fine and put in a pan with a bit of butter over a slow flame until thoroughly heated. Add equal parts of lemon juice and sugar, seasoned with salt, celery seed, freshly ground white pepper, and minced parsley and stir until thoroughly mixed and well heated. Serve immediately.

Italian Mushroom and Lima Bean Salad. Mix equal parts of cooked Fordhook lima beans and freshly cooked sliced mushrooms together with a bit of finely chopped onion, minced parsley, and half a teaspoon of oregano. Marinate in a tangy garlic French dressing. Serve on greens garnished with thinly sliced onion rings.

Italian Style Salad. Marinate oranges, onion rings, and peeled tomato slices in French dressing. Serve on bed of finely chopped greens. Top with a few rolled anchovies.

Japanese Salad. Arrange a raw broccoli floweret (marinated in bland French dressing), a radish fan, a mound of molded crabmeat salad, and a mound of thin sliced cucumber on each salad.

Lettuce and Watercress Salad. Toss lettuce and watercress sprigs with pickled beets, onion rings, and small flowerets of cauliflower. Oil and wine vinegar with freshly ground black pepper and salt add zest to this salad.

Low-Calorie Blue Cheese Salad. On a bed of coarsely chopped watercress, pile a mixture of cottage cheese and lumps of blue cheese on thinly sliced crisp cucumbers. Stick wedges of black olives and slices of pimento-stuffed green olives in the mound. Garnish with sprigs of watercress.

Luncheon Salad. Mix equal parts of cooked peas, toasted broken salted pecans, and a generous amount of chopped pickle relish, held together with salad dressing or mayonnaise. Serve in lettuce cups garnished with strips of pimento.

Macaroni Cream Slaw. Add equal parts of cooled cooked macaroni and shredded cabbage to your sour-cream cole slaw recipe. Also add thinly sliced green onions, some finely grated carrot, and slivered green pepper. Use plenty of freshly ground black pepper.

Main-Dish Green Salad. A main-dish salad without meat or chicken, but substantial. Mix your choice of greens (watercress improves the flavor) with anchovy filets, hard-cooked egg wedges, peeled tomato quarters, and cubes of avocado. Add crumbled blue cheese to French dressing.

Mexican Potato Salad. Add whole-kernel corn, ground green pepper, chopped pimento, and chili powder to potato salad. Serve with hot chili peppers.

Mustard-Butter Cole Slaw. Combine 1 teaspoon of mustard, 1 teaspoon of granulated sugar, 1/2 teaspoon of salt, 6 tablespoons of butter in saucepan and heat. When smooth, add 2 teaspoons of lemon juice. Pour over finely grated green cabbage.

Near East Salad. This is a perfect accompaniment for lamb. Thoroughly wash and drain your choice of greens. The dressing is equal parts of lemon juice and pure olive oil, well salted and peppered. Sprinkle minced fresh mint or crumbled dried mint over the greens. Top with black olives (the big ones) and peeled, quartered tomatoes. To make the salad really elegant, add some luscious herb-stuffed baby eggplants.

New Potato Salad with Herbs. Cook new potatoes, then peel and slice while hot. Season with garlic French dressing, chopped chives, and fresh tarragon. Serve on bed of crisp lettuce while potatoes are still warm. Good on a cold meat plate.

Orange and Asparagus Salad. Alternate green asparagus spears and orange segments on lettuce leaf. Decorate with slices of stuffed olive or pimento strips. Serve with French dressing.

Pineapple Slaw. Add 1/2 cup of drained crushed pineapple to 3 cups of finely shredded crisp cabbage. Moisten with mild salad dressing or boiled dressing spiked with a bit of lemon juice.

Potato Salad Cups. Fill custard cups with potato salad. Turn out on a salad plate. Frost with mayonnaise and garnish attractively with pimento, olives, hard-cooked eggs, or capers.

Potato Salad 1800. Add minced anchovies, sweet basil, chopped parsley, and chives to creamy potato salad.

Potato Salad with Snappy Cream Dressing. Chop potatoes, onions, hard-cooked eggs, and cucumbers. Mix 2 parts of sour cream with 1 part of mayonnaise and flavor with a yellow mustard and a generous sprinkling of poppy seeds. This dressing is also good on cold meat or cabbage salad.

Potato Salad with Sour Cream. Stir 2 tablespoons of tarragon vinegar and 1 teaspoon of salt into a cup of sour cream. Add coarsely ground black pepper. The addition of chopped fresh tarragon makes this really delicious. Pour dressing over about 2 cups of thin tomato wedges and onions sliced in rings.

Pumpkin Salad Bowl. For a fall buffet cut the top off a pumpkin, scoop out the seeds and membrane, and hollow out pulp. (Pulp can be cooked for old-fashioned pumpkin pie or cooked, mashed, and buttered and served as a vegetable.) Line shell with cabbage leaves and fill with Waldorf salad, cole slaw, or Waldorf slaw.

Quick Garlic Cream Dressing. Mix frozen lemonade concentrate with sour cream. Season with salt, freshly ground black pepper, and crushed garlic. Great on sliced cucumbers with onions.

Radish Supreme Salad. Add 1 part sliced, salted, crisp red radishes to 4 parts boiled potatoes sliced and sautéed (not browned) in butter with salt and freshly ground black pepper. For dressing, use sour cream, sprinkled with sugar and thinned with vinegar.

Raw Mushroom Salad. Slice fresh, white mushrooms very thin. Mix with an equal amount of sliced celery hearts. Add lemon juice and 2 chopped hard-boiled egg yolks to French dressing. Mix mushrooms, celery, and dressing and serve on leaf lettuce with chives sprinkled over the top.

Raw Spinach Salad No. 1. Chop 6 hard-cooked eggs, 1 pound raw of spinach, and 2 green onions very fine. Moisten with salad dressing or mayonnaise.

Raw Spinach Salad No. 2. Sprinkle a teaspoon of salt over chopped spinach. Turn into a salad bowl with 2 tablespoons each of lemon juice and olive oil. Toss lightly. Sprinkle with 1/2 cup of chopped salted pecans, a tablespoon of raw wheat germ, and freshly ground black pepper. Serve at once.

Raw Vegetable Salad California Style. Cover a slice of head lettuce with marinated, sliced carrots, beets, and cucumbers and with half an avocado filled with green peas and French string beans marinated in a tangy garlic dressing. Crumble blue or Roquefort cheese over all if desired.

Roast Pepper Salad. Bake whole sweet green or red peppers in hot oven for about 20 or 30 minutes until the skin blisters. Peel and seed. Cut in eighths, lengthwise. Serve with crisp sweet onion rings on shredded lettuce with an oil and wine vinegar dressing seasoned with salt and freshly ground black pepper.

Roquefort Cream Dressing No. 1. Use 1 part cream cheese and 2 parts Roquefort or blue cheese. Blend the cheeses and thin to desired consistency with French dressing.

Roquefort Cream Dressing No. 2. Add crumbled Roquefort, a dash of Worcestershire, and a pinch of salt and raw sugar to equal parts of mayonnaise and buttermilk.

Salad Boheme. Toss equal parts of watercress and celery cabbage with a spicy herb French dressing and hard-cooked eggs, chopped anchovies, chives, and marjoram. Garnish with small whole pickled beets and anchovy filets.

Salad in a Crystal Bowl. Interesting first course or buffet salad. Make tomato juice ice cubes with well-seasoned tomato juice spiked with a dash of wine vinegar. Prepare thin slices of scored cucumber and slices of solid, peeled tomatoes and lemon cut in wedges (1 side of each lemon wedge dipped in minced parsley). At serving time, crush the tomato ice cubes and pile them in a handsome crystal bowl. Arrange the cucumbers, tomatoes, and lemon wedges on top. Sprinkle with chopped chives or parsley. Serve French dressing in a separate bowl.

Salads for the Buffet. Serve an assortment of individual salads in wooden or Chinese bowls. Each bowl should have a border of parsley or watercress—some filled with thinly sliced pickled beets and onions with hard-boiled egg slices; some with cold cooked lentils in French dressing, topped with minced green onion and walnut bits; and some with cooked green peas with capers and anchovies in lemon French dressing.

Sauerkraut Salad. Drain a can of sauerkraut and chop. Add drained pineapple chunks. Place a mound of the mixture in the center of a peeled tomato cut in quarters petal fashion. Serve on a large leaf of romaine. Top with a spoonful of mayonnaise and sprinkle with chopped chives. Fine for health food buffs.

Sesame Wedges. Soft and fresh in a crispy jacket as a salad accompaniment. Cut top and side crusts from an unsliced loaf of white bread. Place on an ungreased baking sheet and cut zigzag into 8 wedges, *almost to the bottom crust*. Blend equal parts of sharp cheese spread and butter with a few drops of Tabasco. Spread between wedges and over top and sides of loaf. Sprinkle with sesame seeds. Tie string around sides. Bake in moderate oven for 20 minutes.

Sour Cream-Garlic Dressing. Mix 1/2 cup each of mayonnaise and sour cream. Gradually stir in 3/4 cup of garlic French dressing. Add a squeeze of fresh lime and some seasoning mix.

Southern Crisp Green Salad. Grind together 1/2 small head cabbage, 2 green and 2 red bell peppers, 4 small carrots, 2 dill pickles, 3 stalks of crisp celery, and 2 crisp, tart apples. Add 1 cup of black walnut meats. Mix with tart French dressing or mayonnaise. Top with grated cheese and crumbled crisp bacon. Old-time recipe.

Spicy Tomato-Potato Salad. Add slightly cooked and drained frozen peas, celery, and minced onion to diced potatoes. Mix with dressing made of equal parts of French dressing, tomato sauce, and mayonnaise, well spiked with Tabasco and seasoned with salt to taste.

Spinach Salad. Serve sliced pickled beets and slices of hard-cooked eggs on a bed of finely shredded raw spinach. Top with a dab of mayonnaise or boiled dressing.

Spinach Slaw with Celery Seed Dressing. Mix equal parts of finely shredded cabbage, shredded raw spinach, and chopped celery. Toss with French dressing to which is added catsup, celery seed, and a crushed clove of garlic.

Spring Salad. Season cottage cheese with onion juice, Worcestershire sauce, and slivered almonds or Brazil nuts. Toss the mixture with watercress, leaf lettuce, and sliced radishes. Additional French dressing may be served with the salad. Garnish with radish roses and green onions.

Sprout Salad. Prepare a salad of fresh bean sprouts, or cooked frozen bean sprouts, minced onion, chopped pimento, and vinaigrette sauce. Serve on a lettuce leaf. An elegant and unusual accompaniment for roast beef or steak.

Stuffed Avocados à la Mexico. Cut avocados in half. Scoop out almost all the pulp and mash with lime or lemon juice. Add peeled and diced tomato, finely minced green onion, minced green hot chili pepper, salt, olive oil, and 1/2 teaspoon of ground coriander. Stuff the shells and serve on lettuce with a wedge of lime or lemon (one side of the wedge dipped in paprika).

Stuffed Cabbage Buffet Salad. Remove outside leaves of a large head of new cabbage and place them around the edge of a large round platter. Remove the heart of the cabbage head and make a well-seasoned slaw by grating the piece taken out. Place cabbage head in the center of the plate and fill with the slaw. Arrange small celery hearts, carrot sticks, radish roses, and green and red pepper rings on the cabbage leaves. Put small green stuffed and black olives on picks and stick in the sides of the stuffed cabbage head.

Sunburst Potato Salad Platter. Mold cottage cheese potato salad in springform pan and turn out in the center of a large platter. Place a mound of chopped egg yolk in the center and arrange sardines in a circle around it. Then arrange chopped egg white around the edge of the mold. Press minced parsley into sides of the mold and arrange cucumber and tomato slices alternately to make the last circle in the sunburst. Serve with sherry mayonnaise.

Sweet-and-Sour Cucumbers. Pare cucumbers very thinly so that only the waxy outer coating is removed. Score lengthwise with fork before slicing thinly. Add several green onions that have been sliced thinly to form miniature onion rings. Marinate in dressing of equal parts lemon juice and sugar, well-seasoned with salt, pepper, and celery seed. This same dressing also makes a delicious grated cabbage slaw.

Sweet Potato Salad. Elegant with cold sliced turkey or chicken. Dice cold boiled or baked sweet potatoes and add drained pineapple chunks, chopped celery, and giant, whole pecans. Moisten with mayonnaise or salad dressing.

Sweet-Sour Kidney Bean Slaw. Good picnic or patio salad. Drain and chill 1 can of red kidney beans. Toss with 3 cups of shredded cabbage, 1/4 cup of sweet pickle relish, 1/4 cup of thinly sliced green onions or chopped chives, 1/2 cup of plump golden raisins, 1/2 teaspoon of celery seed, and a cup of Russian dressing.

Tomato Asparagus Salad. Serve a fairly thick slice of peeled beefsteak tomato on a bed of coarsely shredded head lettuce. Garnish with canned green asparagus spears and a sprig of parsley. Dress with a mixture of equal parts mayonnaise and chili sauce.

Tomato Roquefort Dressing. Combine 4 tablespoons of Roquefort or blue cheese, 1/4 cup of chili sauce, 1/4 cup of olive oil, 1 tablespoon of lemon juice, 1 teaspoon of Worcestershire, 1/2 teaspoon of dry mustard, salt, pepper, and paprika.

Tomato Rose Salad Deluxe. Stuff small, whole peeled tomatoes with chopped black olives and minced celery mixed with salad dressing. Mold pink-tinted cream cheese in a teaspoon and place around sides to form rose petals. Garnish center with chopped egg yolk.

Tomato Stuffed with Artichoke Hearts. Peel small tomatoes. Hollow out center. Sprinkle inside and out with salt, pepper, and crushed dill weed. Place a cooked artichoke heart in the hollowed-out tomato and mask with a thick sour cream-mustard dressing flavored with curry powder. Sprinkle top with paprika. Save the scooped-out tomato centers for another dish.

Tomato Towers. Peel uniform-size tomatoes and cut each in 3 thick slices. Reassemble, top down, with an egg salad or tuna fish salad filling between the slices. Skewer and put a pitted black olive on each toothpick. Arrange tomatoes on lettuce laid out in a circle a little larger than the tomato towers. Several tomato towers on a large platter make an attractive buffet salad.

Tossed Bacon Salad. Toss equal parts of chopped fresh spinach and shredded head lettuce with chopped, crisp bacon, chopped egg whites and a sweet-and-sour French-style dressing. Then sieve the yolks of the hard-cooked eggs over all just before serving.

Tossed Cheese and Corned Beef Salad. Toss greens with slivers of very sharp cheddar cheese and corned beef in a garlic-flavored French dressing.

Tossed Meat Salad. Toss iceberg lettuce and chicory with cubes of ham and turkey or chicken. A French dressing sharpened with horseradish and a dash or two of Tabasco makes an intriguing accent.

Touch-of-Avocado Potato Salad. Use about 1/4 part of cubed avocado to 3 parts of potato in potato salad.

Turnip Cole Slaw. Make the same as sour-cream cole slaw, substituting finely grated small turnips for shredded cabbage.

Turnip-Stuffed Tomato Surprise. Peel tomatoes and hollow out. Chop the scooped-out core with celery, walnuts, and minced parsley. Add an equal part of finely grated raw turnip. Moisten with mayonnaise and refill the tomatoes. Serve on a bed of watercress.

Variety of Salad Greens. Chinese or celery cabbage, young raw spinach, cabbage, young dandelion greens, celery tops, chicory or American endive, watercress, romaine, Belgian or French endive, escarole, turnip greens, mustard greens, young Swiss chard, young beet greens, iceberg lettuce, head lettuce, Boston lettuce, Bibb lettuce, rugala.

Vegetable Bouquet Buffet Salad. In the center of a large plate covered with shredded lettuce place a whole cooked cauliflower. Arrange slices of cooked carrots around the cauliflower, then a circle of pepper relish (made by chopping together one green pepper, a bunch of green onions, and some parsley). Make another circle of tiny pickled whole beets and, finally, around the outside, arrange small leaves of Boston lettuce filled with cooked green peas. Serve with lemon mayonnaise or salad dressing. Be sure to have water well salted while cooking the vegetables.

Waldorf Sweet Potato Salad. Use 2 parts of diced cooked yams, 1 part of chopped apple, 1/2 part of broken walnut meats. Combine with salad dressing or mayonnaise thinned with frozen lemonade concentrate.

Western Way Salad Bowl. Your choice of greens mixed with chunks of avocado and diced chicken, topped with crumbled bacon and large pieces of blue cheese.

White Christmas Salad. Mix one cup of shredded raw cauliflower with 1/4 pound of blue cheese and 1/2 cup of sliced stuffed olives and toss with French dressing. Serve on a small bed of chopped watercress.

Zucchini Boat Salad. Parboil small whole unpeeled zucchini in salted water for about 5 minutes. Cut the zucchini in half lengthwise and scoop out centers. Lay the zucchini cut side up in a shallow dish; cover with French dressing, spiked with oregano; add slices of onion and halved cloves of garlic. Cover the dish tightly and refrigerate for 24 hours. To serve, remove onion and garlic and discard. Save the liquid for dressing a tossed green salad. Serve the zucchini halves, hollows filled with diced peeled tomato and topped with a spoonful of salad dressing sprinkled generously with fresh grated Parmesan cheese.

Sandwiches

Cooking Tip: When packing sandwiches with moist fillings, don't lay them flat in the lunch box. Stand them on edge and they will not soak the bread.

Cold Sandwiches

Anchovy and Cheese on Rye. Mix chopped anchovies with cream-style cottage cheese. Pile on thin slices of buttered dark rye bread. Garnish with watercress.

Chicken Bengal. Grind one cup of cooked chicken and 3 tablespoons of chutney. Moisten with a bit of mayonnaise and season with curry to taste. Make a sandwich on fresh white bread. Trim crusts. Serve on plate with watercress, chilled Mandarin orange sections, and pineapple chunks sprinkled with fresh lime juice.

China Girl Sandwich. Mash tuna and mix with chopped canned water chestnuts, held together with equal parts of chili sauce and mayonnaise. Serve on toast with salted almonds or peanuts and tiny sweet pickles on the side.

Club Sandwich Plate. Set a cup of hot soup in the center of a large service plate. Arrange quarters of club sandwiches around the cup. In between the quarters use a garnish of watercress, a whole spiced apricot, a radish rose, a pickle fan, and a small stuffed celery heart.

Confetti Cream Cheese. Add crumbled cooked bacon and chopped green olives to cream cheese thinned to spreading consistency with mayonnaise.

Diet Delight Sandwich. Make an open-faced sandwich of tongue, lean roast beef, or poached fish on 1 slice of protein bread, spread thinly with equal parts of mustard and yogurt. Serve with a hard-cooked egg, crisp relishes, and a glass of buttermilk.

Easy-to-Make and Easy-to-Eat Variety Sandwiches. (Can be frozen.) Mix equal parts of soft butter and cream cheese and spread thickly on both slices of sandwich bread as the base spread for the following mixtures.

    Chopped nuts and chopped olives.

    Chopped pimento and chopped rolled anchovies.

    Canned tuna fish and chopped mustard pickle.

    Finely grated raw carrot and orange.

    Mashed liverwurst and chopped pecans.

    Chopped chicken, chopped almonds, chopped raisins.

    Ground ham or corned beef and chopped dill pickles.

    Ground lamb and fresh chopped mint, parsley, and chives.

    Ground cheddar cheese and caraway seeds.

    Deviled ham, chopped mustard pickle, and mashed egg yolks.

    Peanut butter and crumbled bacon.

    Peanut butter and raisins.

    Mashed kidney beans and chopped dill pickle.

    Any cold roast meat and/or cheese sprinkled with salt and freshly ground black pepper.

Friday Club Sandwich. Cover 2 slices of white toast with crabmeat, shrimp, or tuna fish salad. Spread top with salad dressing. Top with a slice of Swiss cheese and a third slice of toast spread on underside with Russian dressing.

Frozen Sandwiches from Leftovers. Use ground cooked roast beef, lamb, pork, veal, or chicken, moistened with a bit of gravy and seasoned with grated onion and Worcestershire sauce. May be thawed and heated in a hot oven.

Hearty Lunch. Dip a salmon patty in cracker crumbs and beaten egg and brown in butter. Place on buttered hamburger bun. Serve with tartar sauce, pickled egg, and beets.

He-Man Ham Salad Sandwich. Make a generous bowlful. Mix equal parts of extra-sharp cheese spread and coarsely chopped baked ham. Season with minced onion, mustard, Worcestershire, and Tabasco. Serve with a plate of buttered dark rye bread and a bowl of radishes, celery hearts, and olives.

Lamby Pie Sandwiches. Grind leftover lamb. Add a few tablespoons of grated Parmesan cheese. Moisten with mayonnaise or salad dressing. Season with mustard, horseradish, salt, and pepper.

Lunch Box Extras. For a cold spicy dish in the lunch box, try any of these treats, packed in waxed paper-covered cups: Baked beans with bologna cubes; corned beef hash topped with hard-cooked egg salad and sprinkled with paprika; chili con carne thickened with added ground cooked meat topped with shredded lettuce and diced tomato (Mexican style); macaroni shells and minced clams in a rémoulade sauce, sprinkled with extra cubes of sharp cheese and several tiny sweet pickles. As an added treat include a covered paper cup of mustard pickles or pickled beets tucked in with hearty corned beef or tongue sandwiches on rye bread.

Mike's Club Sandwich. Cut a large, soft onion roll in half. Place a slice of sharp cheese, a slice of smoked turkey, a slice of tomato, and a slice of sweet onion on the roll. Serve with a bottle of cold beer.

Nut Bread Sandwiches. Make with jellied cranberry sauce as the filling. Good with hot chicken soup.

Pineapple Club Sandwich. Substitute a sautéed pineapple slice for the tomato slices in the traditional club sandwich.

Sandwich and Split Pea Soup. Serve hot split pea soup with a sandwich on dark pumpernickel bread made of equal parts of liverwurst and cream cheese mashed together and highly seasoned. Garnish with crisp radishes.

Shrimp Savory. Combine a jar of pimento cheese spread with a bit of chili sauce. Add 1 can of shrimp, mashed. Make a sandwich on fresh white bread. Trim crusts. Serve on Boston lettuce with peeled tomato slices, scored cucumber slices, and green onions, with a tart French dressing.

Smoked Turkey and Mushroom Sandwich. Watercress, sliced tomatoes, and sliced, scored cucumbers. Place sliced turkey on buttered round of toast or toasted English muffin. Mask generously with small whole button mushrooms in a sour-cream sauce seasoned with a bit of scraped onion and freshly ground pepper.

Walnut Salmon Salad Sandwich. Add chopped toasted English walnuts to salmon salad. Make an open-faced sandwich by spreading a piece of toast with butter and mayonnaise, and adding a leaf of lettuce, a thick slice of peeled tomato, then a mound of the walnut salmon salad. Top with a dab of salad dressing and a toasted walnut half.

SANDWICHES WITHOUT MEAT

Avocado and Pure Old-Fashioned Peanut Butter. Serve on a whole wheat bun with a leaf of romaine. A small tossed salad may be served with this sandwich.

California Sandwich. Mix 2 parts of chopped cooked prunes with 1 part of chopped English walnuts and a bit of orange marmalade, adding a squeeze of lemon juice. Spread between buttered slices of whole wheat bread.

Crisp, Crunchy Lunch-Box Accompaniments. Pack an apple and walnut halves, celery hearts, 2 or 3 pitted black olives strung on a thin carrot stick, and a thin wedge of crisp raw cabbage.

Lunch-Box Dessert. Include a spicy gingerbread square, split and filled with cream cheese and orange marmalade. On the side, a ripe pear.

Double Sandwich. Spread horseradish and mustard between 2 slices of cheese. Put the filled cheese slices between buttered slices of bread.

Goat Cream Cheese. Put a thick slice of goat cream cheese on whole wheat bread or on a whole wheat bun spread with whipped sweet butter. Top cheese with steamed muscat raisins and broken (not chopped) English walnuts.

Peanut Butter Fruit Sandwich. Combine equal parts of ground seedless raisins, ground dates, peanut butter, and cream cheese. Spread generously between slices of whole wheat bread and add a crisp green lettuce leaf.

Shoe-Box Lunch. Shoe-boxes make handy disposable lunch boxes for motor trips. Use one for each person, and put his or her name on it. You can enclose a plastic knife, fork, and spoon with individual salt, pepper, and sugar packets as well as a tea bag, powdered cream, and an envelope of instant coffee. A small can of fruit juice can be brought and chilled along the way. For refreshers, cut a tomato into quarters, or a peeled or unpeeled navel orange into sections. Fit them together again tightly and wrap in foil or pack in a plastic sandwich bag.

Shredded Cheese Sandwich Filling. Mix coarsely shredded cheddar cheese with chopped nuts, sliced stuffed olives, and salad dressing.

DAINTY COLD SANDWICHES

Crown Jewels Tea Sandwiches. Cut an equal number of whole wheat and white bread slices into 1-1/2-inch rounds with doughnut cutter. Remove the centers and butter the slices. Fill the whole wheat sandwiches with chicken salad, placing a dab of cranberry jelly in the hole. On white bread sandwiches use ground lamb salad, placing a dab of mint jelly in the hole, or use ham salad, placing a dab of apricot jam in the hole.

French Pastry Party Sandwiches. They look like individual French pastries but are hearty sandwiches. For each you will need 2 slices of buttered thin-sliced bread, crusts removed. Cut each slice in half and spread with salad dressing. Make two small oblong sandwiches, one with a thin slice of tomato the other with a small lettuce leaf. Spread the top of the tomato sandwich with a generous amount of creamy pimento cheese spread or ground smoked turkey salad. Place the lettuce sandwich on top of the cheese spread sandwich, forming a miniature 4-layer stack. Frost each stack with whipped thinned cream cheese and garnish with stuffed olive slices. Serve on lettuce with radish roses and black olives.

Horn-of-Plenty Sandwiches. Spread thin slices of bread, crusts removed, with soft butter. Roll into cornucopias and fasten with toothpicks, cover with a damp cloth and chill. Just before serving fill with crabmeat salad and garnish with a sprig of watercress. Serve two on a salad plate.

Pinwheel Sandwich Fillings. Blend cream cheese with soft butter. Combine equal parts of this mixture and any of the following: crisp bacon bits and chopped chutney; minced smoked turkey; or minced clams flavored with fresh onion juice.

DAINTY SANDWICHES WITHOUT MEAT

Apple Snack Sandwiches. Cut firm, juicy unpeeled apples into rings. Cover with soft cheese spread and sprinkle chopped salted nuts on top.

Avocado Pineapple Rounds. Spread rounds of fresh whole wheat bread with a mixture of mashed avocado, drained crushed pineapple, fresh lime juice, and a bit of salad dressing. Garnish with a flower made of slivers from a slice of pineapple.

Banana Fingers. Cut bananas in half lengthwise and spread with peanut butter softened with a bit of honey or marmalade.

Brandy Tea Tidbits. Serve thin slices of fruit cake filled with a thin layer of brandied hard sauce or marzipan filling.

Canned Date-Nut Bread Sandwiches. Fill sandwiches with cream cheese and chutney or thinly sliced bananas with mayonnaise.

Exotic 3-Decker Finger Sandwich. Use sweet butter. Spread one thin slice of bread, crust removed, with ground crystallized ginger, mixed with honey. For the second slice use coarsely ground black walnuts. Top with a third slice of bread, buttered side down, and cut into 4-inch finger strips. Place half an English walnut on each finger when served.

Feast-of-the-Gods Tea Sandwiches. Cream cheese, ground nuts, and chopped olives.

Fruity Tea Sandwiches. Grind raisins or any uncooked, dried fruit. Moisten with orange juice or sherry wine, if necessary. Add an equal part of broken nuts. Butter bread (white or whole wheat) and spread generously with the mixture. Remove crusts and cut into triangles.

Ginger Cream Tea Sandwiches. Moisten one 3-ounce package of cream cheese with a bit of cream. Add 2 tablespoons of chopped crystallized ginger and some finely ground almonds. Make sandwich with fresh white bread. Trim off crusts and cut each sandwich into 4 triangles.

Merry-Go-Round. Spread nut bread rounds with pineapple and cream cheese spread. Place a thin slice of green olive in the center, radiate several thin strips of pimento from stuffed olive to edge of sandwich like the spokes of a wheel.

Orange Butter for Nut Bread Sandwiches. Mix 2 parts of sweet butter with 1 part of orange marmalade.

Orange Pecan Spread Tea Sandwiches. Soften one 3-ounce package of cream cheese with a bit of cream. Add a dash of salt, 2 tablespoons of ground candied orange rind, and 1/3 cup of finely chopped toasted pecans. Spread on white bread. Trim off crusts and cut in 4 squares.

Peanut Lettuce Rolls. Fewer calories. Spread crisp lettuce leaves with peanut butter. Roll up and fasten with toothpick. Eat as you would a rolled sandwich.

Pistachio Cheese Sandwiches. Combine equal parts of mashed avocado and cream cheese, seasoned with onion salt and freshly ground white pepper, and spread over open-faced rounds. Top with finely chopped pistachio nuts.

Relish Sandwiches. Spread thinly sliced fresh white or whole wheat bread with a mixture of equal parts of soft butter and cream cheese. Roll a tiny tender nib of celery, a small green onion, a sprig of parsley, a carrot curl, or a lengthwise slice of green pepper in each slice. Place seam side down on waxed paper in refrigerator. Cover with a damp cloth or aluminum foil.

Roquefort Pecan Sandwich. Soften 2 parts of cream cheese to 1 part of Roquefort cheese with a bit of cream. Add generous portion of broken toasted walnut or pecan halves. Make sandwich with fresh wheat-germ bread. Trim crusts. Cut in four finger lengths.

Sweet Tea Sandwiches. Cut buttered bread in small fancy shapes. Fill with chopped English walnuts and ground raisins; dates and grated lemon rind; or make open rounds, spread with peanut butter and slivers of dates pressed down in pinwheel fashion; dates and chopped blanched almonds; mashed egg yolks and ground sweet pickles; or chopped watercress and ground figs.

Hearty Hot Sandwiches

Banana Nut Grilled Sandwich. Spread whole wheat toast generously with peanut butter and cover with sliced bananas. Top with 1/2 slice of thinly sliced bacon. Broil until bacon is crisp. Serve open or with another slice of toast. Mugs of hot tomato juice go well with these sandwiches.

Broiled Shrimp Salad Sandwiches. Split hamburger buns, toast on cut side, butter, and spread with a generous portion of shrimp salad. Top with grated cheese and broil. Serve with cole slaw, sliced tomatoes, watercress, and potato chips.

Chuckers. Rub a small chuck steak with garlic. Cut into small cubes and put on small skewers. Wrap in bacon strip and broil. Serve in a split, warm hoagie bun with steak sauce and a mixture of sautéed chopped onions and chopped mushrooms.

Elegant Turkey Cream. Place thin slices of buttered toast on cookie tray. Add several cooked asparagus or cooked broccoli spears, then a slice of white turkey meat. Cover with sauce made of a can of condensed cream of chicken soup spiked with 2 tablespoons of sherry. Sprinkle generously with grated Parmesan cheese and bake in moderate oven for 20 minutes or until cheese bubbles.

Fiesta Buns. Moisten chopped cooked turkey dark meat with heated spaghetti sauce. Season with Worcestershire sauce and chili powder. Fill split frankfurter buns generously. Wrap in foil and bake in a hot oven for about 15 minutes. Serve with shredded lettuce and tomato.

French Toast Sandwiches. Make a sandwich with your choice of spread. Dip in egg and milk mixture as for French toast. Sauté or grill sandwich on both sides in butter or oil. Try salad mixtures of tuna, salmon, chicken, or ham made this way.

Grilled Devils. Mix grated cheddar cheese and deviled ham to fill a sandwich. Butter the outside of it and grill.

Grilled Ham and Swiss Cheese with Sour Cream-Mustard Sauce. Place a slice of baked or boiled ham and a slice of Swiss cheese between two slices of square rye bread. Sauté in butter or bacon fat. Serve with a sauce made by mixing 1 teaspoon of mustard and 1/2 cup of sour cream. Garnish with creamed cole slaw, sweet pickles, and herbed tomato slices.

Grilled Pastrami Sandwich. Place a slice or two of hot pastrami between 2 slices of square rye bread, and spread with chopped liver. Remove crusts. Sauté on both sides in oil. Serve with Kosher dill pickles, sweet-and-sour cole slaw, and sliced tomatoes.

Grilled Turkey and Blue Cheese. Make a sandwich of sliced turkey and a thick slab of blue cheese. Butter the outside of the sandwich and grill. Serve immediately with sliced tomatoes and large black olives.

Missouri Club Sandwich. If your freezer holds a supply of generously filled meat sandwiches—the meat sliced thin, of course, for quick thawing—you are ready to make this super fare. Dip slightly thawed sandwiches in egg and milk mixture as for French toast. Brown on both sides in hot oil about 1/2-inch deep, or grill in oiled skillet for about 4 minutes on each side. Serve with crisp garden relishes: carrots, cauliflower flowerets, onions, quartered tomatoes.

No Bread Sandwiches. These sandwiches can be served hot for dinner or lunch or cold in a lunch box. Cut thinly sliced veal into long rectangles. Sprinkle with salt and freshly ground black pepper. Cut slices of Swiss cheese a little less than half the size of the veal slices. Lay the cheese on the veal, fold over, and fasten with toothpicks. Dip in slightly beaten egg and then in seasoned cracker meal. Deep fry until golden brown. Drain on paper towels. Serve with a thin slice of peeled lemon and a lemon cup filled with chili sauce.

Pantry-Shelf Grilled Ham and Cheese Sandwich. Mix canned deviled ham with sharp cheese spread. Make sandwich, removing crusts. Sauté in butter or bacon fat. Serve with sliced tomatoes, lettuce, stuffed green olives, and any pickles on hand.

Polish Hot Dogs. Bake sauerkraut with hot dogs. Serve on split buttered and toasted hot dog buns.

Tacos. Sauté a tortilla in oil or butter until golden brown but still flexible, or heat a prepared tortilla. Fill with finely shredded lettuce, finely chopped tomato, and a portion of barbecued beef seasoned with chili sauce.

Tart Apple Relish. This makes a wonderful relish spread for hamburgers or cold turkey sandwiches. Quarter and core (don't peel) 2 large Winesap or Jonathan apples. Put through food chopper with 2 dill pickles and 1 medium-size onion. Add 1/2 cup of brown sugar and 1/4 cup of mild cider vinegar. Mix well. May be kept in refrigerator for several days.

HOT SANDWICHES WITHOUT MEAT

Cinnamon Sandwiches. Make bread and butter sandwiches, sprinkling butter with brown sugar and cinnamon. Toast in waffle iron or sauté lightly in oil and serve hot with applesauce or canned freestone peaches.

Hot Tomato Sandwich. Place a slice of peeled tomato and slices of hard-cooked egg on buttered toast, and cut in 1/2 diagonally. Pour hot tomato cheese sauce over top of tomatoes and eggs. Serve at once. Make sauce by combining some sautéed green pepper, parsley and onion, and a cupful of grated sharp cheese with condensed cream of tomato soup.

Mexican Sandwich. Place a thick slice of Monterey jack cheese and 1/2 canned green chili pepper diced lengthwise on half a tortilla. Fold tortilla in half over the cheese. Sauté the sandwich on both sides in butter. Serve with cold beer or limeade.

Toasted Onion Cheese Sandwich. For each two sandwiches sauté a medium-size sliced onion in butter (don't brown). Salt well. Spread toasted bread with the sautéed onion slices and top with a spoon of chili sauce. Lay a thick slice of cheddar cheese on top. Broil until cheese melts. A glass of ice-cold milk goes well with this.

Breads

Note: These are not, for the most part, recipes for baking bread, rolls, biscuits, and muffins. The suggestions are for using pre-baked or premixed baked goods in unusual and delicious ways.

Biscuits and Muffins

Butter Sticks. Shape biscuits into 8 long, narrow rolls, like salt sticks. Melt 1/4 cup of butter in an 8-inch square pan. Roll the sticks in the melted butter and arrange in the pan. Sprinkle with poppy seeds or toasted sesame seeds and a little coarse salt, if desired. Bake in hot oven.

Cheese and Mustard Biscuits. The perfect hearty salad accompaniment. Cut biscuit dough into 2-inch rounds. Slit the tops before baking, and insert in each a 1/2-inch cube of cheddar cheese, coated lightly with mustard. Bake in a very hot oven for 12 to 15 minutes.

Chive Biscuits. Add 2 tablespoons chopped chives for each 2 cups of flour in a standard biscuit recipe, or use with 2 cups biscuit mix.

Confetti Biscuits. For the teenagers or the bridge luncheon—something fancy without extra calories. Add one tablespoon each of finely chopped pimento and finely minced green pepper to rich biscuit dough before baking.

Crisp Biscuits. Prepare biscuit dough and knead lightly, rolling out 1/2 inch thick. Cut with doughnut cutter, leaving a hole in the middle of each biscuit. Place on cookie sheets about an inch apart and bake in hot oven. Use as a garnish for platter of creamed oysters, chicken, or salmon.

Onion Corn Muffins. Add 1 teaspoon of chopped onion to corn muffin batter, and use 1/3 cup of cream-style canned corn for that amount of liquid in the recipe. Bake in muffin pans in hot oven for 12 minutes.

Pinwheel Butter Biscuits. Roll rich biscuit dough into a rectangle 1/4 inch thick. Spread with softened, but not melted, butter. Roll up like jelly roll. Cut in pieces one inch wide and bake in muffin pans in a hot oven for 12 minutes. Any pinwheel biscuits can be baked in muffin pans instead of on a baking sheet for a different texture and appearance. For variety, bake both ways and use different fillings.

Roquefort Glazed Biscuits. To serve with a crisp, green salad. Cool and split small baked biscuits and spread with a mixture of Roquefort or blue cheese smoothed with just a bit of cream cheese. Sprinkle the cheese-covered halves with paprika and glaze under the broiler. Serve immediately. This is an elegant way to serve fresh or leftover biscuits.

Salad Biscuits. Add 1/2 cup of finely chopped watercress or parsley to rich biscuit dough.

Spanish Biscuits. Press ready-to-bake biscuits down in center. Fill the indentation with a mixture of grated cheese, chopped olives, and chili sauce.

SWEET BISCUITS AND MUFFINS

Applesauce Pinwheel Biscuits. Roll out biscuit dough to form a rectangle. Spread thinly with applesauce, sprinkle with brown sugar, and dot with butter (a light sprinkling of cinnamon too, if desired). Roll up and cut into 1-inch slices. Place in oiled muffin tins and bake in a very hot oven.

Assorted Upside-Down Fruit Muffins. Drain a can of fruits for salad (not canned fruit cocktail, which is diced). Place pieces of the fruits in the bottom of muffin pans (pears in one, peaches in another, pineapple in another, and so on). Add 1/2 teaspoon of melted butter and 1 teaspoon of sugar to each muffin cup. Cover with plain muffin batter. Bake in hot oven. Turn pan upside-down to cool. Warm before serving.

Baby Bismarcks. Make biscuit dough and drop biscuits into hot fat (350°) about 1-1/2 inches deep. Turn when golden brown, after about 1 minute. Remove from fat and drain. Cut a short slit in the side of each and insert a spoonful of jelly. Press sides together and sprinkle with powdered sugar.

Banana Corn Muffins. Add 3 mashed bananas, 1/2 cup of sugar, 1/4 teaspoon of baking powder, 1/4 cup of warm water, and 1 egg to corn muffin mix. Bake in large muffin tins. Sprinkle with equal parts of cinnamon and granulated sugar mixed together.

Glaze for Doughnuts or Coffee Cake. Heat 1/4 cup of milk or fruit juice and add enough confectioners' sugar to make it of spreading consistency. Spread on doughnuts or coffee cake while they are still slightly warm. This glaze could also be used on slightly cooled dried fruit or nut muffins.

Jam-Packed Muffins. Prepare plain or corn muffin dough. Pour batter into muffin tins and place 1/2 teaspoon of preserves or jam in the center of each muffin. Bake in hot oven. The jam will sink in a bit and you will have a jam-filled muffin.

Muffin Pep-Ups. To standard muffin recipe for 12 medium or 6 large muffins, add: 3/4 cup of grated sharp cheese; or 1/2 cup of dates, figs, raisins, or dried apricots, chopped finely or ground; or 3/4 cup of chopped nuts; or 1/3 cup of crumbled cooked bacon; or 3/4 cup of ground raw cranberries combined with 1/4 cup of sugar; or 1 cup of blueberries combined with 1 tablespoon of sugar; or 3/4 cup of finely diced banana; or 3/4 cup of finely chopped or coarsely grated peeled, raw apple. Try grinding the dried fruits instead of chopping them—a delicious difference in texture and flavor.

Orange-Almond Wedges. Pour orange muffin batter in a deep 9-inch round cake pan. Top with a mixture of 1/2 cup each of brown sugar and flour, 1/4 cup each of butter and thinly sliced almonds, and a teaspoon of grated orange rind. Bake. To serve, cut in wedges like a pie.

Orange-Pecan Biscuits. Make biscuit dough with orange juice instead of the required liquid and add 2 tablespoons of finely grated orange rind and 1/2 cup of ground or finely chopped pecans. Dip tops in sugar before baking. Fine with fruit salad.

Orange Rolls. Roll biscuit dough into a rectangle about 1/2 inch thick. Spread the dough with equal parts of sugar, melted butter, and grated orange peel (about 1/4 cup of each). Roll up like a jelly roll and cut off in 1-inch pieces. Put fairly close together, and bake on cookie sheet.

Orange Tea Biscuits. Stir 1 tablespoon of grated orange rind into biscuit batter. Then dip sugar cubes in frozen orange juice concentrate and press one on each biscuit. Bake.

Prune-Bran Muffins. Make all-bran muffins, adding 1/2 cup of chopped, cooked prunes to the batter. Makes the muffins tasty and much more moist.

Prune Pinwheels. Cover a rectangle of biscuit dough with a mixture of equal parts of small prunes, sugar, and chopped nuts. Roll up, slice, and bake. This is the nearest thing to a prune Danish, without the work.

Sour Cream Biscuits. In buttermilk biscuit recipe substitute sour cream for buttermilk. Thin the cream with a little heavy cream if it is too thick. A few spoonfuls of ground, seeded raisins or soft currants added to the flour mixture make the biscuits very special. Dust the tops with powdered sugar when done.

Upside-Down Marmalade Muffins. Place 1 teaspoon of melted butter and 1 teaspoon of orange marmalade in the bottom of each

BREADS   **149**

muffin pan. Place muffin batter on top and bake. Turn pan upside down to cool a bit before removing muffins.

Upside-Down Pecan Muffins. In each muffin cup place 3 or 4 large
pecan halves, rounded side down on a mixture of 1 teaspoon
each of melted butter and brown sugar. Place muffin batter on
top and bake. Turn pan upside-down to cool.

Variety Refrigerator Turnovers. Use those wonderful, already cut,
ready-to-bake refrigerator biscuits. Flatten the biscuits and put a
dab of jam, peanut butter, or cheese in the center. Fold over and
press edges to seal. Bake like biscuits or fry in hot oil for fried
pies.

Your Very Own Coffee Cake. Individual coffee cakes are fun to eat
and easy to make. Just make biscuit dough and turn it out into
paper-cup-lined muffin pans till half full. Sprinkle with a mixture of grated orange rind, brown sugar, cinnamon, chopped
walnuts, and melted butter. Bake in a hot oven for 15 minutes.

Breads and Rolls

Anchovy Rolls. Cut crusts off thinly sliced fresh white bread.
Spread each slice with mustard and sprinkle with grated Parmesan cheese. Place a filet of anchovy on each slice and roll up.
Brush lightly with melted butter and bake on lightly greased
baking sheet in very hot oven about 7 minutes. Can be prepared
ahead of time. Keep rolls in refrigerator covered with a damp
cloth until ready to bake and then serve immediately.

Curried Rolled Toast. Delicious served with a crisp, green salad or
with a bland soup. Mix softened butter, a dash of curry powder,
salt and crushed garlic. Spread thinly sliced, fine-textured white
bread (crust removed) with the curry butter. Roll each slice and
fasten with a toothpick. Place rolls on a baking sheet, lightly
oiled with butter or oil. Bake in a hot oven until golden brown,
about 10 minutes.

Date-Nut Bread Sandwiches. Cover slices of date-nut bread with a
slice of cheese. Place under broiler until cheese melts. Serve with
fruit salad.

Filled Toast. Make sandwiches of wafer-thin slices of bread with a layer of cream cheese and a thin layer of tart jelly. Cut each sandwich in 2 triangles. Toast both sides of the sandwiches under the broiler. Serve with Waldorf salad.

French Roll-Ups. Remove crusts from a loaf of unsliced, day-old bread. Slice lengthwise into 6 or 8 slices. Dip each slice in French toast batter and brown lightly on both sides. Spread with any spicy meat or fish sandwich filling. Roll up jelly-roll fashion and secure with toothpicks. Brush with oil or melted butter and bake on lightly greased baking sheet in moderately hot oven for about 5 minutes or until heated through. Serve one roll on each dinner plate with a generous helping of salad.

French Sesame Bread. A family favorite and ready to serve in a jiffy. Sprinkle sesame seeds thickly on the bottom of a baking sheet and toast in moderate oven for 5 minutes (don't burn). Slice fresh French bread 1/2-inch thick and brush one side of each slice with melted butter. Place bread on top of the toasted sesame seeds, buttered side down. Transfer bread, buttered side up, to the other end of the baking sheet. When ready to serve, toast under the broiler for about 1 minute, or heat in very hot oven for 2 or 3 minutes.

Herbed French Rolls. Split hard rolls. Spread cut side with herb butter, laced with a dash of Tabasco sauce. Toast in oven, cut side up, just before serving.

Herb Toast Cups. Remove crusts from thin-sliced sandwich bread, brush with melted butter and your choice of dry or fresh herbs. Press the slices, herb side up, into buttered muffin tins. Bake in moderate oven for about 12 minutes. Spoon creamed vegetables, meat, or fish into the cups.

Jiffy Bread Sticks. Remove crusts from slices of white bread. Butter both sides, cut in 6 strips, roll in poppy seeds, and heat on baking sheet for about 12 minutes.

Parsley Bread. A round loaf of French or Italian bread makes an attractive buffet bread when cut in 12 to 16 wedges (depending on size of the loaf). Before cutting wedges, slice bottom crust off in a circular slice. Spread parsley butter between the wedges; replace the buttered wedges on the circle of bottom crust. Wrap in foil and warm in the oven. When hot, fold foil down and crumple it around the bread to form a serving container. Butter the top of each wedge and sprinkle chopped parsley in the center of the loaf. This same method can be used for a round loaf of pumpernickel, using plain sweet butter. The pumpernickel need not be heated.

Quick French Onion Bread. Split a loaf of sourdough French bread lengthwise. Mix well 1/2 package of onion soup mix and 1 stick of soft butter. Spread the cut sides of the bread and put halves together. Wrap in aluminum foil, leaving foil open a bit at top to keep bread crisp. Heat in moderate oven for 20 minutes. Slice at the table.

Salad Squares. Split cornbread squares. Spread cut surfaces with topping made of grated cheddar cheese, finely minced onion, minced green olives and mayonnaise. Place in moderate oven until browned.

Toasted Herb Loaf. Trim all crusts but the bottom one from a loaf of unsliced white bread. Cut into slices about 1-inch thick, but don't cut through the bottom crust. Spread slices on both sides with a mixture of softened butter, finely chopped chives, parsley, and tarragon. Cut through the middle lengthwise, still not cutting through bottom crust. Wrap loaf in aluminum foil or place in a slightly damp brown paper bag. Before serving, heat in moderate oven, then remove paper or foil and place under broiler until loaf is light brown on top.

Toasty Cheese Rolls. Split French hard rolls lengthwise. Spread with soft butter to which you have added grated Parmesan cheese. Slip under broiler for a minute to melt cheese and toast the rolls. Serve immediately.

SWEET BREADS AND ROLLS

Cinnamon Buns Extraordinary. Form large, uneven balls of ready-to-bake refrigerated rolls. Coat the balls with a mixture of 2 parts cinnamon and 1 part granulated sugar. Place 3 balls of the dough (clover leaf fashion) in each greased muffin tin. Bake in hot oven. While the buns are still warm, ice them with a thin butter icing, flavored strongly with cinnamon.

Cinnamon Toast. Make a thick paste of soft butter, sugar, and cinnamon (be generous with the cinnamon). Spread on lightly toasted bread or split English muffins. Pop under the broiler until the mixture bubbles. Good for after-school or TV snacks, as well as for breakfast. A batch of the mixture will keep in a covered container in the refrigerator.

Cinnamon Twists. Roll hot roll dough into a 12-x6-inch rectangle. Sprinkle with a mixture of 1/3 cup of brown sugar and 1/4 cup of cinnamon. Fold over in half to form a 6-x6-inch square. Cut into 1-inch strips and twist each strip. Bake. Cool and frost with confectioners' icing.

Hot Currant Breakfast Bread. Place biscuit dough in an 8-inch square pan and sprinkle top with 1/3 cup of soft currants (can be plumped in hot water) which have been mixed with 1/2 teaspoon of cinnamon and 2 tablespoons of sugar. Press currants down lightly into top of the dough.

Indian Bread. In Iowa long ago, young braves from a friendly Indian tribe used to stop at a pioneer family's home for breakfast. They loved biscuits which were baked in a large iron frying pan on top of the stove. The wood-fed stove was not always hot enough, on such short notice, to bake the biscuits in the oven. A modern version of Indian bread made with biscuit mix is loved by children, especially if the story of the original Indian bread is told with the serving. Heat several tablespoons of oil in a medium-size skillet. Roll out the dough to fit your skillet and make some slits in the top as you would in the top of a pie crust. Place the round of dough in the sizzling pan and lower the heat. Cook, uncovered, until brown on one side; then turn and brown the other side, adding more oil if needed. Cut in wedges. Serve with butter and syrup.

Lemon Sticky Buns. Use brown-and-serve rolls. Place 3 tablespoons of butter, 1/4 cup of light brown sugar, 1/2 teaspoon of grated lemon rind, and 1 tablespoon of frozen lemonade concentrate in the bottom of an 8-inch pie pan. Put brown-and-serve rolls on top of the mixture. Bake for 7 minutes in a hot oven. Turn, baste the rolls, and bake for 7 or 8 minutes longer. Serve with fried ham or sausage and apple rings.

Maple Toast. Toast bread on one side. Spread the other side with a mixture of butter, a sprinkling of flour, and maple syrup. Dust with cinnamon and place under the broiler until bubbly and brown.

Quick Apricot-Nut Bread. Prepare biscuit dough, using orange juice for the required liquid. Add 1 cup of ground soft dried apricots, 1/4 cup of sugar, and 1/2 cup of crushed (not chopped) pecans. Bake in a loaf pan.

Rosebud Rolls. Roll out roll mix to 1/3-inch thickness. Cut into rounds with 1-inch biscuit cutter. Arrange 5 small rounds of dough in each greased muffin tin. Press firmly in center to hold the 5 petals together and to make an indentation in the center of each roll. Fill the center with a mixture of crushed whole cranberry sauce, crushed pineapple, and grated orange rind. Cover and let rise. Bake. When baked, brush with butter, or frost lightly with thin confectioners' icing, tinted light pink. Can be made with layers of refrigerator butterflake rolls.

Streusel Coffee Cake. Bake plain biscuit coffee cake for 10 minutes before sprinkling on the topping. Dry bread crumbs added to the streusel topping give it an interesting texture and flavor.

Streusel Ginger Cake. Bake gingerbread batter for 10 minutes. Make the following spiced streusel topping and sprinkle on the cake: combine 1/4 cup of brown sugar, 2 tablespoons of flour, 2 teaspoons of cinnamon, 2 tablespoons of firm butter, and 1/2 cup of chopped nuts. Finish baking.

Yule Coffee Cake. Can be baked in a tube cake pan, but if the angel food cake pan is busy or if you need 2 or 3 coffee cakes, the following makeshift works very well for a coffee cake ring. Butter a nine-inch layer-cake pan. Place an empty soup can, buttered on the outside, in the center of the pan. Arrange 8 smooth balls of coffee cake dough around the can. Space balls evenly so an attractive cake ring will result. Bake, ice, and decorate for Christmas brunch.

Sunday Breakfasts

FRENCH TOAST

Dutch Cheese Toast. Fry French toast light brown on one side. Turn. Place a dollop of cream cheese, whipped cottage cheese, or ricotta cheese on each slice. Cover the pan. Cook until the cheese melts. Sprinkle with minced parsley and serve immediately.

Eggnog French Toast. Flavor egg and milk mixture with nutmeg, vanilla, and a dash of dark rum, if desired. Use slices of raisin bread for the toast. Serve 2 slices, sandwich style, with jam or marmalade between and powdered sugar on top, or serve with rum-flavored sugar syrup.

French Luncheon Toast. Make French toast, 2 slices for each person. Serve buttered and piping hot with hot applesauce between the layers. Spread the top slice with currant jelly and sprinkle lightly with powdered sugar.

French Toasted Shredded Wheat. Dip shredded wheat biscuits in a mixture of beaten egg and milk. Let soak a few minutes. Fry in butter or oil. Serve with maple syrup.

French Toast Variation. Serve French toast with stewed or dried fruit, or put warm, thick applesauce between two slices and sprinkle top with equal parts of cinnamon and powdered sugar.

FRITTERS

Carrot Fritters. A welcome change from potatoes. Finely grate 4 or 5 carrots. Mix with 1 beaten egg, salt, pepper, and about 1/3 cup of flour. Drop from a tablespoon on greased pancake griddle.

Creamed Corn Fritters. Mix together 1 cup of cream-style corn, 2 whole eggs, and salt and pepper to taste. Stir in 1 teaspoon of baking powder and just enough flour to make a heavy batter. Drop by spoonfuls into 1/2 inch of hot oil. Cook only a few at a time and drain on absorbent paper. Serve piping hot. Delicious with fried chicken.

Date Fritters. Pit dates and stuff with walnut halves. Dip in fairly thin fritter batter. Fry in hot oil at about 370°. Drain. Serve with powdered sugar.

Deviled Egg Fritters. Use deviled eggs, seasoned with a bit of anchovy paste and a dash of Tabasco. Dip deviled eggs in fritter batter and fry in hot oil. Make cheese sauce by adding grated cheese to a can of condensed cream of mushroom or cream of celery soup.

Fruit Fritters. Dip drained, stewed fruit in a thin fritter batter. Fry in hot oil. Slices of canned pineapple and halves of peaches are particularly good this way. Serve with meat or chicken.

Main Dish Fritters. Add 2 cups of corn, 1/4 cup of finely chopped or ground green pepper, and 1/2 cup of grated cheese to your fritter batter. Fry by spoonfuls in hot oil. Drain. Serve with tomato sauce.

Pear Fritters. Before dipping drained, canned pears in thin fritter batter, roll in flour. Fry in hot oil. Serve with cheese sauce and Canadian bacon or smoked turkey.

PANCAKES

Almond-Rice Pancakes. Add cooked rice and finely chopped, toasted, blanched almonds to a thin pancake batter. Serve with a honey butter topping made by heating 4 parts of honey with 1 part of butter.

Apple Pancakes with Brandy Syrup. Add 1 cup of finely chopped, peeled apple to pancake batter. Heat syrup with a piece of butter and brandy or pure brandy extract. Serve syrup and pancakes warm.

Banana Pancakes. Add 1 cup of mashed banana to 2 cups of pancake batter. Make small pancakes and serve with hot lemon sauce. For hot lemon sauce, add 1/2 cup of extra water, the juice of 1/2 lemon, and a bit of grated lemon rind to lemon pudding.

Blini with Sour Cream and Red Caviar. Make thin, eggy pancakes. Put red caviar between two pancakes and serve with melted butter and a bowl of sour cream.

Buttermilk Pancakes. Serve with honey and sweet butter.

Dollar-Size Pancakes. Serve 5 or 6 small pancakes with sour cream and plenty of sugar and cinnamon.

Eastern Version of Hot Tamales. Cook large, 5-inch corn pancakes made with corn muffin batter. Fill with chili con carne and fold over. More chili can be poured over the top.

Fruit and Ham Kebabs with Pancakes. Alternate pineapple chunks and chunks of ham on skewers. Dip in a mixture of the pineapple syrup, melted butter, and a little brown sugar. Broil the kebabs and serve with pancakes for a fancy Sunday brunch.

Griddle Cakes with Hot Applesauce and Brown Sugar. After generously buttering the griddle cakes, top with hot applesauce and a generous sprinkling of brown or maple sugar.

Onion Pancakes. Add 1 cup of finely chopped and sautéed onion to 2 cups of pancake batter. Bake the pancakes and serve hot, topped with browned ground beef in gravy.

Pennsylvania Dutch Baked Cornmeal Mush. Slice cornmeal mush or scrapple about 1/4 inch thick. Brush with milk and dust with fine bread crumbs. Place the slices on a well-buttered cookie sheet. Bake in a very hot oven until brown. Turn once, if desired. Serve with butter and maple syrup; with gravy, or tomato sauce if served as a vegetable. Good with pot roast instead of potato pancakes. Or serve for breakfast with fried tomato slices and fried eggs, with a brown sauce over all.

Rich Corn Pancakes. Add 1 cup of cream-style corn to pancakes made with buttermilk pancake batter. Serve with crisp bacon or thin slices of ham.

WAFFLES

Cheese Waffles and Apple Butter. Make waffle batter, adding 1/2 cup of grated, very sharp cheese to the dry ingredients. Bake, and serve with melted butter and apple butter instead of syrup. Or serve with melted butter and warm, poached apples.

Chocolate Nut Waffles. This is a first cousin in flavor to a chocolate soufflé. Add 1/2 cup of sugar and 2 squares of melted chocolate to biscuit mix recipe. Also add 1/3 cup of broken nut meats and 1 teaspoon of vanilla. Bake on waffle iron. Serve hot with sweetened mocha whipped cream or coffee ice cream. To make the mocha whipped cream, add 1 teaspoon of instant coffee and 1 tablespoon of instant cocoa mix to a pint of heavy cream and whip.

Corn Waffles. Corn-frittery good and not so much fat. Add 1 cup cooked whole-kernel corn (well drained) and 1/2 teaspoon of paprika to waffle batter. The corn liquid can be used as part of the liquid called for in the recipe.

Deviled Waffle Butter. Spread equal parts of canned, smoked, deviled ham and butter on hot waffles and serve with hot maple syrup.

Thrifty Filling-Station Waffles. Bacon waffles with creamed green peas. Cut cooked bacon in small pieces and sprinkle over the waffle batter just before baking. For a vegetarian version, use chopped soybean bacon-substitute bits instead of bacon.

Preserves
and Relishes

Preserves

Damson Plum Conserve. Add broken English walnuts and steamed raisins to ready-made damson plum preserve.

Date Butter. Contains no cane sugar. Mix equal parts of date crystals or date sugar and water. Add grated lemon rind. Bring to a boil, then simmer, stirring, until thickened. Delicious on muffins or as a cake or pie filling.

Quick Honey Marmalade. Soak dried apricots in boiling water for 5 or 10 minutes. Drain and run through fine blade of food chopper. To each cup of ground apricots add 1-1/2 cups of mild honey. Blend thoroughly. Store in sterilized jars at least 2 weeks before using. This forms a spread of marmalade texture. Delicious on toast.

158

Strawberry Conserve. Add grated orange rind, drained crushed pineapple, and halved blanched almonds to a jar of good strawberry preserves. Heat just to the boiling point. Cool and serve.

Relishes

Chili-Prune Relish for One Meal. Chop 1/2 pound of steamed prunes. Combine with 3 tablespoons of light brown sugar, 3 tablespoons of cider vinegar, 2 tablespoons of minced candied ginger, 1/3 teaspoon of chili powder, 1/2 small hot chili pepper finely minced, 1/4 teaspoon of salt, 1 teaspoon of mustard seed, 3 tablespoons of diced pimento, and 1/2 cup of crushed English walnuts.

Pickled Bing Cherries. Cover 2 pounds of black bing cherries with 2 cups of cider vinegar. Let stand overnight. Drain, saving juice, and remove pits from cherries. Mix juice, pitted cherries, 2 pounds of sugar, 1 stick of cinnamon broken into pieces, and 1 teaspoon each of whole pickling spice and whole cloves. Bring to boil, remove from fire and pour into a small crock. Cool at room temperature for several hours. Refrigerate. Will keep for several weeks. Pineapple chunks or fresh apricots can also be pickled and kept this way.

Raw Cranberry-Orange Relish. Put 1 pound washed and drained cranberries and a quartered, unpeeled navel orange through food chopper. Add 1-1/2 cups of granulated sugar, 1/4 cup of finely chopped English walnuts, and 1/4 cup of minced celery heart. Refrigerate in a covered crock or bowl for several days.

Raw Papaya Chutney. Coarsely grind a peeled large Florida papaya and a canned green hot chili pepper. Mix with a tablespoon of finely minced preserved ginger and 1/4 cup of finely grated coconut. Serve as an accompaniment to chicken or shrimp curry or in lemon peel cups with fried chicken.

Red Pepper Jam. Delicious alone as a relish or grand mixed with cream cheese, cottage cheese, or potato salad. Remove the seeds from 12 large sweet red peppers. Put peppers through food grinder and mix with 1 tablespoon of salt. Let stand for 3 hours and drain well. Add 2 cups of vinegar and 3 cups of sugar. Simmer slowly until consistency of jam, about 1 hour. Pour into small glasses. Or make less and use as soon as cooled.

Spiced Cherry Relish. Grind 2 cups of pitted fresh Bing cherries. Prepare a package of black cherry-flavored gelatine with 1 cup of water instead of the usual 2 cups. Add 1 tablespoon of lemon juice and 1/4 teaspoon each of cloves, allspice, and cinnamon. Fold in the ground cherries and chill. Serve with smoked turkey or any meat.

Spiced Vegetables. Drain liquid from a one-pound jar of any vegetable—such as carrots, beets, asparagus spears, or a combination of sliced carrots with whole kernel corn and French-cut green beans—or use cooked frozen vegetables. To the vegetable liquid (about 3/4 cup) add 1/4 cup of vinegar, 2 tablespoons of sugar, and 1 tablespoon of mixed pickling spices. Bring to a boil and simmer for 10 minutes. Pour through small strainer over the vegetables in a jar or crock. Cool, replace lid and refrigerate.

Tart Apple Relish. Peel, core, and quarter 2 large Winesap or Jonathan apples and put through a food chopper, together with 2 dill pickles and 1 medium-size onion. Add 1/2 cup brown sugar and 1/4 cup mild vinegar and mix well. Let stand overnight. May be used immediately or kept for several days in the refrigerator. Delicious as a relish spread for hamburgers, cold turkey sandwiches, or a cold meat plate.

Desserts

Fruit Desserts

Tip: To prepare segments of grapefruit, tangerine or seedless oranges, cut a thick layer of peel off the top and bottom of the fruit, then cut sections of peel from sides, cutting deep enough to remove all the white membrane, leaving the fruit exposed. With a sharp knife (preferably with a serrated edge), cut out each section separately. Do this over a bowl to save the juice.

APPLE DESSERTS

Apple Baked Alaska. Place a baked apple on a round slice of sponge or angel food cake cut larger than the apple. Put a spoonful of ice cream on top of the apple. Cover with very stiff meringue and broil or bake for a few minutes until light brown. Serve immediately.

Apple Crunch Dessert. Half fill a square or oblong baking dish with sliced, peeled apples. Cover with a topping made of 3/4 cup of quick-cooking oatmeal, 3/4 cup of sugar, 1/4 cup of butter, 1/4 cup of flour, and 1/2 teaspoon of cinnamon. Cover and bake until apples are tender and top is brown and crisp. Remove cover during the last half of baking time.

Applesauce and Cookies. Serve soft spice cookies frosted with lemon icing or crisp peanut butter cookies with applesauce chilled icy cold.

Danish Apple Macaroon. Place two soft macaroons in each sherbet glass. Sprinkle with sherry and maraschino cherry juice. While the macaroons are soaking, poach halves of cored and peeled apples in sugar syrup. Place a poached half of apple on top of the soaked macaroons. Put a teaspoonful of red currant jelly in the hollow of the apple half and top with slightly sweetened whipped cream flavored with almond. Crown with a few toasted almond slivers.

Fancy Baked Apples. Wash, core, and peel apples two-thirds of the way down. Place in baking dish and pour thin sugar syrup or maple syrup over the apples. Bake for at least an hour in a covered baking dish to keep them from shriveling. Uncover for the last 10 minutes of baking. Try stuffing apples with mincemeat, with raisins and brown sugar, or with crumbled ginger snaps and peanut butter.

Honey Apples. Poach peeled apples in equal parts of honey and water. Serve with a dab of sour cream and a sprinkling of cinnamon.

Lemon Baked Apples. Serve baked apples with lemon sauce instead of cream.

Light-of-Life Brandied Baked Apples. Pile a mound of whipped cream in the bottom of each dessert dish and then place a warm baked apple on top of the cream. Pour a tablespoon of warmed brandy over each apple and place a lump of sugar that has been dipped in vanilla or orange extract on top. Light the sugar cube and serve. The flame never fails to burn brightly.

Orange Applesauce. Make fresh applesauce by cooking 1/2 cup of orange marmalade and 1 teaspoon of water with 5 cupfuls of sliced cooking apples. Serve warm or cold for dessert with plain orange wafers.

Party Baked Apples. Warm or bake the apples. When done, top with a meringue made of 2 tablespoons of sugar to each egg white. Place slivers of blanched almonds and bits of maraschino cherries in the meringue and bake for 15 minutes or until delicately browned.

Spiced Baked Apples with Ice Cream. Arrange unpeeled, seedless orange slices in the bottom of the pan in which you bake the apples. Fill apples with mincemeat and pour maple syrup or cinnamon-and-nutmeg-flavored sugar syrup around the apples. Bake. Cool slightly. Serve while still warm. Top with a scoop of vanilla ice cream.

Super Applesauce. Flavor warm applesauce with cinnamon and lemon rind and juice. Stir in a generous amount of steamed seedless raisins. Serve with plain sugar cookies.

Surprise Fresh Fruit Dessert. Serve whole apples or pears (the fanciest), peeled or unpeeled but cored (use a round wheel-shaped cutter that leaves the fruit "intact" but cut into 8 sections). Arrange a few halves of fancy unsalted walnuts or pecans or several slices of cheese on the same plate. Camembert or Brie is delicious with pears; sharp or American cheese with apples.

Sweetie Apple Betty. Make Apple Betty with wheat germ instead of bread crumbs. Serve with cinnamon-flecked thin cream slightly sweetened with maple syrup.

APRICOT DESSERTS

Apricot Ambrosia. Serve halves of fresh apricots and canned or fresh pineapple chunks in apricot nectar. Sprinkle with freshly grated coconut just before serving.

Apricot Rum Whip. Drain and puree 1 large can of apricots and combine with 3 stiffly beaten egg whites, 3/4 cup of heavy cream whipped, and 1 tablespoon of dark rum. Sweeten if desired. Pile in sherbet glasses and serve immediately. You can use the strained apricots and apple baby food for the apricots, but not the apricot-tapioca version as it is too bland.

Ginger Apricots. Drain stewed or canned apricots and serve in a fruit dish or sherbet glass. Cover with a jigger of ginger brandy.

AVOCADO DESSERTS

Avocado Supreme. Cut three avocados in cubes and toss with the pineapple and part of the juice from a can of pineapple chunks. Lace with fresh lime juice. Serve in the avocado shells or in sherbet glasses (the edges of which have been dipped in lemon juice and then in powdered sugar). Chill thoroughly. Garnish with very fine freshly grated coconut and slivered almonds.

Whipped Avocado Dessert. Whip the pulp of three soft, but not brown, avocados and the juice of 1/2 a lime with 1 cup of confectioners' sugar and 1/2 cup of any liqueur. Pile in the avocado shells and serve immediately with wedges of lime. This dessert can be made in an electric blender.

BANANA DESSERTS

Jamaican Bananas. Bake bananas, split lengthwise, with equal parts of rum, apricot brandy, and melted butter. Serve warm with icy cold fresh coconut whipped cream (add very finely grated fresh coconut to unsweetened whipped cream). The bananas need no further sweetening.

Pantry Dessert. In a sherbet glass, put a spoonful of strawberry jam then a double layer of sliced bananas. Sprinkle bananas with coarsely chopped or crushed pecans. Cover all with sweetened whipped cream flavored with a generous amount of grated lemon rind.

Paradise Banana Fritters Delicious. Cut a ripe banana into 4 pieces, crosswise. Dip in sour cream flavored with grated lemon peel, powdered sugar, and a little chopped candied ginger. Roll in freshly grated or flaked coconut. Serve two fritters to a person. Garnish with several large whole strawberries if desired.

BERRY DESSERTS

Almond Berry Fritters. Wash and hull strawberries. Force apricot jam through a sieve or food mill and cover the berries with the jam. Roll in finely chopped almonds. Dip in beaten egg and then cracker meal. Chill for at least an hour. Fry four or five berries at a time in oil heated to 360° for one or two minutes, or until golden brown. Drain. Serve hot, dusted with powdered sugar.

Berries for Dessert. Serve in unusual combinations such as half black raspberries and half red raspberries with cream sweetened lightly with maple syrup. Or, in hot weather, serve both kinds of berry over raspberry ice.

Cranberry Cheese Dessert. Serve a slice of canned jellied cranberry sauce and a generous slice of cream cheese with saltines.

Cranberry Whip. Let 1/3 cup of ground cranberries (part of those you grind for raw cranberry relish before the other ingredients are added) stand with 1/3 cup of honey overnight. Add 2/3 cup of sliced green seedless grapes and fold all into whipped cream. Serve immediately in sherbet glasses lined with lady fingers.

Fresh Strawberries in Fluffy Sour Cream. Combine a pint of hulled, sliced fresh strawberries with 1 tablespoon of sugar. Fold 1/4 pound of diced marshmallows (pink ones if you have them) into 1/4 pint of sour cream. Fold in the lightly sugared strawberries. Refrigerate for several hours before serving. Serve in sherbet glasses topped with a whole unhulled strawberry.

Ice Cream Version of Strawberries Romanoff. Gives the dish more body and tastes delicious. Mix together a pint of vanilla ice cream, a cup of heavy cream whipped, and 1-1/2 ounces each of rum and Cointreau. Pour over whole berries and garnish the top with a choice whole berry.

Molded Fresh Berry Custard. Bake sweet custard cups without nutmeg. Turn out upside down in sauce dishes. Surround with sweetened red and black raspberries. Top with a dab of sweetened whipped cream.

Quick All-Blueberry Pie. When blueberry sauce is cool (see Thick Hot Blueberry Sauce), add and gently fold in another pint of fresh blueberries. Pour all gently into baked pie shell. Top with sour cream or serve with ice cream or whipped cream.

Quick Strawberry Tarts. Bake rich pie crust in fluted tart shells. Just before serving, fill with 1/4 part of sweetened strawberries folded into 3/4 parts of whipped cream. Top with a whole berry.

Rhubarb Strawberry Sauce. Cook 1 pound of fresh rhubarb with a little sugar. When cool, add a package of partially defrosted frozen sliced strawberries. Serve as is or over a chilled cup of custard or over a scoop of vanilla ice cream.

Strawberries California. Pour fresh orange juice over whole strawberries in sherbet glasses. Serve with lady fingers.

Strawberries in the Snow. Wash and dry whole strawberries thoroughly, dip in butter frosting and then in finely grated fresh coconut or in canned, shredded coconut. Store in refrigerator. Serve four or five strawberries on a salad or dessert plate covered with a paper lace doily.

Thick Hot Blueberry Sauce. Spoon over waffles or cake for dessert. Blend 1/4 cup of water, 1/4 cup of maple syrup, and 1 tablespoon of cornstarch in a small pan. Cook and stir over low heat until sauce bubbles and begins to thicken. Add 1 pint of blueberries and cook a few seconds more.

CHERRY DESSERTS

Black Bing Cherries Royale. Soak fresh large pitted Bing cherries in kirsch. Serve in sherbet glass with slightly sweetened whipped cream spiced with nutmeg, ginger, and cinnamon.

Brandied Cherries and Cheese. Pile whipped cream-cottage cheese in sherbet glasses. Garnish with brandied Bing cherries.

Cherry Almond Dessert. Add a dash of almond extract to canned cherries. Serve with almond cookies or add three or four blanched almonds.

Raspberry Sherbet with Pitted Black Bing Cherries. Marinate pitted black Bing cherries in Triple Sec. Serve over a scoop of raspberry sherbet.

Very French Dessert. Pit and sweeten large black cherries and let stand in refrigerator until thoroughly chilled. Serve topped with sour cream.

DRIED FRUIT DESSERTS

Exotic Steamed Figs. Stuff large dried figs with chopped nuts and dates. Store in tightly closed tin container. When needed, steam the figs in the top of a double boiler for 20 minutes. Serve hot with whipped cream.

Little Jack Horner Pies. Butter individual dessert dishes and sprinkle thickly with graham cracker crumbs, pressing down smoothly. Fill with baby-food strained prunes. Cover with more crumbs. Put in refrigerator for several hours. Stick a maraschino cherry on the end of a thin pretzel stick and push it down into the pie so a child can easily pull it out.

Prunes in Jelly. Flavor 1-3/4 cups of prune juice with sherry and lemon juice. Soften one envelope of unflavored gelatine in 1/4 cup of cold water. Bring the prune juice mixture to a boil and add the gelatine. Cool. When mixture begins to thicken, pour into individual molds in which you have placed two stewed prunes stuffed with blanched almonds. Chill. Unmold and serve plain or with thin custard sauce.

Prune Whip Baked Alaska. Split a layer of spice cake. Put lemon ice cream or lemon sherbet between the layers. (The ice cream can be molded in a waxed-paper-lined layer-cake pan of the same size and then turned out on the cake layer without crumbling it and without the ice cream getting too soft.) Sprinkle the ice cream with finely grated lemon rind. Cover cake thickly and completely with prune meringue (1/2 cup of chopped prunes, four egg whites, and 8 tablespoons of sugar). Bake in hot oven for 3 to 5 minutes. Serve immediately.

Spiced Stewed Prunes. Prunes can be interesting for dessert if, while cooking, you add a stick of cinnamon and a few thin slices of lemon. Let the prunes chill in their syrup for a day or so and they will be juicy and plump. No sugar is needed in cooking.

Spicy Fruit Compote. Cook an 11-ounce package of mixed dried fruits with 1/2 cup of light brown sugar, two or three thin slices of lemon, 1 teaspoon of whole cloves, and a 1-inch stick of cinnamon. Use about 2 cups of water to cover. Cool in the liquid.

Stuffed Jumbo Prunes. Stuff pitted jumbo prunes with ground nut and raisin mixture. Cover the stuffed prunes with a mixture of

equal parts of sherry and boiling water. Let stand in refrigerator
for several days. Serve with some of the marinade and with
whipped cream on the side.

Summer Fig Pudding. Prepare lemon gelatine. When slightly thickened, add 1 cup of canned Kadota figs, mashed. Then whip 1 cup
of heavy cream and fold it into the fig mixture. Chill and serve
garnished with a whole fig.

Thanksgiving Day or Halloween Sherbet. Serve a scoop of orange
ice cream or ice with a sauce of ground raisins steamed with a bit
of water and lemon juice.

GRAPEFRUIT DESSERTS

Dessert for a Curry Dinner. Citrus parfait: Remove the membranes
from a grapefruit half, leaving the sections intact. Top with a
scoop of orange sherbet and Mandarin orange sections soaked in
rum.

Grapefruit Crème de Menthe. Fill the small cut-out center of carefully prepared halves of grapefruit with crushed ice. Pour green
crème de menthe over the ice. Serve on a bed of fresh mint or
other attractive leaves. Place a small bunch of frosted seedless
grapes on the plate. (See Frosted Grapes.)

GRAPE DESSERTS

Frosted Grapes. Choose well-formed, firm, small bunches of seedless
grapes. Dip each bunch in water. Drain on a paper towel. Shake
lightly in a paper bag that contains powdered sugar, or dip
thoroughly dried bunches in slightly beaten egg white, then in
granulated sugar. Put on waxed paper on wire rack to dry.

White Grapes and Sour Cream. Wash and dry white seedless grapes.
Pull off the stems and chill thoroughly. Serve with sour cream
and a generous sprinkling of brown sugar. Warm spice cake goes
well with this, if you don't mind the calories.

MELON DESSERTS

Honeydew Ball Halves. Use small honeydews. Fill halves with pitted black cherries and sliced peaches, adding a sprinkling of lime juice and a sprig of fresh mint.

Honeydew Melon Cooler. Cut circles of peeled honeydew melon and serve with a scoop of lime sherbet, garnished with fresh mint leaves.

Watermelon for Picnics. Square off your melon in a rindless block and cut into pieces about 5 inches long and 2 inches wide. Insert a wooden skewer lengthwise in each piece of melon for a handle.

MIXED FRUIT DESSERTS

Baked Fruit with Sour Cream. Place drained canned pears, freestone peaches, and large black Bing cherries in a baking dish. Sprinkle with light brown sugar and about 1/2 cup of light rum. Heat in a very hot oven. Serve hot, with a bowl of cold sour cream.

California Fruit Bowl. Put three or four halves of fresh figs in a dessert dish. Surround with large pitted Bing cherries. Chill. Add California champagne and serve.

Children's Fruit Kebab Dessert. Stuff soft, pitted uncooked prunes with peanut butter. Put prunes, banana chunks, and pineapple chunks alternately on small skewers or picks. Or alternate strawberries, pineapple chunks, and orange sections.

Dessert for a Chinese Dinner. Serve chilled, canned lichee nuts and Mandarin orange sections. Or, as the Peking Restaurant in New York does it, serve a large mound of crushed ice with preserved kumquats and chunks of fresh pineapple stuck in it on small picks.

Dessert for an Italian Dinner. Serve Bel Paese and Gorgonzola cheeses, little chunks of bread, and crispy bread sticks with a bowl of ice-cold assorted fruit.

Edible Autumn Centerpiece. Slice the top off a large, well-shaped pumpkin about one-third of the way down. Hollow out the pumpkin and line it with foil. Fill it with well-shaped fall fruits and set it on a bed of colorful autumn leaves in the center of the table or buffet.

Exotic Pantry Dessert. Fold chopped nuts, dried figs, preserved ginger, and a few maraschino cherries into lemon gelatine, just as it begins to thicken. Pour into sherbet glasses. Serve with a dab of sweetened whipped cream sprinkled with a bit of grated lemon rind.

Flaming Fruits. Place any sweetened cooked fruit (apricots, apples, pears, peaches, bananas) in a flameproof shallow dish. Heat in the oven. Pour 3 or 4 ounces of rum or brandy over the fruit while still hot. Ignite the liquor and bring the flaming fruits to the table. Serve with a cold custard sauce.

Fruit and Cheese for Dessert. Interesting combinations: yellow Delicious apples with sharp cheese; pears with Camembert or Brie; whole red tart-cherry preserves with sharp cheese and saltines; a mound of whipped cream cheese studded with seedless grapes; dates with sharp cheese.

Fruit Cointreau. Marinate whole fresh grapefruit sections, whole fresh strawberries, and canned Mandarin orange sections for several hours in Cointreau. Serve with tiny rich nut cookies for a tantalizing and refreshing dessert.

Fruit Gelatine Variations. Ambrosia: orange gelatine with Mandarin orange segments and flaked coconut; strawberry gelatine with halved strawberries and bananas; lemon gelatine with seedless grapes and sliced bananas.

Fruit on Ice. Press crushed ice into a large bowl and freeze for about 15 minutes. Remove to room temperature for a few minutes to loosen ice. Unmold on a deep tray lined with grape leaves or other appropriate greens. Place a variety of fresh fruits on wooden picks or skewers and stick in the ice. Strawberries dipped in sugar, pineapple chunks, preserved kumquats, honeydew balls, apricot halves, large frosted grapes, watermelon cubes—take your choice.

Fruit Sauce with Water Chestnuts. Drain a can of water chestnuts. Slice and sauté the chestnuts in 2 tablespoons of butter until lightly browned. Cool. Then make a fruit sauce of equal parts of frozen tangerine juice and canned unsweetened pineapple juice flavored with a stick of cinnamon, some chopped crystallized ginger, and lemon rind (no sugar needed) mixed with cornstarch and brought to a boil until clear (1 level teaspoon of cornstarch to 1 cup juice). Add 1 tablespoon of butter. Remove cinnamon sticks. Chill. Just before serving, add the sautéed water chestnuts. Serve over fresh fruit chunks (pineapple, apple slices, melon balls, seedless grapes).

Fruits Tempura (Japanese). A conversation piece party dessert that will be enjoyed even by nondessert eaters. Have a variety of bite-size pieces of fruit ready (banana chunks, whole strawberries, thin rings of apple, chunks of seedless orange, halves of apricots). Prepare thin fritter batter. Dip each piece of fruit into the batter, and hold over a bowl to drain. Drop into 1/2-inch depth of oil heated to 375°F. Fry, turning once. Drain on absorbent paper and sprinkle with powdered sugar. Serve hot with a bowl of slivered, preserved ginger and a bowl of toasted sesame seeds for guests to use as a dip.

Hawaii Fruit Float. Float chilled Mandarin orange sections, canned pineapple chunks, and sliced papaya or mango (fresh or canned) in chilled orange juice. Put a scoop of vanilla ice cream in the middle. Use flaked coconut for topping on the ice cream if desired. Serve in soup plates.

Italian Fresh Fruit Dessert. Serve this dessert in a large market-style basket with a handle. Fill the bottom of the basket with assorted unshelled nuts, and hang nutcrackers from the sides. Cover the nuts with a layer of the most elegant fruits: perfect peaches, grapes, and plums. Carry the basket to the table and let each guest help himself. Dessert plates and fruit knives complete the service.

Port Wine with Walnuts. A bottle of good port, a lovely bowl of semicracked and warmed walnuts, glasses, and salad plates.

Two-Tone Ambrosia. Old but new. Serve orange and grapefruit sections with coconut in a grapefruit shell. Garnish with white seedless grapes or plumped white seedless raisins.

Western Fruit Compote. In handsome individual glass bowls, place a pineapple slice, pear half, whole fig, whole prune, and a few boysenberries or raspberries. Include some syrup from all the fruits except the berries. Chill. Top each serving with a sprinkling of nutmeg.

ORANGE DESSERTS

Baked Orange Sections. Remove white membrane from peeled orange sections. Arrange close together in a pie plate or shallow baking dish. Cover thickly with meringue to which you have added grated orange rind. Bake in a hot oven for about 5 minutes, or until lightly browned. Serve immediately, sauced with chilled orange juice.

Crème de Menthe à l'Orange. Cut 1/3 of the top off a seedless orange and hollow it out. Put a scoop of orange sherbet in the orange shell. Pour over it a generous jigger of green crème de menthe. Garnish with frosted mint leaves and a half slice of orange, and provide short straws for sipping.

Dessert Araby. Prepare peeled, thinly sliced, seedless oranges, mixed with sliced fresh dates, orange juice, brandy, and some slivered toasted almonds. Chill thoroughly and serve in sherbet glasses.

Mandarin Oranges Flambé. Place Mandarin orange sections with a bit of the thin syrup in a chafing dish. Add brown sugar and cinnamon and heat. Add cognac or rum and light. Serve immediately, either plain or on a scoop of vanilla ice cream.

Orange Baskets Filled with Fruit Salad. Marinate diced fruits in sweet white wine. Fill orange shells. Serve with crisp, plain sugar cookies.

Oranges in Wine. Peel and slice seedless oranges. Sprinkle with sugar and barely cover with red wine. Chill overnight.

Orange Waffle. Use a quarter of a waffle for each portion. Heap the center with drained Mandarin oranges or fresh oranges peeled and with membranes removed. Cover with a sauce made by blending the juice of two oranges with 3/4 cup of confectioners' sugar. Top with stiffly whipped cream.

Sweets After a Chinese Dinner. Top off the dinner with Mandarin orange sections, fresh dates, and blanched almonds marinated in brandy.

PEACH DESSERTS

Peaches Almond. Moisten almond paste with a little orange juice and spoon into fresh, ripe peach halves (or canned freestone peach halves). Broil fruit until just heated and serve with orange juice poured around it.

Peaches Imperial. Drench ripe sugared peach halves with fresh, sweetened, and crushed red raspberries or thawed frozen red raspberries. Top with a sauce of equal parts of cream cheese and sour cream whipped together.

Peaches with Rum Butterscotch Sauce. Put an oversized sugar cookie on a dessert plate. Top it with a fresh peach half or a drained canned freestone peach half. Top with rum butterscotch sauce made by adding a tablespoon of rum or a teaspoon of rum extract to butterscotch sundae sauce.

PEAR DESSERTS

Jiffy Spiced Canned Pears. Drain pear syrup into a saucepan. Add several cloves and 1/4 cup of red cinnamon candies. Boil for 3 minutes. Pour hot syrup over pears. Cool, then chill. Serve with whipped cream tinted and flavored with a teaspoonful of the syrup.

Memorable Dessert. Whole peeled and cored jarred Bartlett pears dipped in waffle batter and baked in a hot oven. Serve with almond-flavored whipped cream or brandy sauce.

Pear Belle Hélène. Scoop vanilla ice cream into a dessert dish for each portion. Bank the ice cream with two chilled canned pear halves or peeled, ripe, fresh pear halves and drown in chocolate sauce.

Pear Melba. Fill canned pear halves with frozen red raspberries, almost thawed. Lace the berries with Cointreau if desired.

Pears with Apricot Sauce. Thoroughly chill cored pear halves, fresh or canned. Serve with a sauce of apricot puree (baby-food strained apricots and apples), laced if you like with a bit of rum or brandy.

Poached Pears Avocado. Use fresh poached pears or canned pear halves. Arrange several halves in each dish. Sprinkle with lime juice and Curaçao. Chill. Top with 1 cup of whipped cream mixed with 1/2 cup of confectioners' sugar, 1/8 teaspoon salt, and 3/4 cup of sieved avocado.

Spiced Pear Snowballs. Drain canned pears. Prepare sauce of 2 parts of sour cream to 1 part of softened vanilla ice cream, seasoned with cinnamon and nutmeg. Refrigerate the sauce until serving time.

PINEAPPLE DESSERTS

Gingered Pineapple. Drain a can of pineapple chunks or use fresh or thawed frozen pineapple chunks. Marinate in 1/4 cup of dark Jamaica rum and 2 tablespoons of the pineapple juice. Place marinated pineapple chunks and a bit of the marinade in sherbet glasses. Top with slightly sweetened whipped cream to which you have added some finely chopped crystallized or candied ginger.

Ginger Sauce. Fold crushed pineapple and candied ginger into applesauce. Serve with ginger snaps for a quick dessert.

Lime Sherbet with Pineapple Sauce. Boil a can of crushed pineapple to thicken syrup. Add a squeeze of fresh lime juice. Serve the sauce warm over lime sherbet.

Pineapple Anisette. Arrange thawed frozen pineapple chunks on a scoop of pineapple sherbet. Sprinkle with fresh coconut and spoon on a sauce made by mixing the thawed pineapple juice and equal parts of anisette over the top. Serve with almond cookies.

Pineapple Compote. Serve a slice of canned pineapple with steamed, soft, seeded muscat raisins.

Pineapple Sherbet Sputnik. A scoop of pineapple sherbet stuck with 4 or 5 toothpicks; some toothpicks spear chunks of fresh pineapple, some frosted, seeded Ribier grapes and red Tokay grapes (see Frosted Grapes), and some strawberries dipped in granulated sugar. Perfect after a hot curry dinner.

Pineapple Supreme. Cut a fresh pineapple into sixths, lengthwise, cutting through the green top, too, so that each section has its share. Cut pineapple meat away from shell with grapefruit knife, leaving the shells intact. Core and cube the pineapple meat. Sprinkle with Cointreau. Keep both cubes and shells cold. Just before serving, arrange cubes of pineapple in the pineapple shells. Top with coconut whipped cream and one beautiful, un-hulled strawberry. To make the coconut whipped cream, fold canned flaked coconut into whipped cream flavored with a few drops of Cointreau.

Strawberry-Pineapple Dessert. Serve thawed frozen pineapple chunks topped with partially thawed sliced strawberries. Top all with a large dollop of sour cream and spoon maple syrup into the center of the sour cream.

SAUCES FOR DESSERTS

Emergency (but Real) Whipped Cream. I belong to the pure whipped cream school, but even I enjoy this. Add 4 tablespoons of instant vanilla pudding mix to 1 cup of cold light cream and whip. Serve on fresh or stewed fruit.

Fruit Flair Toppings. Try one of these toppings on chilled, drained, canned fruit: whipped cream flavored with almond extract and sprinkled with sliced, toasted almonds or sweetened whipped cream sprinkled with nutmeg. Or try your choice of fruits topped with ice cream, softened cream cheese, or thin custard sauce. Fruit served on top of plain tapioca pudding or in a meringue shell with whipped cream topping is also a real treat. (Raggedy free-stone peaches, fresh or canned; strawberries; or grated raw apple or pear are particularly delicious to use with the above ideas.)

Frozen Desserts

HOMEMADE FROZEN DESSERTS

Angel Parfait with Red Raspberries. Heat 1 cup of light corn syrup to 238°F. Pour the hot syrup over 3 stiff, but not dry, beaten egg whites. Cool. Fold in 1 cup of heavy cream, whipped, and 2 teaspoons of vanilla. Freeze in small molds or in refrigerator tray, without stirring, for about three hours. Serve with sweetened red raspberries.

Easy Coffee Mousse. Melt 1/2 pound of marshmallows in 2 cups of strong coffee. Cool. Fold the mixture into 1 pint of whipped cream. Freeze without stirring.

Frozen Prune Whip. Make prune whip with a jar of junior-food prunes. Fold the whip into 1 cup of heavy cream whipped. Freeze without stirring.

Graham Cracker Mousse. Fold 1 cup of graham cracker crumbs into sweetened whipped cream flavored with vanilla. Freeze without stirring. Serve with hot fudge sauce.

Pineapple-Rhubarb Ice Cream. Simmer 5 cups of chopped rhubarb with 2 cups of undrained crushed pineapple until rhubarb is tender. Add 1 cup of sugar. Cool and chill. Whip 1 pint of heavy cream. Fold the chilled fruit mixture into the whipped cream. Pour into two 1-quart-size freezer trays and freeze until firm.

READY-MADE ICE CREAM DESSERTS

Apricot-Macaroon Melbas. Press two soft coconut macaroons into muffin-pan cups to make shallow shells. Remove. Fill shells with ice cream. Top with a canned, peeled apricot, spread open and seed removed. Place a spoon of seedless red raspberry jam or other red jam or jelly on top of the opened apricot.

Black-and-White Party Dessert. Put layers of vanilla ice cream, fudge sauce, more ice cream, and marshmallow sauce in sherbet or parfait glasses. Top with chopped nuts. Freeze. Thaw slightly before serving.

Cantaloupe Rings with Mint Ice Cream. Wash cantaloupe and slice into rings about 1 inch thick. Peel the rings quite thickly and evenly. Place on chilled dessert plates. Fill the center of each ring with a scoop of mint ice cream and garnish with frosted mint leaves.

Caramel Nut Topping for Ice Cream or Cake. Melt 1/2 pound of caramels in 1 tablespoon of butter and 1/2 cup of hot water. Add 1/3 cup of walnut or pecan halves. Use on loaf cake or on a scoop of vanilla ice cream.

Children's Party Dessert. Serve scoops of tutti-frutti ice cream studded with thin pretzel sticks.

Chocolate Ice Cream with Lemon Queens. Serve chocolate ice cream with lemon sponge cake or lemon chiffon cake baked in muffin pans and iced with a thin lemon confectioners' frosting (not buttery).

Coffee Ice Cream Balls. Roll balls of coffee ice cream in chocolate sprinkles or grated semisweet chocolate. Serve in a little pool of maple syrup heated and flavored with instant coffee and then cooled.

Coupe Deluxe. Put a scoop of ice cream in a glass. Cover with tiny melon balls soaked in white wine with a dash of Curaçao. Top with ground toasted almonds.

Coupe Madeleine. Place 1 tablespoonful of crushed pineapple in the bottom of each parfait glass or slender pilsener beer glass. Half fill the glass with soft vanilla ice cream. Add another tablespoon of crushed pineapple, 1 teaspoonful of apricot jam, and 1 teaspoonful of kirsch or light rum. Top with whipped cream and a dab of apricot jam.

Date-Nut Ice Cream. Stir broken nut meats, chopped dates, a bit of grated orange rind, and 1 tablespoon of brandy into slightly softened vanilla ice cream. Return to freezer until ready to serve.

Date Parfait. Combine 1 cup of chopped, pitted dates with 1/2 cup of brown sugar, 1 cup of water, and 1-1/4 cups of brandy. Simmer for about 10 minutes until slightly thickened. Add 1/2 cup of chopped nuts. Place alternate spoonfuls of date sauce, vanilla ice cream, and whipped cream in sherbet or parfait glasses. Finish with a dab of whipped cream and a sliver of pitted date.

Easy Homemade Spumoni. Press toasted almond or butter pecan ice cream all around the sides of a large mold. Mix 1/4 cup of ground, mixed glacéed fruits with strawberry ice cream and fill the middle of the mold. Freeze until ready to use. Unmold and cut in wedges. Good dessert with an Italian dinner.

Fresh Coconut Ice Cream. Fold a generous amount of finely grated fresh coconut rather unevenly into vanilla ice cream and return to freezer. Roll large scoops of the coconut ice cream in grated coconut. Serve in deep sherbet glasses on top of thawed frozen raspberries or strawberries.

Frosted Ambrosia. Roll scoops of vanilla ice cream in freshly grated or canned flaked coconut. Put balls in sherbet glasses. Pour a little defrosted but not diluted orange juice concentrate around the ice cream balls.

Ice Cream Tarts. Bake rich pie crust in fluted tart shells. Just before serving, fill with vanilla ice cream topped with a generous dab of fudge sauce or strawberry preserve.

Maple Marshmallow Sundae. Melt 8 marshmallows in 1/2 cup of maple syrup. Add 1/2 cup of crushed (not chopped) English walnuts. Cool slightly. Serve over 3 small balls of vanilla ice cream in a sherbet glass.

Orange Blossom Sundae. Cover vanilla ice cream with sections of orange and a spoonful of orange blossom honey. Top with a fresh or candied orange blossom if available.

Parfait au Rhum. Make thin rum sauce by boiling equal parts of sugar and dark rum for a few minutes. Almost fill parfait glasses with coffee ice cream. Float a tablespoonful of the rum sauce on top. No whipped cream. Some of the sauce can be put in the bottom of the glass before the ice cream.

Peach Melba Parfait. In parfait glasses put alternate layers of ice cream, sliced freestone peaches, and melba sauce (which can be bought in jars). Top with whipped cream and garnish with a peach slice. Or make your own melba sauce by combining one package of frozen red raspberries, thawed, and 1/2 cup of currant jelly. Add 1-1/2 teaspoons of cornstarch mixed with 1 tablespoon of water. Cook until thick and clear, stirring constantly. Strain and cool.

Peach Parfait. Alternate peach ice cream, whipped cream, and red raspberries in a parfait glass. Top with a rosette of whipped cream.

Peanut Ball Sundae. Cover vanilla ice cream balls with coarsely ground salted peanuts. Keep in freezer until serving time. Place in dessert dishes or sherbet glasses and surround with warm butterscotch sauce.

Pear Melba. Make a mousse by folding 1/2 cup of seedless red raspberry jam into 1 cup of heavy cream, whipped. Serve a scoop of the frozen mousse with 2 pear halves (one pressed on each side of the mousse). Top with a dab of raspberry jam or red raspberries.

Peppermint Chocolate Ice Cream. Melt 2 ounces of chocolate-covered mint patties in 2 tablespoons of cream. Stir into 1 quart of slightly softened chocolate ice cream. Return to freezer until serving time.

Pineapple and Strawberry Coupe. Line sherbet glasses with grated fresh pineapple, sugared and well chilled, or with drained crushed pineapple if absolutely necessary. Fill with vanilla ice cream, covered with crushed, sweetened strawberries. Top with whipped cream.

Sherried Cranberry Sundae. Cook 1/2 pound of fresh cranberries with 3/4 cup of sherry and 1/2 cup of water for 10 minutes, or until skins pop. Add 1 cup of sugar and 1/4 cup of white seedless raisins. Cook for 15 minutes more. Cool. Serve on vanilla ice cream.

Strawberry Casserole. Put generous spoonfuls of sliced, sugared strawberries and a spoon of brandy, rum, or Cointreau in bottom of earthenware ramekins or individual casseroles. Cover with hard vanilla ice cream. Top with a meringue made by beating 2 tablespoons of confectioners' sugar with each egg white used. Brown quickly under the broiler and serve at once.

Swiss Chocolate Parfait. Serve in medium-size brandy snifter. Place fudge sauce in bottom, then uneven chunks of chocolate ice cream, then small irregular chunks of block milk chocolate (the old-fashioned kind), and whole toasted almonds (be generous with the almonds). Top with a dab of fudge sauce and cocoa-flavored whipped cream, a blanched almond, and a small chunk of the chocolate.

Thanksgiving Dinner Dessert. Heat mincemeat in chafing dish at the table. Allow 2 tablespoons of warmed brandy to each cup of mincemeat. Light the brandy and spoon the mixture over vanilla or rum ice cream.

True Maple Walnut Sundae. Serve ice cream with maple syrup and walnut halves.

SHERBET DESSERTS

Blueberry Sundae. Add a whisper of cinnamon to fresh or canned sweetened blueberries. Serve over lemon sherbet. A perfect summer dessert.

China Sundae. Cover a scoop of orange sherbet with Mandarin orange sections. Serve with Chinese fortune cookies.

Christmas Cup. Put 1 tablespoon of Nesselrode sauce or tutti-frutti sauce in the bottom of a sherbet glass. Add a small scoop of raspberry sherbet and one of pistachio ice cream. Garnish with whipped cream, sprinkled with red and green sugar if desired.

Mint-Lemon Sherbet. Top lemon sherbet with green crème de menthe. Delicious after a fish dinner.

Orange Dessert Squares. Cut slices of orange chiffon cake about 1/2-inch thick. Place a slice on each serving plate, followed by a slice of orange sherbet, then another slice of cake. Top with whipped cream or frost with whipped cream and garnish with fresh orange sections or Mandarin orange sections.

Puddings

ABC Dessert. Spell names of children on top of chocolate pudding with cereal letters.

American Version of Custard Brûlée. Put a soft candy caramel in the bottom of each custard cup, then pour on custard mixture. Bake as usual. When inverted, you have a dessert with a delicious caramel sauce.

Chocolate Peppermint Floating Island. Prepare chocolate pudding as directed on package, using an extra cup of milk. Put the pudding in serving dish and top with an island of pink-tinted, peppermint-flavored whipped cream. Garnish with chocolate sprinkles.

Cranberry Cream. Fold 1 cup of crushed jellied cranberry sauce into chilled tapioca pudding. Serve with whipped cream.

Dainty. Make uncooked lemon custard with a can of sweetened condensed milk. Fold in 3/4 cup of crushed lemon snaps and 1 cup of sliced strawberries. Place in sherbet glasses and sprinkle with lemon-snap crumbs. Serve with a dollop of whipped cream.

Double Chocolate Pudding. Make chocolate pudding according to package directions, adding an extra 1/4 cup of milk. Remove from fire and add 1/2 cup of chocolate bits or 2 squares of broken semisweet chocolate, stirring until melted. Cool, and add 1 teaspoon of vanilla. Fold in 1 cup heavy cream, whipped, and pile into sherbet glasses. Top with a few chocolate chips or with curls of semisweet chocolate. (Chocolate curls can be made by using a vegetable peeler to cut curls off slightly warm chocolate.)

Festive Quick Family Orange Dessert. Chill 2 packages of orange gelatine (made with part orange juice) in ring mold. Turn out. Fill center with sweetened whipped cream with cubes of cake folded into it.

French Dessert. Make a regular floating island pudding: that is, a thin egg custard sauce with poached puffs of meringue. Sprinkle toasted, slivered almonds over the meringue islands when they are floated on the custard sauce. For a taste thrill, serve with a bowl of fresh cut-up fruits that have been soaked briefly in Cointreau.

Heavenly Rice. Combine chilled cooked rice with crushed pineapple, finely cut marshmallows, crushed walnuts, chopped maraschino cherries, and enough sweetened whipped cream to hold them together. Chill thoroughly before serving. Top with a maraschino cherry and a walnut half.

Louisiana Rice Pudding. Fold cooked rice into a vanilla-flavored thin boiled custard made with egg yolks. Turn into a baking dish. Sprinkle top of custard generously with nutmeg. Top with a high meringue that touches all sides of the baking dish. Bake in a slow oven until meringue is delicately brown and firm. Chill and serve with thin cream or a pureed apricot sauce.

Mint-Lemon Pudding. Garnish packaged lemon pudding with a dab of apple-mint jelly and a sprig of fresh mint.

Minute Rice Imperial. Make butterscotch pudding according to package directions. When pudding is cold, add 2 cups of cold, cooked rice and 1 cup of whipped cream (that is, 1/2 cup of cream, whipped). Serve in sherbet glasses, top with whipped cream, and sprinkle with a dash of nutmeg.

Mocha Nut Pudding. Add 1 teaspoon of instant coffee to chocolate pudding mix. Pour the hot pudding over beaten egg yolk and return to the pan for a few minutes. Alternate layers of the pudding and crushed nuts in sherbet glasses. Top with sweetened whipped cream flavored with a little cocoa and 1/4 teaspoon of instant coffee.

Orange Tapioca Elegant. Pile orange tapioca or any orange custard pudding unevenly in parfait glasses alternately with whipped cream, tiny shreds of orange rind, and a Mandarin orange section here and there. Top with a dab of whipped cream and 1 or 2 Mandarin orange sections.

Red, White, and Blue Pudding. Fill individual custard cups or sherbet glasses 2/3 full of vanilla pudding. Arrange a circle of sliced strawberries around the edge, then a circle of blueberries, with a dab of whipped cream in the center. Stick a tiny paper flag in a strawberry and place on the whipped cream.

FRUIT AND NUT CONCOCTIONS

Apple-Butterscotch Pudding. Make a Brown Betty with crushed cornflake crumbs instead of bread. Serve with a butterscotch sauce made from a package of butterscotch pudding thinned with milk and flavored with a bit of browned butter.

Apple Potpie. Make a recipe of rich biscuit dough. Roll thin and cut into 2-inch squares. Dice pared tart apples and sprinkle generously with sugar, cinnamon, and a dash of nutmeg. Arrange the biscuit dough squares and the apples alternately in a buttered, deep glass casserole, adding light brown sugar between the layers. Put 3 or 4 tablespoons of butter on top. Fill the casserole half full of water. Cover and bake until apples are done. Serve hot with a big pitcher of cream. Old-time and delicious.

Apple Scallop. Put alternate layers of sliced apples and broken graham crackers or buttered toast cubes in a baking dish. Sprinkle each layer of apples with sugar, cinnamon, nutmeg, and bits of butter. Bake for 30 minutes in a moderate oven. Serve with cream.

Baked Blueberry Cake. Swedish accent. Put a rich shortcake dough (made from biscuit mix with added butter) in a baking dish and cover dough liberally with fresh blueberries, sweetened and sprinkled lightly with lemon juice and a dash of nutmeg. Bake in a hot oven until the shortcake dough is done and the berries have formed a heavenly thick sauce on top. Serve with heavy cream in a pitcher.

Baked Fig Pudding. Make Brown Betty without the usual cinnamon and use canned, cut-up Kadota figs instead of apples. Serve warm with whipped cream sweetened with brown sugar.

Blueberry Boiled Dumplings. Poach biscuit mix dumplings in a sauce made of 1-1/2 cups of blueberries, 3/4 cup of water, 1/4 cup of sugar, a dash of salt, and 1 teaspoon of lemon juice. Bring the sauce to a boil. Drop spoonfuls of dumpling batter on top. Reduce heat and gently boil, uncovered, for 10 minutes. Cover and cook without peeking for 10 minutes more. Serve immediately with lots of cream.

Blueberry Roll with Ice Cream. Make rich biscuit dough and roll out a rectangle. Spread it thickly with blueberry preserves. Roll up like jelly roll. Brush top of the roll with cream and bake in a hot oven for 25 to 30 minutes. While still warm, serve sliced with ice cream and a blueberry sauce made by thinning blueberry preserves with water, adding a little lemon juice and a bit of butter.

Corn Topping for Peach Pudding. Lay sliced, sweetened peaches in a shallow buttered baking dish. Sprinkle with 1/2 cup of corn muffin mix, 1/4 cup of light brown sugar, and 1/4 cup of butter. Bake in a moderate oven for about 40 minutes. Serve warm with cream.

Orange Baked Apple Dumplings. Cover small peeled and cored apples with rich biscuit dough. Place in 12 x 7 x 2-inch baking dish. Cover with syrup made of 1-1/2 cups of sugar, 2 cups of orange juice, 1/4 teaspoon of nutmeg, and 1/4 cup of butter. Bake in a hot oven, basting dumplings occasionally with the syrup.

Quick Brown Betty. Mix together 1 container of bread crumbs, 3/4 cup of butter, 1 beaten egg, 1 cup of milk, 3/4 cup of brown sugar, 4 cups of chopped apples, and a dash of nutmeg. Place in a frying pan or electric skillet. Cover and cook over medium heat for 10 to 20 minutes. Serve with cream flavored with cinnamon.

Sauce for the Dumpling. Apple dumplings or apple cobbler are especially delicious when sprinkled with cinnamon or nutmeg and served in a bowl with slightly sweetened, thin cream, or with a thin custard sauce.

Sherried Fruit Cake Pudding. Soak leftover fruit cake in sherry wine. (Heat the soaked cake in the top of a double boiler if desired.) Serve with custard sauce and a dab of whipped cream or a puff of poached meringue.

Slip-Easy Pudding. Put equal amounts of whole-wheat bread crumbs and fresh rhubarb, generously sugared, in layers in a buttered casserole. The top layer should be crumbs. Dot with butter and pour a generous amount of milk over the top. Bake slowly until golden brown. For sauce, mix 1 cup of brown sugar, 2 tablespoons of vinegar, 1 cup of hot water, and 1 tablespoon of flour. Boil until creamy. Serve sauce warm or cold on the warm pudding.

Other Unusual Desserts

Almond Strawberry Shortcake. Add 1/2 cup of thinly sliced almonds to rich shortcake dough. When baked, split and serve with sugared strawberries and almond-flavored whipped cream. Top with a few toasted, sliced almonds.

Apple Dessert Sauce. Sauce: equal parts of cream cheese and sour cream, sweetened and seasoned with a little cinnamon and a lot of nutmeg. A delicious sauce for apple strudel, apple pie, or Brown Betty.

Banana au Confiture. Place a vanilla wafer on a plate. Spread with whipped cream and add a slice of banana first dipped in orange juice. Repeat, using 4 wafers to a portion. Top with 1 teaspoon of strawberry jam or preserves. Cover sides with whipped cream. Very pretty.

Blueberry Blini. For dessert or brunch, spread 1/3 cup of cottage cheese between 2 thin pancakes and top with hot blueberry sauce, made by thinning whole blueberry preserves with a few tablespoons of water.

Caramel Whipped Cream Puffs. Prepare and bake cream puffs. Fill with cream whipped with brown sugar. Serve the filled puffs with caramel glaze made by melting 1/2 pound of soft caramels with 1/4 cup of water in a double boiler. While glaze is still warm (not hot), pour it over the cool puffs and serve.

Cheese Cake with Sour-Cream Topping. Topping: Add 3 tablespoons of sugar and 1/2 teaspoon of vanilla to 1 pint of sour cream and spread over hot cheese cake immediately upon removing from the oven. Or, if using a bakery cheese cake, heat and spread with the mixture. Sprinkle with slivered, toasted almonds. Return to a very hot oven for just 5 minutes. Chill thoroughly before serving.

Chocolate Angel. Melt 7 small milk-chocolate-almond candy bars with 1 square of unsweetened chocolate. Cool slightly. Fold into 1/2 pint of heavy cream, whipped. Split an angel food cake crosswise. Use chocolate mixture as filling and frosting, covering top and sides of cake. Chill overnight.

Chocolate Mint Cups. Put paper baking cups in muffin tins. Melt semisweet chocolate bits with 2 tablespoons of butter and lightly coat the entire inside surface of the cups with the chocolate mixture. Chill. When chocolate is hard, tear off paper. Fill chocolate cups with mint ice cream. Make several extra cups in case one breaks or one is a little too thick. The broken or thick cups can be grated and used as a garnish or melted for flavoring.

Chocolate Peppermint Rolls. Add a few drops of peppermint extract and pink food coloring to the whipped cream with which you put chocolate wafers together for icebox dessert. Cover tops and sides with the whipped cream. Chill overnight. Garnish with peppermint candies or small candy canes for Christmas.

Crêpes Annette. Make thin, small pancakes, using a thin batter. Spread with blackberry jam; roll up and sprinkle with powdered sugar. Serve hot.

Dessert Garnishes or Ingredients. Cut candied fruits, marshmallows, dates, and so on with scissors. Dip the scissors in hot water occasionally as you go along.

Double Chocolate Torte. Line an 8-inch square cake pan with graham cracker crust mixture. Fill with chocolate pudding, adding 1 tablespoon of unflavored gelatine and a cup of chocolate chips while pudding is hot. Chill until firm and top with whipped cream. Cut into squares to serve.

Easy Crêpes. You can make tender, thin dessert pancakes with pancake mix if you want to. Heat 1-1/3 cups of milk and 3 tablespoons of butter until the butter melts. Cool to lukewarm. Beat an egg thoroughly and add the cooled milk and egg to 3/4 cup of pancake mix. Beat with electric mixer or rotary beater until smooth. Bake on a hot griddle, using only about 2 tablespoons of batter for each pancake. Stack by fours and cover to keep moist until filled and rolled for crêpes suzette, or fill with sweetened cream cheese thinned with orange juice and grated orange rind. Roll each pancake around the filling and place in shallow baking pan, folded side down. Heat in oven at 400° for 10 minutes. Serve with hot blueberry sauce or hot whole cranberry sauce.

French Crullers. Add grated orange rind to packaged cream puff mix, and bake in the shape of eclairs. When cool, split and fill with cocoa-flavored sweetened whipped cream or with double-chocolate pudding from mix. Coat with orange frosting made by thinning confectioners' sugar with a bit of fresh or frozen orange juice.

Fresh Strawberry Cream Puffs. Fill cream puffs with sweetened whipped cream into which you have folded a generous amount of sliced, sugared strawberries. Dust puffs with confectioners' sugar and place a pretty unhulled strawberry on the plate beside each puff.

Holiday Dessert. Serve slices of fruit cake with crisp salted nuts and port.

Individual Baked Alaskas. Place sponge cake dessert shells on baking sheet. Spoon strawberry preserves into the shells. Place firmly frozen scoops of ice cream (scooped out ahead of time and kept in freezing compartment on waxed paper) in the center of each dessert shell on top of the preserves. Cover top and sides thickly with meringue made of 6 egg whites and 3/4 cup of sugar. Brown in hot oven (400°) for 3 to 5 minutes. Serve on chilled dessert plates.

Last-Minute Dessert. Crush the contents of a can of Kadota figs. Add the crushed figs to a pint of cream which has been whipped very stiff and flavored with almond extract. Place in sherbet glasses lined with lady fingers, cut in half with the rounded ends up. Chill.

Lemon Angel Torte. Bake meringue in two well-buttered 8-inch pie plates. Put the two layers together with a generous coating of whipped cream mixed with a package of lemon pudding to which you have added a teaspoon of finely grated lemon peel and a tablespoon of fresh lemon juice. Top with whipped cream and garnish with thin lemon slices dipped in granulated sugar. Cut lemon slices from center to rind and twist into an S shape.

Lemon Cream-Topped Blueberry Shortcake. Fill baked sponge cake cups with sweetened fresh blueberries. Top with lemon whipped cream. Whip 1 cup of heavy cream. Mix 1 teaspoon of lemon juice, 1 tablespoon of powdered sugar, and 1/2 teaspoon of finely grated lemon rind. Fold the lemon mixture into the whipped cream just before serving.

Meringue Marron. Buy or make 6 vanilla-flavored meringues. Whip 1 pint of heavy cream very stiff. Fold in 1 ounce of sauce from preserved marrons and 2 tablespoons of brandy. Pile high on meringues. Force the drained marrons through a ricer onto the whipped cream, covering each dessert generously. Serve ice cold.

Mincemeat Dessert Waffles. Serve a quarter of a hot waffle with a mound of hard sauce in the center, surrounded by warm mincemeat.

No-Bake Chocolate Torte. Fill an 8-inch cake tin with alternate layers of crushed graham crackers mixed with butter (as for graham cracker pie crust) and chocolate fudge sauce, with the chocolate fudge sauce on top. Sprinkle top with crushed (not chopped) walnuts. Chill overnight. Cut in squares and serve with whipped cream.

Orange-Chocolate Cream Cake. Mix 1/4 cup of instant (ready-mixed) cocoa with 1-3/4 cup of chocolate cookie crumbs. Whip 1 quart of heavy cream. Fold in 1-1/4 cups of confectioners' sugar, 1/4 cup of orange juice, the grated rind of 1 orange, and 2 teaspoons of vanilla. In two refrigerator trays or square cake pans, put alternate thin layers of crumbs and cream mixture, making the top layer cream. Chill until firm. Cut in squares. Garnish with drained Mandarin orange sections.

Peaches in Blankets. Wrap fresh peach halves filled with mincemeat in extra-rich pastry squares. Bake and serve warm with sherry-flavored, sweetened whipped cream.

Sponge Cake Shell Variations. With individual sponge cakes, usually used for shortcake, you can make many interesting and delicious variations. For example:

Pineapple Dainty: Toast and crumble half of the sponge cakes. Whip 1 cup of heavy cream, add the cake crumbs and some drained, crushed pineapple. Moisten the other sponge cakes with pineapple juice and fill with the cream mixture. Make a hollow in the filling and put in a dab of strawberry preserves.

Lemon Tarts: Fill sponge cakes with cooled lemon pie filling. Cover sides and a narrow border on top edge with meringue. Bake at 375° for a few minutes, until tips of meringue are lightly browned. (Meringue: 2 tablespoons of sugar to each egg white.)

Cherry Pudding: Cream 1/3 cup of butter with 1 cup of powdered sugar. Fold in 1/2 cup of tart red canned cherries, drained. Steam the sponge cakes in top of a double boiler. When ready to serve, put cherry mixture in the center and garnish with cherries. Serve with cream.

Raspberry Creams: Fill center of each sponge cake with red raspberry (or any other) jam. Cover with sweetened whipped cream. Place a dab of jam on top and sprinkle with chopped nuts. Chill for several hours.

Swiss Chocolate Puffs. Make or buy small cream puffs. For chocolate sauce, melt 6 ounces of a Swiss milk chocolate bar with 1/2 cup of light cream. Whip 1 pint of heavy cream. At serving time, split and fill the cream puffs with Swiss chocolate ice cream or chocolate ice cream to which you have added 2 toasted salted almonds for each puff. Place whipped cream in bottom of large sherbet glasses or brandy snifters. Drop several ice-cream-filled puffs into the whipped cream and drizzle chocolate sauce over the top. Fold very gently to get a marbled effect.

Thanksgiving Buffet Dessert. Serve a sliced ice cream roll with a bowl of warm mincemeat laced with brandy and another bowl of spiced whipped cream.

Trifle. Cover the bottom of a shallow glass serving dish with almond macaroons. Pour on 1/4 cup of sherry wine and let stand until macaroons are soft. Line sides of dish with lady fingers which have been split and put back together with red raspberry jam. Pour in cold, soft egg custard (you may make the custard by adding an extra 1/2 cup of milk and the yolk of 1 egg to a package of vanilla pudding mix). Chill well. Garnish with dollops of whipped cream topped with a bit of raspberry jam.

Pies and Tarts

Cooking Tips: Secrets for Good Fruit Pies. Make a rich crust. Use a small amount of some thickening agent and some butter in the filling (2 tablespoons of flour, 1 tablespoon of cornstarch, or 1 tablespoon of tapioca). Make sure there are no holes in the bottom crust, not even the tiniest ones. Four or 5 slashes in the top crust will allow steam to escape without forcing sides open. Set oven at a very high baking temperature at first, so the crust can set before juices begin escaping from the fruit. Set on bottom rack or very bottom of the oven. Lower temperature during the last 20 minutes of baking so juices do not boil over. Cool pie in pan on cake rack to prevent sogginess of bottom crust from steam.

Cream Pies

Ambrosia Pie. Bake a rich pie shell. When cool, fill with orange custard to which you have added flaked coconut and grated orange rind. Top with meringue. Sprinkle with more flaked coconut. Bake in a hot oven for about 8 minutes or until top is just slightly golden.

Avocado Strawberry Pie. Cover baked pastry shells with sliced strawberries until 3/4 full. Pour partially thickened, strawberry-flavored gelatine over the berries to fill pie shell. Chill until filling is firm. Serve with avocado cream made by beating until light 3/4 cup of sieved avocado, 1/2 cup of confectioners' sugar, and 1 drop of green food coloring. Fold into 1 cup of heavy cream, whipped.

Black-Bottom Coconut Cream Pie. Bake a rich 9-inch pie shell. Cool. Melt 4 ounces of dipping chocolate or chocolate bits and 4 teaspoons of butter in a double boiler. Remove from heat and brush chocolate on bottom and sides of pie crust. Let harden. Fill chocolate-coated crust with cooled coconut-cream filling (add freshly grated or canned flaked coconut and 2 egg yolks to 2 packages of vanilla pudding). Sprinkle top of filling with grated coconut and shavings of sweet chocolate.

Orange Cream Tarts. Bake graham cracker crumb crust in tart shells. Prepare packaged vanilla pudding according to directions, but use 3 tablespoons less liquid than called for. Pour the thickened hot pudding over the slightly beaten yolk of 1 egg and return to pan for a few minutes. Then add 3 tablespoons of thawed orange juice concentrate. Cool. Pour into tart shells. Serve with whipped cream flavored with 1 tablespoon of the thawed orange juice concentrate. Garnish with drained Mandarin orange sections or finely grated orange rind.

Rum and Butterscotch Pie. Add 1 teaspoon of rum flavoring to butterscotch pudding mix. Pour into baked pie shell. Top with sweetened whipped cream flavored with an additional 1/2 teaspoon of rum flavoring.

Strawberry Napoleon Pie. Roll three 9-inch circles of rich pie crust about 1/4 inch thick. Before baking, prick all the circles well and cut around the inside of one circle, 1-1/2 inches from the edge, leaving a deep mark. Remove from oven and take the center circle out of the ringed piece. Sprinkle with powdered sugar. Cool pie crust rounds. Make a rich cream filling from vanilla pudding mix, adding 1 egg yolk for each package of mix. Cool filling. Put cream filling between the 2 baked crusts and on top of the second. Top that with the pastry ring and fill the center of the ring with sweetened, choice strawberries. Garnish the bottom outside edge of the torte with whipped cream.

Strawberry Tarts Chantilly. Bake tart shells from rich pie dough. Pile full with Chantilly cream (whipped cream well sweetened with sifted powdered sugar and flavored with a dash of almond extract) into which you have folded whole, ripe sweet strawberries. Place a plump whole strawberry on top.

Tortoni Pie. Fill rich baked pie crust with vanilla pudding mix made with an added egg yolk and flavored with 1 teaspoon of almond extract and a cup of crumbled almond macaroons. Top with additional crumbled macaroons and a few finely chopped toasted almonds.

Frozen Pies

Crème de Menthe Pie. Bake a chocolate wafer crust. When cool, fill crust with vanilla ice cream which has been softened by folding in 1/2 pint of whipped cream. Place pie in the freezer until serving time. Serve with whipped cream and green crème de menthe poured over each piece. For the children, pour chocolate mint sauce over the pie instead of the crème de menthe.

Ginger Peachy Pie. Make a gingersnap crumb crust in a metal pie pan. Chill it. Fill with peach ice cream, leaving the top uneven, and put it in the freezer. Just before serving, place slices of fresh peaches on the ice cream. Cover with meringue and sprinkle with a bit of powdered ginger. Bake in a very hot oven for 3 to 5 minutes to lightly brown the meringue peaks.

Mincemeat Ice Cream Pie. Slightly soften vanilla ice cream and lace with mincemeat flavored with light rum. Turn into a baked graham cracker crumb crust. Keep in the freezer until just before serving time. Garnish with sweetened, rum-flavored whipped cream.

Peach Pie Alaska. Bake a rich pie shell. Spread the shell with a thin layer of a stiff meringue (5 egg whites and 3/4 cup of sugar). Cover meringue with sliced freestone peaches and fill with peach ice cream. Top with the rest of the meringue, making dents for the addition of garnish peaches later. Brown meringue quickly under broiler just before serving. Place sweetened peach halves and slices in the dents in the meringue. Serve immediately.

Red Raspberry Ice Cream Pie. Bake a graham cracker crust in a deep pie pan. Beat 1 cup of heavy cream until stiff and fold into 1 quart of partially softened vanilla ice cream. Fill crust and place pie in the freezer until serving time. Cut in wedges and top with almost-thawed frozen red raspberries and a dab of whipped cream.

Rummy Mincemeat Ice Cream Pie. Fold 1-1/2 cups of mincemeat and 2 tablespoons of dark rum or brandy into 1 quart of softened vanilla ice cream. Fill pie shell and freeze. Just before serving, cut in wedges and serve with a sauce of hot mincemeat laced with rum or brandy.

Surprise Frozen Lemon Pie. Make a rich pie crust. Fill half full with vanilla ice cream. Keep in freezer. Prepare tart lemon pie filling. Chill. Just before serving, cover the ice cream with the chilled lemon pie filling. Return to freezer and make meringue, adding a bit of grated lemon rind. Spread meringue on pie top. Place under the broiler for 3 to 5 minutes to lightly brown meringue.

Fruit Pies

Apple and Cheese Pie. Add 2/3 cup of grated extra-sharp cheese to the apple filling for the pie. Add 1 teaspoon of cinnamon to the dry ingredients of the pie crust. You may make a lattice top crust for the pie if desired. Try arranging the lattice top crust on waxed paper (a little bigger than the pie) and then turning it over on top of the pie.

Apple-Orange Pie. Add 1 can of drained Mandarin oranges or peeled fresh orange sections (white membranes removed) to apple pie filling before baking.

Blueberry Pie à la Mode. Make the pie with 2 tablespoons of lemon juice and 3 tablespoons of quick-cooking tapioca to thicken the filling. Flavor with a dash of cinnamon if desired. Rich crust, hot oven. Serve with vanilla ice cream.

Blackberry Pie with Blackberry Hard Sauce. Bake a two-crust black-berry pie. Serve slightly warm with a small scoop of blackberry hard sauce made by creaming 1 cup of butter with 2 cups of confectioners' sugar and adding 1 tablespoonful of blackberry jam and 1 tablespoon of cognac. You may use any combination of fruit and jam—strawberries, cherries, and so on.

Blueberry Sundae Pie. Bake graham cracker crumb shell. Fill with unbaked gelatine-type cheese cake filling. Top with fresh blue-berries mixed gently with melted blueberry jam or red currant jelly.

California Dried-Fruit Pie. Bake a rich pie shell. Fill with pitted cooked prunes and cooked dried apricots that have been mixed with crumbs made of 1/2 cup each of sugar and graham cracker crumbs and 1/4 cup each of flour and chopped English walnuts mixed with 1/3 cup of melted butter. Bake until golden brown and set.

Cranberry Mincemeat Tarts. Cook 1 cup of cranberries with 1/4 cup of sugar and 1/2 cup of water until soft. Add 1 cup of mince-meat. Fill unbaked tart shells and put strips of pastry on top. Bake in hot oven.

Cranberry Strudel. Put 2 cups of raw cranberries and 1/2 cup of raisins through a food chopper. Add 2/3 cup of sugar and 1 cup of chopped nuts. Roll pie crust in 5-inch squares and brush with melted butter. Spread cranberry mixture on squares and roll up like small jelly rolls. Place on a cookie sheet and bake in a very hot oven for about 20 minutes.

Date and Gooseberry Pie. Sweeten and thicken 2 cups of cooked gooseberries and juice and 1 cup of sliced dates. Add a dash of salt. Pour into a baked pie crust. Chill. Cover with slightly sweet-ened whipped cream and sprinkle with cinnamon.

Devonshire Tarts. Shape rich pie crust into tarts and bake. Spread a thick layer of cream cheese, thinned with cream, on the bottom. Cover with fresh or canned fruit—strawberries, cherries, apri-cots, bananas, seedless or seeded grapes, or a slice of pineapple with a large strawberry in the middle. Pour melted red currant jelly over fruit to glaze.

Dutch Apple Cream Pie. Fill a partially baked rich pie shell with poached, sweetened, and thickened apple slices. Cover with a thin custard made of 1 package of vanilla pudding mix, 2-1/2 cups of milk and 2 well-beaten egg yolks added just before pouring the custard over the apples. Sprinkle custard generously with nutmeg. Bake until custard is set but still soft. Cool before serving.

Fresh Fruit Cake-Pie. Add 5 tablespoons of milk to 1 package of yellow layer-cake mix to form stiff dough. Handle lightly with pastry blender. Roll out between sheets of waxed paper. Line greased and floured 10-inch pie plate with the dough. Flute the edges. Pierce bottom and sides with a fork. Bake in a moderate oven for 25 to 30 minutes, or until golden brown. Cool. Just before serving, fill with sliced fresh fruit (peeled peaches and apricots, sliced bananas, and seedless grapes mixed). Melt and sieve apricot jam. Cool a little and pour over the fruit. Garnish the pie with whipped cream.

Frosted Plum Pie. Steam 2 pounds of fresh Italian prune plums with 1/3 cup of water. Add 3/4 cup of sugar and 1/4 teaspoon of salt. Thicken with 2 tablespoons of cornstarch, and add 1/4 cup of slivered, blanched almonds. Place unbaked bottom crust in a pie plate and cover with orange marmalade. Top with the fruit mixture. Put top crust on, seal and bake in a very hot oven for 35 to 45 minutes. Brush when almost cool with vanilla-flavored confectioners' frosting.

Fruit Custard Pie. Spread pitted, canned sweet cherries or sliced, canned freestone peaches on the bottom of a pie crust before covering with a custard mixture. Sprinkle top with nutmeg. Bake as you would a custard pie.

Glazed Cherry Pie. Line a 9-inch pie plate with crust. Sweeten and thicken sour red cherries. Add 1 tablespoon of lemon juice. Pour into pie crust. Dot with 2 tablespoons of butter. Bake without top crust at 450° for 10 minutes. Lower heat to moderate and bake for 1/2 hour longer. When pie is cool, pour glaze over the top: melt 3/4 cup of red currant jelly with a dash of cloves and cinnamon. Spoon over cherries and let cool. Serve with whipped cream.

Glazing Fruit Tarts. Cook the fruit juice down with sugar and a little cornstarch. Pour over the filled tarts and cool.

Kirsch Pie. Add 2 jiggers of kirsch and a tablespoon of tapioca to canned, tart cherry pie filling before placing it in the crust. Serve with whipped cream tinted and flavored with a little maraschino-cherry juice.

Mincemeat Cheese Crescents. On circles of rolled rich pastry, place 1 spoonful of mincemeat and top with a thin slice of cheese. Fold over and press edges together to form crescents. Bake on cookie sheet in a hot oven for about 20 minutes, or until brown. Serve with coffee.

Mincemeat Moderne. Put mincemeat filling in unbaked rich pastry shell. Bake without top crust. When cool, top with sour cream and sprinkle with finely grated lemon rind.

Palm Springs Date Pie. Make as pecan pie, substituting 1 cup of chopped pitted dates and 1/2 cup of chopped English walnuts for the pecans. Top with whipped cream.

Pumpkin-Mince Pie. Fill unbaked pie shell half full of mincemeat and bake for 15 minutes in a very hot oven. While this bakes, prepare pumpkin custard pie filling. Lower the oven temperature to moderate and pour the pumpkin mixture over the mincemeat. Continue baking until the pumpkin custard is set. No need to make a momentous decision for Thanksgiving dinner when you can have both in one—pumpkin and mince.

Quickest Fresh Strawberry Pie. Fill a baked pie crust with fresh, hulled, washed, and thoroughly drained whole strawberries. Melt a cup of clear red currant jelly or clear apple jelly over low heat. Do not boil. Pour the melted jelly over the strawberries to sweeten and glaze.

Rhubarb Tarts. Cook 2 pounds of rhubarb with a little water until tender. Drain and beat pulp with a spoon until smooth. Beat 3 egg yolks with 1/2 cup of sugar until fluffy and light. Add the rhubarb pulp. Beat 3 egg whites until stiff and fold in 1/2 cup of sugar. Add the rhubarb mixture. Fill baked tart shells and place in a slow oven until filling is firm, about 30 minutes.

Sour-Cream Apple Pie. Fill an unbaked pie shell with sliced apples prepared as for regular apple pie. Top with 1 cup of sour cream and sprinkle raw pie crust crumbs, sugar, and cinnamon thickly over top. Bake as a regular apple pie.

Strawberry Angel Pie. Make packaged vanilla pudding adding a beaten egg yolk just before removing from the fire. Pour the pudding into a baked pie crust. Cover the custard with sliced fresh strawberries (no sugar needed). Top with strawberry fluff made by combining 1 egg white, 2/4 cup of sugar, a dash of lemon juice, a pinch of salt, and a few berries. Beat in electric mixer bowl until thick. Chill.

Strawberry Rose-Petal Pie. Wash, hull, and drain strawberries. Wash fresh rose petals and shake dry. Mix 2 tablespoons of flour and 1 cup of sugar. Put half of the flour-sugar mixture on bottom crust. Add berries, then a layer of rose petals, then more berries, and sprinkle the remaining flour and sugar over all. Dot with butter and cover with strips of pastry, lattice fashion. Bake on the bottom of a very hot oven for 15 minutes, then reduce to moderate heat for slow baking until done. Cool and serve. The fragrance is most tantalizing!

Unique Lemon Pie. When you have a peeled lemon on hand, use it as the main ingredient of this 8-inch pie. (To peel a lemon perfectly for use in mixed drinks, cut a slice off of each end; run an ice pick or skewer around under the skin and push the whole peeled lemon out one end.) Line a pie plate with pastry dough. Partially bake the crust. Blend 1-1/2 cups of sugar and 3/4 cup of flour. Sprinkle this dry mixture over the pie crust and on it lay 1/2 cup of very thin slices of the peeled lemon. Pour 1 cup of cold water over all and dot with 1 tablespoon of butter. Cover top with strips of pastry, lattice fashion. Bake in very hot oven for 15 minutes; reduce heat to moderately slow and bake for 50 minutes. Serve the pie warm with sweetened whipped cream if desired.

Upside-Down Pecan-Apple Pie. Spread 4 tablespoons of softened butter evenly over the bottom and sides of a 9-inch pie plate. Arrange 3/4 cup of pecan halves evenly, round side down, in the butter. Sprinkle the nuts with 2/3 cup of firmly packed light-brown sugar. Roll out bottom crust and fit it in the pan over the sugar-nut mixture. Fill with apple pie filling and cover with top crust. Bake as regular apple pie (very hot oven for the first 10 minutes, then with heat reduced for moderately slow baking). Remove pie from oven. Let stand a few minutes. Loosen edge. Invert pie on cake plate and remove pan from top. Cool. Cut in wedges to serve.

Unusual Crusts and Toppings

Baked Custard Pie. Sesame seed crust: Toast 4 tablespoons of sesame seeds on a pie plate in a slow oven until slightly browned. Add the toasted seeds to pie crust mix before liquid is added. Line a pie plate with crust and partially bake. Fill with egg custard and bake until custard is set. When done, sprinkle with brown sugar mixed with a bit of butter, and more sesame seeds (untoasted). Place under broiler for a few minutes to melt the sugar and toast the seeds.

Banana Split Pie. Delicious uncooked filling made with electric mixer or blender. Cream 1/2 cup of butter, 1 teaspoon of vanilla, and 1-1/2 cups of sifted confectioners' sugar until fluffy. Add 2 eggs, one at a time, beating well after each addition. Slice 2 bananas and sprinkle with 1 tablespoon of lemon juice. Grate 1 square of chocolate. Fold sliced bananas and grated chocolate into the sugar mixture. Pile into a baked pie shell. Chill for 2 or 3 hours. Just before serving, garnish with walnut halves and maraschino cherries, with more banana slices and a dab of whipped cream.

Brown-Sugar Hard Sauce for Apple or Blueberry Pie. With electric mixer, beat 1-1/2 cups of sifted brown sugar and 1/2 cup of butter. Flavor with a drop of almond extract. Form a roll. Chill. Serve a slice of the hard sauce on a piece of warm pie.

Café au Lait Pie. Make a gingersnap crust. Make vanilla pudding, adding 2 teaspoons of instant coffee to the dry mix. Cool. Pour in pie shell and top with sweetened, stiffly whipped cream to which you have added 1/4 teaspoon of instant coffee dissolved in 1 teaspoon of boiling water and cooled.

Cheese Cake Pie. Bake cheese cake (a half recipe will probably be enough) in a pie plate lined with graham cracker crust. When almost done (10 minutes before), spread 1/2 inch of sour cream on top. Cool. Serve with a spoonful of strawberry preserves on each piece of pie.

Cheese Wheels for Apple Pie. Spread cream cheese thickly over a slice of sharp or American cheese. Roll up and chill. Slice roll into 3/4-inch-thick wheels and serve on crusty warm apple pie.

Chocolate-Coconut Crust. Melt 2 unsweetened chocolate squares and 2 tablespoons of butter in the top of a double boiler. Combine 2 tablespoons of hot milk and 2/3 cup of sifted confectioners' sugar. Add the chocolate mixture and stir well. Add 1-1/2 cups of shredded coconut. Spread on bottom and sides of a 9-inch pan. Chill until firm. Fill with ice cream or chiffon pie filling.

Coconut Apple Pie. Spread 1 cup of shredded coconut over apple filling before covering with top crust.

Coconut-Crowned Pumpkin Pie. Mix 1/2 cup of flaked coconut with 1 tablespoon of softened butter. Sprinkle over pumpkin pie filling when partially baked. Press lightly into the filling.

Coconut Tarts. (Similar to French macaroon tarts.) Line tart pans with rich pastry. For filling, cream 1 cup of butter with 3/4 cup of sugar. Beat in 3 egg yolks, one at a time; stir in 1/3 cup of sherry or cognac and 1 teaspoon of vanilla; then fold in 2 cups of freshly grated coconut or canned flaked coconut. Beat the 3 egg whites until stiff but not dry. Fold beaten egg whites into the coconut mixture. Spoon it into the unbaked tart shells and bake for 10 minutes in a hot oven; then reduce heat to moderate and bake for 25 to 30 minutes longer.

Cranberry-Cream Cheese Tarts. Bake tart shells of rich pie crust flavored with several tablespoons of grated orange rind. Cool. Make filling by mashing 1 small package of cream cheese with 1/4 cup of confectioners' sugar and folding the mixture into 1 cup of heavy cream, whipped. Fold in 1 cup of miniature marshmallows, 1/2 cup of chopped English walnuts, then gently fold in 2 cups of mashed, jellied cranberry sauce. Pile in shells. Garnish with a frosted English walnut half (dip walnut halves in thick, hot, sugar syrup and then in granulated sugar. Dry on waxed paper on cake rack).

Crunchy Dutch Apple Pie. Prepare pie crust. Instead of rolling out the top crust, crumble the dough and sprinkle it over the apples. Then sprinkle the pie with brown or white sugar and bake as usual.

Elegant Meringue Crust for Pie. Line a 9-inch pie plate with very heavy brown paper. Fit perfectly. Make meringue of 3 egg whites, 3/4 cup of sugar, a dash of salt, and 1/2 teaspoon of vanilla. Beat very stiff. Spread in pie pan, hollowing out middle somewhat. Arrange some blanched almonds around the edge. Bake in a very slow oven for 1-1/2 to 2 hours, until meringue is crisp throughout and very slightly brown. Remove from pan and pull off paper. This shell will keep for several days. When ready to serve, fill with chocolate ice cream, fudge sauce, and whole toasted, blanched almonds. Top with almond-flavored whipped cream or alternate dabs of whipped cream flavored with orange or lemon concentrate and a bit of grated rind. Or fill with lemon pie filling and top with whipped cream.

Fruit Glaze for Fruit Pies. Run heated apricot jam through a sieve and spread on top of a hot pie as it comes from the oven.

Ginger Topping for Pumpkin Pie. Combine 1 large package of cream cheese with 1/4 cup of chopped preserved ginger. Soften with a little of the ginger syrup, and beat until fluffy. Serve on pumpkin pie.

Italian Cheese Pie. Mix ricotta cheese, sugar, vanilla, and eggs as for cheese cake. Place in an unbaked pie shell. Garnish with thin slivers of orange peel, chocolate chips, and sliced maraschino cherries. Bake in moderate oven for 1 hour or until set.

Lemon Macaroon Pie. Fold 1/2 cup of macaroon crumbs into lemon custard pie filling and sprinkle the meringue with another 1/2 cup of the macaroon crumbs. Bake in a moderately hot oven for about 12 minutes or until lightly browned.

Meringue Magic. For stiff, high, and tender meringue, beat 3 egg whites with 1/4 teaspoon of salt until frothy. Gradually add 6 tablespoons of sugar and beat again until moist, stiff peaks are formed. Be sure that meringue touches all edges of a pie crust, or completely covers the cake or pudding on which it is to bake, so there will be no shrinkage. Bake in moderate oven for 15 minutes.

More Flavor for Your Favorite Lemon Meringue Pie. Add a teaspoonful of finely grated lemon rind to the meringue before baking.

No-Bake Pumpkin Pie with Walnut Crust. Mix 1 cup of ground walnuts with 2/3 cup of gingersnap crumbs. Press into 8-inch

pie pan which is coated with 2 tablespoons of soft butter. For
filling, cook 1 cup of canned mashed pumpkin and 1 cup of milk
with 1 package of butterscotch pudding mix, adding spices and
brown sugar to taste. Cool and pour into crumb crust. Chill
thoroughly for at least 4 hours. Garnish with dabs of whipped
cream or top with walnut halves.

Old-Fashioned Jam Custard Pie. Bake a custard in a rich pie crust.
Let cool until just slightly warm. Spread with red raspberry jam
or grape preserve, then with a layer of unsweetened whipped
cream.

Paradise Pie. Bake graham cracker crumb crust. Combine 1/2 cup of
sugar, a dash of salt, 1 cup of stiff apple sauce, and 1 cup of
heavy cream, whipped. Mix well. Pour into the crumb crust.
Sprinkle with 1/2 cup of ground English walnuts. Chill until set.

Peanut Butter Pie in Chocolate Crust. Make chocolate wafer crumb
crust. Paint the inside of the crust with chocolate morsels melted
with butter. Make vanilla pudding, adding 3 tablespoons of
smooth peanut butter. Cool and pour into crust. Top with
ground, salted peanuts.

Pink Parfait Pie. Make coconut crust by adding 3 tablespoons of
butter and 1 package of shredded coconut to pie crust mix. Prepare strawberry gelatine using 1-1/2 cups of water, instead of
the usual 2 cups. Mix with 1 pint of vanilla ice cream. Fill the coconut crust with the gelatine and ice cream mixture. Garnish
with whipped cream and whole strawberries. Chill.

Pumpkin Chiffon Pie with Walnut Crust. Add 1 cup of ground English walnuts and 2 tablespoons of granulated sugar to pie crust
mix. Press in a thin layer over the bottom and sides of a well-
buttered pie plate. Bake. Chill. Then fill with pumpkin chiffon
filling.

Spiced Whipped Cream for Plain Pumpkin or Mince Pie. Flavor 1
cup of heavy cream, whipped with 1/4 teaspoon each of cinnamon, nutmeg, and vanilla, and powdered sugar to taste.

Sugar-Nut Glaze with Pumpkin or Custard Pie. When pie is baked,
cover crust with silver foil to keep from burning. Cover top of
pie with brown sugar and chopped nuts. Broil for a few minutes
until sugar melts. (Try mixing sugar with a little melted butter.)

Surprise Pie. Line a pie plate with rich pastry dough. Beat 3 egg whites until stiff. Fold in 20 crushed Ritz crackers, 1 cup of light brown sugar, 1 teaspoon of baking powder, 1/2 cup of chopped English walnuts, and 1 teaspoon of vanilla. Pour the filling into the pie shell and bake in a moderately slow oven for 30 minutes or until puffy and brown. The filling will settle as it cools. Serve in thin wedges with an eggnog sauce made from 3 yolks beaten together with 1/4 cup of powdered sugar, 1/2 teaspoon of rum extract and folded into 1/2 cup of heavy cream, whipped stiff.

Topping with Christmas Hard Sauce Stars. Make firm hard sauce. Spread 1/2 inch thick in flat pan or plate. Chill. Cut into stars with cookie cutter. On each piece of mincemeat pie or serving of plum pudding, serve 1 star topped with a lighted, tiny, red birthday candle stuck in a maraschino cherry and pressed into the hard sauce star.

Topping for Apricot or Raisin Pie. Soften a 3-ounce package of cream cheese. Mix it with 1 tablespoon of sugar and 1 tablespoon of frozen orange juice concentrate. Spoon on top of warm pie (not hot). Even a bakery pie becomes a gourmet's delight with this glorious crown.

Wheat Germ Pie Crust. For a nutritious as well as delectable crunchy pie crust, substitute 1/2 cup of raw wheat germ for 1/2 cup of the flour in pie crust recipe.

Cakes

Filled and Upside-Down Cakes

Ambrosia Cream Cake. Put orange sauce (see recipe for Orange Sauce) between 2 thin sponge cake layers. Ice the top with orange butter frosting sprinkled with shredded coconut.

Arithmetic Chocolate Cakes. Prepare chocolate cake mix batter. Pour one half the batter over a mixture of 1/4 cup of butter, 1/2 cup of light brown sugar, and 1/2 cup of whole fat pecans arranged in the bottom of an 8-inch pan. Bake for 35 to 40 minutes in a moderate oven. Turn the pan upside down when it is slightly cooled. Bake the remaining batter plain in an 8-inch greased and floured pan. Serve the second cake the next day, split, with a filling of instant chocolate pudding and the top iced with a thin butter frosting or whipped cream.

Chocolate Cream Cake. Bake a chocolate cake. When cool, split each layer in half. Spread sweetened whipped cream (1-1/2 cups of heavy cream and 1/4 cup of powdered sugar) between the layers. Frost with chocolate butter frosting. Cake will keep in the refrigerator for several days.

Cracker Cake. Make a torte or layer cake from either graham crackers or finely rolled unsalted soda crackers (cracker meal). Put alternate layers of crumbs together with raspberry jam and whipped cream (pure whipped cream, please, not from a can). Put a layer of jam and then one of whipped cream between the layers and frost the top and sides of the cake with the whipped cream that is left. You will need at least a pint of heavy cream, whipped, for an eight-inch cake. It must be thick.

Double Date Cake. Make a date-nut filling from 1 cup of brown sugar, 1 cup of chopped dates, 1/2 cup of water, and 1/2 cup of chopped nuts, boiled together for about 15 minutes. Add a dash of salt and 1 teaspoon of lemon juice. Make a brown-sugar seven-minute frosting. Fold the date-nut filling into two-thirds of the frosting and use between the layers and on top of cake. Use the rest of the plain frosting to cover the sides of cake thickly.

Dutch Upside-Down Cake. Melt 1/4 cup of butter in a 13 x 9 x 2-inch oblong pan. Blend in 1/2 cup of brown sugar and 1/2 teaspoon of cinnamon. Next, arrange about 4 cups of thinly sliced apples evenly over the sugar mixture and pour in a batter made from the full package of spice-cake mix. Bake for 45 to 50 minutes in a moderate oven. Serve warm with whipped cream.

Gingerbread Upside-Down Cake. Place apple slices, sugar, cinnamon, butter, and some chopped nuts in the bottom of a 9-inch square pan. Cover with gingerbread mix batter. Bake. Turn baking pan upside down to cool slightly. Serve warm with plain or whipped cream.

Lemon Angel Food Torte. Cut angel food cake in three or four layers. Spread cooked lemon pudding filling between the layers (not too much or it will run). Frost with fluffy white frosting into which you mix 1 tablespoon of finely grated lemon rind, and in which you have used fresh lemon juice for part of the liquid. Chill until serving time.

Orange Cake à la Mode. Serve orange chiffon cake with a scoop of half orange sherbet and half vanilla ice cream.

Orange Sauce for Ambrosia Cream Cake or for Gingerbread. Prepare lemon pudding using orange juice instead of water for the liquid and add 1 teaspoon of finely grated orange rind.

Poppy Seed Cake. Soak 1/2 cup of poppy seeds overnight in 1/3 cup of milk. Add the mixture to white cake batter and bake. When cake is cold, put layers together with nut-cream filling and dust thickly with confectioners' sugar. Make nut-cream filling by adding 1/2 cup of chopped nuts, 1 teaspoon of vanilla, and a beaten egg yolk to a package of vanilla pudding mix, or use thick custard filling.

Rhubarb Upside-Down Cakes. Cover bottom of individual buttered cupcake pans with several pieces of rhubarb and some granulated sugar. Drop white cake batter on top and bake. Turn pan upside down for a few minutes after removing from oven. Serve with slightly sweetened whipped cream.

Strawberry Cakes. Bake yellow cupcakes (don't overbake). Cut a cone out of each center when they are cool and dip the top of each cone in powdered sugar. Fill hollows to running over with sliced sweetened strawberries. Top strawberries with a generous dollop of whipped cream and stick cone of cake back into the whipped cream.

Swiss Chocolate Almond Cake. Split an angel food cake into four. Melt 1 large chocolate almond candy bar (at least 6 ounces) with 1 square of unsweetened chocolate. Cool slightly and fold into 1 cup of whipped cream. Chill overnight. Put between layers and use for frosting. Garnish with additional toasted almonds.

The General's Cake. Prepare orange chiffon cake mix. Bake in four 9-inch layer-cake pans. Cool. Prepare a package of lemon pudding mix and when cool, spread it between the layers. Make a butter frosting, substituting equal parts of orange and lemon juice for the liquid and adding the grated rind of 1 lemon and the grated rind of 2 oranges. Frost the top and sides of the cake.

Frostings and Toppings

Ambrosia Cake. Add 1/2 cup of flaked coconut to yellow cake mix. When baked and cooled, frost cake with orange butter frosting and sprinkle additional coconut on top and sides. Put a ring of drained Mandarin orange sections around the bottom edge of the cake, pressing them into the icing so that each serving of cake will have an orange section.

Arabian Spice Cake. Bake spice cake. Frost with fudge frosting, adding about 1/2 cup of finely chopped dates to the frosting. Decorate the top with halved, pitted fresh soft dates.

Baba Au Rhum. Buy baba at your favorite French bakery. Serve with this simple sauce and a generous dab of whipped cream. Boil 1/2 cup of water and 1-1/4 cups of granulated sugar for 2 or 3 minutes. Add a dash of salt. Cool to lukewarm. Stir in 1/2 cup of light rum and pour over the cake.

Banana Nut Cupcakes. Make yellow batter cupcakes with chopped nuts in the batter. Frost with banana frosting made by mashing a ripe banana with 1/2 teaspoon of lemon juice and adding 3-1/2 cups of confectioners' sugar for 2 or 3 minutes. Add a dash of salt. Cool to lukewarm. Stir in 1/2 cup of light rum and pour over the cake.

Butter Pecan Self-Made Frosting. As soon as a cake comes from the oven, sprinkle butterscotch chips on top. When melted, spread over the cake and sprinkle with chopped toasted pecans.

Candy Cake. Frost a cake with pink seven-minute frosting. Cut thin round pastel cream wafers or mints in half. Stand halves in the frosting at a slant about 1/2 inch apart around the top edge of the cake to form a colorful border.

Chocolate Curls. For frosting decoration, shave slightly soft chocolate with a vegetable peeler.

Chocolate Mint Cake Squares. Bake chocolate cake in 13 x 9 x 2-inch pan. When done, place 4 thin chocolate bars on top. Return to the oven for 2 or 3 minutes. Spread the melted chocolate evenly with a spatula and cool completely (overnight is best) so chocolate will harden. Tint fluffy white frosting pink and flavor with peppermint extract. Cut the cake into squares to serve.

Cinnamon Almond Cake. Use white cake mix, adding 2 teaspoons of cinnamon to the dry ingredients. Frost with butter frosting flavored with grated lemon rind. Garnish with whole blanched almonds.

Confetti Frosting. Delicious on a prune or spice cake. You may use fluffy white frosting mix. Add 1/2 cup of finely chopped or ground mixed candied fruit and 1 teaspoon of rum flavoring.

Creamy Gingerbread. Bake gingerbread. To make the sauce, prepare pudding as directed on the package, using only 1-1/2 cups of milk. Whip 1/2 cup of heavy cream until stiff and fold into the pudding. Spoon the sauce over the gingerbread and garnish with sliced bananas and canned Mandarin orange sections. Be sure to drain the orange sections thoroughly.

Delicate Jam Frosting. Whip 1 cup of heavy cream until stiff and fold in 1 cup of strawberry, raspberry, or apricot jam. Particularly delicious on sponge cake or angel food split into several layers and frosted.

Easy Marbled Seven-Minute Frosting. Stir and partially blend semisweet chocolate bits into a basic seven-minute frosting after taking it off the fire but while it is still hot.

Frostings Made with Prepared Fluffy White Frosting. Add 1 teaspoon of maple flavoring and 1/3 cup of broken walnuts or pecans (quite large pieces). Fold 2 squares of shaved semisweet chocolate into the warm frosting, stirring until frosting is marbled with the chocolate. For mocha flavor, add 2 teaspoons of instant coffee to the dry ingredients.

Fruit Cake Garnish. To give sides and bottom of baked fruit cakes a shiny glaze, sprinkle granulated sugar in the greased pan before filling. To glaze and decorate a fruit cake, melt apricot jam with a spoon of water. Cool and spread on top of the cake. Press fruit and nut decorations into the glaze while it is still soft. If you add the decorations later, dip each piece in white corn syrup (brought to a full boil) before arranging them on the glaze.

Golden Sponge. Ice a bakery orange chiffon cake or your own sponge cake with lemon icing. Garnish with thin slices of lemon that have been dipped in granulated sugar and dried out a bit.

Maple Butternut Cake. From Vermont. Make white cake, adding 1/2 cup of coarsely chopped butternuts to the batter. Frost with maple sugar frosting made by cooking 3 cups of maple sugar with 1-1/2 cups of cream to 234°F, or soft-ball stage. Cool slightly. Beat and add 1/2 cup sliced butternuts.

Marzipan Icing for Fruit Cake. Blend 1 cup of almond paste, 1 cup of confectioners' sugar, 1/4 teaspoon of almond flavoring, 1 egg yolk, and 1/4 cup of orange juice. If too thin, add a bit more sugar. Spread over cooled, baked fruit cake and let dry until stiff. When icing is partially set, decorate with whole blanched almonds and candied orange peel.

Mocha Cream Topping for Cakes. Whip 1 cup of heavy cream and fold in 1/4 cup of sifted confectioners' sugar, 1 tablespoon of powdered coffee, and 1 tablespoon of instant cocoa mix.

Nutty Spice Cake. Bake a spice cake. Use prepared fluffy white frosting mix. Just before spreading, add 1/2 cup of chopped walnuts, 2 tablespoons of grated orange rind, and 1-1/2 cups plump seedless raisins. (To plump the raisins, pour boiling water over them and drain thoroughly while you are making the icing.) Frost the cake.

Orange Sunburst Cake. Make a yellow layer cake. Put together and frost top with a rich orange butter frosting. Decorate with orange sections dipped in fluffy white frosting and allowed to harden. Place the frosted orange sections on top of the cake, sunburst fashion. Frost the sides and swirl some of the fluffy frosting into the grooves around the orange sections when they are in place. Sprinkle finely grated orange rind over the middle of the top of the cake.

Peanut Butter Chocolate Cake. Bake a chocolate cake. Frost with peanut butter icing and decorate the top of cake with circles of whole salted peanuts.

Peppermint Chocolate Cake. Bake a chocolate cake. Make a very light pink fluffy icing flavored with a few drops of peppermint extract. Make about 1/3 of the icing a darker pink than the rest. Frost the cake first with the lighter icing, then swirl the darker icing around the top and sides.

Polka Dot Cake. Bake a white cake and frost with a fudge icing. Decorate the top and sides of cake with nonpareil candies arranged in polka dot fashion.

Prune Spice Squares. Bake a spice cake in a 9-inch square pan. When cake is done, top with a 3-egg-white meringue into which you have stirred 1 cup of chopped stewed prunes and 1/2 cup of chopped walnuts. Pile the fruited meringue on the hot cake and return to the oven for about 15 minutes.

Rich Old-Fashioned Marble Cake Frosting. Bake marble cake in large 9 x 9 x 2-inch pan. Make a thick butter cream icing, like hard sauce, and spread thickly on the cake while it is still in the pan. Melt 2 squares of unsweetened chocolate. Pour the melted chocolate over the frosting and spread evenly so it is thin as paper. Let cake stand in pan overnight so the chocolate hardens. It's scrumptious.

Rose Marie Cakes. Bake small cup cakes. Cool. Beat 1 cup of currant jelly until frothy and dip cakes in it or spread it over them. Roll cakes in freshly grated or flaked coconut.

Seven-Minute Peppermint Icing. Make white fluffy frosting, folding in 2 drops of peppermint oil or 1/2 teaspoon of peppermint extract and a few drops of red food coloring (not too much—it should be a delicate pink). May be garnished with crushed peppermint candy, tiny candy canes, or red and white peppermint drops.

Soft Brown-Sugar Frosting. Easy frosting for a one-layer oblong cake. Frost the cake while it is cool but still in the pan. Beat 2 egg whites until stiff and dry, gradually adding 6 rounded tablespoons of light-brown sugar. Pile on the cake and spread thickly. Cut the cake into squares and serve.

Sour-Cream Spice Cake or Prune Spice Cake. Frost with coffee icing made by adding 1 teaspoon of instant coffee to vanilla butter frosting mix.

Tropicana Spice Cake. Bake spice cake in 13 x 9 x 2-inch pan. Have ready a mixture of 2 cups of flaked coconut, 1-1/3 cups of brown sugar, 2 tablespoons of grated orange rind, 1/4 cup of light corn syrup, 1/2 stick of butter, 1/4 cup of cream, and 1/2 teaspoon of vanilla. Spread the mixture on top of the baked and partly cooled cake. Broil for 2 or 3 minutes. Cool cake in pan set on rack.

Two-Tone Chocolate Cake. Bake chocolate cake. Make a light chocolate icing and spread between the layers and on the sides of the cake. Add 1/2 cup of cocoa or 2 squares of melted unsweetened chocolate and a bit more cream to the light icing that remains.

Frost the top of the cake with the darker icing, edging it with rosettes of this icing pressed through a pastry tube, or scatter chocolate sprinkle candies on the frosted top.

Unusual Cakes

Black Walnut Butterscotch Cake. Add 1/2 cup of finely chopped black walnuts to yellow cake batter. Frost cake with sea foam (boiled brown-sugar frosting) or with browned-butter frosting. To make the browned-butter frosting, melt and slightly brown (do not burn) the butter for butter icing before mixing it with the powdered sugar.

Chocolate Spice Cake. Make chocolate or devil's food cake. Add 1 teaspoon each of ground ginger and cinnamon to the batter. Frost with a mocha butter frosting.

Cider Cake. Make yellow cake with apple juice or cider instead of water. Fill and frost with fluffy white icing. Crush nut brittle into coarse crumbs with rolling pin and use as a garnish.

Creole Fruit Cakes. The secret is putting most of the mixed fruits through the food chopper. Use orange juice and sour milk for liquid. Garnish with pecan meats and pitted, whole dates. Freeze after baking or keep in refrigerator.

Currant Cake. For those who like a not-too-sweet dessert. Make a yellow cake in a large square or oblong pan, adding 1 cup of soft currants to the batter. Sprinkle granulated sugar over the top of the cake before baking and sprinkle the top with powdered sugar after it is done.

Tweed Cake. Make white cake batter. Before final beating, blend in 3 squares of finely grated unsweetened baking chocolate. Bake. When cool, frost cake with a rich butter icing made with the egg yolks left over from the cake. Melt 3 ounces of semisweet chocolate bits in top of double boiler. Add 2 tablespoons of water and stir until smooth. Cool somewhat and pour the melted chocolate over the top of the frosted cake, allowing some to run down the sides. Let cake stand overnight to set chocolate.

Walnut Applesauce Cake. Use packaged spice cake mix but add 1 teaspoon of baking soda and substitute 1/4 cup more applesauce than the required liquid. Stir into the batter 1/2 cup of crushed walnuts (rolled in a paper bag, not chopped). Bake. Frost lightly with a butter cream icing and garnish with crisp golden walnut halves and glazed, unpeeled apple slices, made by poaching slightly in thick sugar syrup. Cool in the syrup, then drain, dip in granulated sugar, and lay on waxed paper to dry.

Walnut Burnt-Sugar Cake. Fold 1/3 cup of finely chopped walnuts into the batter for a burnt-sugar cake. Frost with burnt-sugar icing and garnish the edge of the cake with a circle of perfect walnut halves. Make burnt-sugar frosting by carmelizing sugar and adding the resulting syrup to butter frosting.

Special Occasion Cakes

Birthday Clock Cake. Bake yellow cake and frost with white fluffy icing. Decorate with a circle of 12 varicolored candles stuck in varicolored gum drops. Press a few gumdrops polka dot fashion in sides of the cake. Use 2 candy sticks, one short and one long, as hands of the clock and set for the child's age.

Circus Cake. Frost a chocolate cake with peanut butter cream icing. Stand chocolate-covered animal crackers around the edge of the top of the cake, and press some around the sides. Place birthday candles, set in peppermint cream candies or gumdrops, between the animals on top.

King-Size Birthday Cake. Bake three 10-inch yellow cake layers. Between layers, spread a thin layer of fudge frosting. Cover the frosting thickly with mashed red currant jelly. Cover top and sides with fluffy white frosting. Press chocolate sprinkles lightly into the frosting on the sides.

Pennsylvania Dutch Black-Walnut Christmas Cake. Add 1/2 cup of chopped black walnuts to yellow cake batter. Bake in an oblong pan. Spread generously with a fluffy white frosting to which you have added 1 cup of broken black walnut meats. Cut in squares to serve.

Valentine Cake. Bake his favorite cake in large heart-shaped pans. Make fluffy pink frosting. Add 1/2 cup each of chopped raisins, nuts, and dates to the frosting before spreading. Bake a large arrow, using cookie or pie dough, and stick the arrow in the top of the cake at an angle.

Cookies

CHEWY COOKIES

Brownie Turtles. Prepare chocolate cookie batter. On greased baking sheet, place groups of 3 walnut halves with tips touching in the center. Drop a level teaspoon of dough in the center of each group of walnuts and bake. Cool slightly before removing from the baking sheet. When turtles are cold, frost with butter icing and dribble melted chocolate over the frosting to make markings on the turtle.

Date Oatmeal Cookies. To butter cookie dough, add 1/3 cup of quick-cooking oatmeal and a few chopped dates soaked in 1/3 cup of buttermilk.

Dates in Cheese Pastry. Wrap pitted dates in small squares or circles of rich cheese pastry and bake.

Dream Drops. Add chopped, cooked prunes and chocolate chips to butter cookie dough.

Fruit Cake in Candied-Orange-Peel Cups. Bake fruit cake batter in orange shells that you have saved and candied after squeezing the breakfast orange juice.

Orange-Nut Ginger Bars. Use 3/4 cup of water in making gingerbread dough. Stir in 1 tablespoon of grated orange rind and 1 cup of chopped walnuts. Bake in two greased square pans. While still slightly warm, spread with orange butter frosting. (Make butter frosting with orange juice or thawed frozen orange juice concentrate instead of any other liquid.)

Stuffed-Date Cookies. Stuff dates with pecans or walnuts. Make a soft cookie batter. Drop the dates in the batter and coat thinly but thoroughly. Then place coated date on a greased and floured cookie sheet. Before baking, sprinkle with chopped nuts, if desired. Bake for 12 to 15 minutes. Or omit the chopped nuts and put a dab of rum butter frosting on each cookie when cool.

CRISP COOKIES

Black Walnut Dreams. Make a cookie batter and add 1 cup of finely ground black walnuts. Bake. While cookies are warm, dust generously with confectioners' sugar.

Christmas Wreaths. Prepare butter cookie dough. Form into small balls. Dip into slightly beaten egg white, then into nuts or flaked coconut. Place on greased baking sheet. Press hole in center with your thumb. Bake in slow oven for 8 minutes. Indent again and continue baking until done. Remove from sheet and fill center with jam or jelly.

Chunky Chocolate Chip Cookies. Make chocolate chip cookie recipe with cut-up (uneven small chunks) of milk chocolate instead of the chips. Use large broken milk chocolate bars for these or cut up some of those big chunks bought in bulk.

Crispy Cookies. Add 1/2 cup of whole cornflakes to the batter for sugar cookies.

Crunchy Orange Cookies. Make butter cookies with orange juice instead of milk and add grated orange rind, bran flakes, and 1 cup of oil to the batter.

Frosted Date Balls. Add 1/4 cup of ground (medium blade of food chopper) pitted dates to dough for those luscious little round nut cookies that are baked and rolled immediately in powdered sugar.

Halloween Cookie Lollipops. Bake butter cookie or sugar cookie batter by shaping into large balls into which you insert wooden skewers. Place on ungreased cookie sheet. Flatten balls. Bake in a moderate oven. Decorate with butter frosting faces, using raisins, jelly beans, nuts, and coconut for features and hair.

Jelly Tarts. Make soft, rich butter cookie dough. Generously butter and half fill fluted tart pans with the dough. Bake for 15 to 20 minutes. Remove cakes from pans to cooling racks. Spread the upturned bottoms of the cakes with 1/3 cup of seedless raspberry jelly or jam. Then sprinkle each with a generous amount of shredded or ground blanched almonds.

Orange Scallops. Make sugar cookie dough with orange juice and 2 tablespoons of oil instead of other liquid and flavor with grated orange rind. Sprinkle rolled dough with grated orange rind mixed with sugar before cutting with a round, scalloped cutter.

Peanut Cookies. Add chopped peanuts and ground raisins to cookie dough.

Peanut Fingers. Cut or press peanut butter cookie dough into 2 1/2-inch oblongs and bake. When cool, dip one end of each cookie in melted chocolate and then in ground salted peanuts.

Seed Cookies. For New Year's Eve—symbol of a bountiful year. Roll rich butter cookie dough into balls. Coat with sesame or poppy seeds. Place on ungreased cookie sheet and flatten in crisscross fashion with a fork. Bake.

Shadow Box Cookies. Let refrigerated cookie dough stand at room temperature until soft enough to handle and roll out, or make a batch of rich sugar dough or butter cookie dough. Roll out. Cut dough into 2-1/2-inch rounds or larger if desired. From half of the rounds, cut out the centers in the shape of Christmas trees, stars, gingerbread men, bunnies, clowns (these small centers can be baked separately as smaller cookies). When the cookies are baked, put a solid round and a cut-out round together with a firm butter cream frosting (like hard sauce). Sprinkle colored sugar crystals into the opening formed in each cookie by the cut-out.

Sugar Almond Balls. Add a generous amount of chopped blanched almonds and flaked coconut to butter cookie dough and shape into long rolls (about 1/2 inch in diameter). Cut into 2-inch lengths and bake. When cool, dip rolls in thin confectioners' sugar frosting flavored with almond extract. Place on waxed paper on cake rack until icing hardens.

Wedding Ring Cookies. Cut butter cookies in circles with doughnut cutter. Bake and cool. Dip in thin lemon-flavored confectioners' sugar icing and sprinkle top of each iced cookie with yellow granulated sugar.

SOFT COOKIES

Christmas Trees in Tubs. With a sharp knife, cut cones from cooled cupcakes and fill the holes with pudding. Roll the cones in pale green frosting, then in green-tinted flaked coconut. Place, pointed end up, on top of the pudding-filled tubs. Frost the pudding-filled part with chocolate icing or dip in melted semisweet chocolate mixed with a bit of melted butter. Trees can be decorated with tiny colorful candies.

Currant Cookie Squares. Add 3/4 cup of soft currants to batter for soft cookies. Bake in 8-inch-square pans for 20 to 25 minutes. Cut into squares or triangles and dredge with granulated sugar while still warm.

Double-Chocolate Brownies. Add 3/4 cup of chocolate chips to brownie batter at the time you add the chopped nuts.

Lemon Sours. Spread a mixture of 1-1/2 tablespoons of lemon juice, 1 teaspoon of grated lemon rind, and about 2/3 cup of confectioners' sugar over pan of bar cookies as soon as pan is taken from the oven. Let cool in pan and cut in squares.

Lemon Spice Cookies. Bake soft spice cookies, flavored with a lot of cinnamon and a little ginger. Ice with lemon butter frosting.

Marmalade Cobbler Cakes. Make yellow cupcake dough and put in cupcake or muffin tins. Place a teaspoonful of orange marmalade on top of the batter. Bake. Serve warm with a dollop of whipped cream cheese and a sauce made by heating orange marmalade with a spoonful or two of water.

Rum Butterscotch Peaks. Cut a large cone out of chocolate cupcakes. Fill with rum custard made with butterscotch pudding generously laced with rum. Place cupcake cone on top of the pudding, wide side down. Frost the whole cupcake generously with rum-flavored whipped cream. Chill several hours before serving.

Sherry Christmas Cakes. Add 1 cup of ground assorted candied fruits and 1 cup of finely chopped nuts to cupcake batter, which should be made with sweet sherry as part of the liquid. Bake in cupcake pans. Frost cakes with a white butter frosting and decorate with poinsettias made from quarters of maraschino cherries, yellow sugar, and angelica (available in gourmet or candy shops).

Treasure Hunt Cookies. Make soft filled sugar cookies with different fillings. Decorate filled cookies before baking with bits of candied cherries, pineapple, orange or lemon rind, and nut meats or maraschino cherries, making a different design on each.

UNBAKED COOKIES

Pantry Cookies. Melt chocolate bits or milk chocolate bars in double boiler. Arrange 4 pecan halves (rounded side up) on waxed paper in four-leaf-clover design. Place a teaspoon of chocolate in center of each group of pecans and top with a vanilla wafer. Frost top of vanilla wafer with a teaspoon of the chocolate.

Pantry-Shelf Jelly Wafers. Put 2 vanilla wafers together with red currant jelly. Dip wafer, sideways about 2/3 of the way, in butter frosting made with confectioners' sugar. Then dip in finely chopped or ground nuts.

Candies

COOKED CANDIES

Chinese Coconut Candy. If you are serving tea or a Chinese dinner, try this inexpensive and easy candy. Cut a fresh coconut in two-inch-long narrow strips with vegetable peeler. Boil in sugar syrup until tender. Dry in a slow oven and roll in powdered sugar. Serve in a Chinese bowl or in individual flower favors.

Chinese Penuche. Add a few tablespoons of finely chopped candied ginger to penuche recipe.

Chinese Surprise Candy. Interesting and inexpensive. Slice small or medium-size potatoes 1/8 inch thick. Boil in sugar syrup until tender but not mushy. Drain. Sprinkle lightly with ginger. Place on foil on a cookie sheet in a slow oven to dry out, then roll in powdered sugar. Guests will be mystified as to what the candy is made of.

Cocoa-Covered Filberts. Melt one 7-ounce package of semisweet chocolate in the top of a double boiler and add 3/4 cup of evaporated milk. Stir and cook until very thick. Chill in refrigerator for 1 hour. Mold 1 teaspoonful of the chocolate mixture around each filbert and drop balls into a mixture of equal parts of cocoa and confectioners' sugar.

Creamier Fudge. Add the juice of half a lemon to your fudge when you add the vanilla for a delightful flavor and a creamier texture.

Crystal Apples. Add red coloring to sugar syrup or make the syrup with sugar and red cinnamon candies. Cook pared apple wedges or slices slowly in the syrup until they are transparent and coated—not too many at a time. Allow cooked slices to stand uncovered on waxed paper on a cake rack for 24 hours. Roll apple slices in granulated sugar to make a thin coating of the sugar crystals. Store in a covered box, but not tightly covered or the apples will become syrupy. Children will love these attractive and colorful apple slices, which have the consistency of jelly beans.

Million Dollar Fudge. This recipe makes 4 or 5 pounds of fudge. Beating is not necessary so it really can't fail. Combine in a saucepan 4-1/2 cups of sugar, 1 large can of evaporated milk, 4 tablespoons of butter, and a dash of salt. Stir over low heat until sugar is dissolved, then cook for 8 minutes, stirring just often enough to prevent sticking. Remove from fire. Add 2 packages of semisweet chocolate bits, 1 jar of marshmallow cream, and 1 teaspoon of vanilla. Stir until the chocolate is melted and the mixture is thoroughly blended. Pour into two 8 x 8-inch pans, well buttered to hold the fudge. When fudge is almost set, mark in generous squares.

Nogada (Mexican Fudge). Just add 1 teaspoon of cinnamon to penuche recipe. Fold in 1-1/2 cups of broken pecan pieces.

UNCOOKED CANDIES

Candy Marbles. Steam dried apricots for 5 minutes. Put through food chopper with flaked coconut and walnuts. Add a trace of lemon juice and grated rind. Shape into tiny balls. Roll in granulated sugar.

Chocolate Crunch. Melt one 6-ounce package of chocolate bits. Stir in 1/2 cup of graham cracker crumbs or cornflake crumbs and 3/4 cup of crushed, not chopped, walnuts. Drop mixture from teaspoon onto waxed paper or into small muffin papers or bon-bon cups until chocolate hardens—overnight, if possible.

Chocolate Flake Candy. Combine 1 cup each of chopped pecan meats and pitted dates, 5 cups of cornflakes, and 1/4 teaspoon of salt. Melt 1 pound of sweet milk chocolate and two 1-ounce squares of unsweetened chocolate. Pour melted chocolate over the cornflake mixture. Stir lightly and drop from teaspoon onto waxed paper.

Chocolate Pears. Cut cores from soft, dried pear halves. Melt semi-sweet chocolate. Dip wide end of pears in chocolate, coating about half the pear. Shake off excess chocolate. Place pears on waxed paper until chocolate is firm—overnight, if possible.

Chocolate Squares. The chocolate left in the pan after dipping need not be wasted. Pour the leftover chocolate into a small pan and press nuts or raisins into it.

Christmas Fruit Patties. Grind equal amounts of figs, dates, raisins, almonds, walnuts, and pecans with a few maraschino cherries. Mix thoroughly and form into small patties or balls. Roll in sugar and keep in a cool place.

Circus Candy. Melt semisweet chocolate in a double boiler. Pour a thin layer into tiny paper cups and stand an animal cracker in each one. Tear off cups before serving. These make a charming decoration on a child's birthday cake.

Miniature Chocolate-Coconut Marshmallows. Dip small marsh-mallows in melted semisweet chocolate. Roll in flaked coconut and place on waxed paper. Cool overnight until chocolate is firm.

Nuts in Sherry. Marinate walnuts and almonds in sherry overnight. Drain and roll in powdered sugar twice. Let dry.

Popcorn Snowmen. Make popcorn balls in two sizes. Press the smaller balls on top of each of the larger ones. For jaunty buttons and features, use small colored candies, jelly beans, raisins, and nuts. A scarf or necktie and a black hat can be made from soft licorice sticks. Festive and edible favors for a party.

Raisin Clusters. Melt 8 ounces of semisweet chocolate. Remove from heat and stir in 2 cups of seedless raisins and 1/2 cup of chopped nuts. Drop mixture in clusters from teaspoon onto waxed paper. Cool until chocolate hardens—overnight, if possible.

Real Quickie Caramel White Caps. Melt 1/2 pound of caramels in 2 tablespoons of water. Dip sides of marshmallows in the caramel and then in chopped nuts. Place on a baking sheet and chill in refrigerator.

Stuffed Dates. Cover small cubes of cheddar cheese with 2 pitted dates and roll in ground almonds. Stuff dates with walnut halves and roll in light-brown sugar. Stuff with peanut butter and roll in ground peanuts, or stuff with pecan halves and roll in grated coconut.

Sugarplum Tree for Christmas Centerpiece or Table Decoration. Prepare various sizes of different colored paper cups by looping string through holes near the top of the cups. Decorate the cups with bright Christmas stickers or gold and silver seals, gay ribbon, and paper doilies. Fill the cups with homemade candies. Wrap candy canes in transparent wrap and tie a loop of string on the handle of the cane. Wrap individual pieces of candy in foil and tie with narrow ribbon, inserting a Christmas tree ornament hook into the ribbon. Hang these sweets on a small tree and use as a centerpiece on dining table or coffee table.

Beverages

Cold Beverages

Banana Milkshake. Blend 1 mashed, ripe banana into a glass of cold milk or mix in an electric blender.

Carrot Freeze. Blend 1 cup of fresh or canned carrot juice and 1 pint of vanilla ice cream in an electric blender. Pour into 3 pilsener glasses. Top with a scoop of vanilla ice cream and garnish with a twisted orange slice and carrot sticks.

Cherry Cubes. Freeze maraschino cherries inside some ice cubes and a mint leaf in others for lemonade, iced tea, or old-fashioneds.

Chocolate-Strawberry Float. Serve a generous scoop of strawberry ice cream in ice-cold chocolate milk. Top with whipped cream and a fresh strawberry.

Cranberry Juice Cocktail. Mix 2 parts of cranberry juice with 1 part of canned, unsweetened pineapple juice. Chill. Serve over cracked ice in an old-fashioned glass, garnished with a canned pineapple spear and short straws.

Cranberry Mist. Combine 2 bottles of cranberry juice cocktail and 1 can of undiluted frozen pineapple juice. Half fill large old-fashioned glasses or highball glasses with crushed ice and fill with the concentrated punch. Put a canned or fresh pineapple spear and 2 short straws in each glass.

Double-Lemon Lemonade. Add a little grated lemon rind to lemonade the next time you make it.

Easy Milk Shakes for the Small Fry. Simply add 6 tablespoons of instant chocolate or vanilla pudding to 2 cups of cold milk, then whip.

Fruit Juice Frappé. Mix equal parts of pineapple, grapefruit, and orange juice (fresh or canned). Add a little lime or lemon juice. Tint the combination pale green with a drop of food coloring and freeze to a mushy consistency, stirring occasionally. Serve in tall glasses garnished with fresh mint and Mandarin orange sections. This can be made in an electric blender by filling the blender 2/3 full of crushed ice, adding these juices, and blending quickly at high speeds.

Fruit Stirrers for Lemonade. Spear a chunk of pineapple, a maraschino cherry, and a watermelon ball on sipping straws or stirrers.

Ginger Lime Rickey. Combine 1-1/2 cups of fresh lime juice and 1/2 cup of sugar. Shake or stir well. Add a quart of ginger ale and a dash of powdered ginger. Stir a bit and serve with wedges of fresh lime.

Health Cocktails from a Can. Canned vegetable juices are not very appetizing alone, but try equal parts of chilled, canned, unsweetened pineapple juice and chilled, canned celery juice. or equal parts of chilled, canned carrot juice and chilled fresh orange juice. Freshly made vegetable juices are delicious alone or in almost any combination.

Iced Coffee Float. Add a scoop of coffee ice cream to each glass of iced coffee. Top with sweetened whipped cream.

Iced Tea on the Rocks. Serve iced tea in a large old-fashioned glass with 2 ice cubes, a lump of sugar soaked in bitters, and a stemmed maraschino cherry.

Junior Glacier. Stir 2 teaspoons of orange marmalade into a tall glass of ice-cold milk. Serve with an iced-tea spoon for scooping out the last bit of orange peel.

Mauna Loa Punch. For a luau or any patio party, set a large metal mixing bowl in a roaster pan with ferns, leaves, or other greens in the roaster around the bowl. Put water on the greens and 2 or 3 chunks of dry ice in the water around the punch bowl. Fill the bowl with a fruit punch.

Milk Lassie. Stir 2 tablespoons of unsulphured molasses into a glass of cold milk. It's healthful, easy to prepare, and delicious. Natural iron in the molasses makes the milk complete.

Minted Chocolate. Add 2 or 3 drops of peppermint extract to chocolate milk. Pour over cracked ice. Top with whipped cream and garnish with a sprig of fresh mint or a candy mint leaf on a straw or stirrer. Serve immediately.

Minute Meals in a Beverage. Make with a hand beater, electric blender, or in a shaker: mashed avocado mixed with fresh, unsweetened grapefruit juice; beaten egg yolk mixed with fresh orange juice or unsweetened grape juice.

Mocha Soda. Large glasses of iced coffee, with a tablespoon of chocolate syrup and a scoop of chocolate ice cream in each.

Orange Zing. Add 2 tablespoons of frozen orange juice concentrate to a tall glass of iced plain soda or cola beverage and spike with a twist of orange peel.

Pineapple Punch. Mix syrup from a can of pineapple chunks with ginger ale and a dash of fresh lemon juice. Serve in tall, well-chilled glasses with several chunks of pineapple stuck on straws or stirrers.

Prune Nog. Equal amounts of prune juice and rich milk with an egg yolk or whole egg added. Serve with a sprinkle of cinnamon on top. Can be made in an electric blender.

Quick-as-a-Wink Iced Tea. Add 1 teaspoon of instant tea to a glass of lemonade, or add several tablespoons of lemonade concentrate to a glass of iced instant tea. With either, serve a slice of fresh lemon and stem cherry if desired.

Snow Blossom Eggnog. Fold 2 stiffly beaten egg whites and 1 cup of whipped cream into a quart of chilled eggnog. Spike with brandy, rum, or whiskey. Sprinkle with nutmeg or mace, and serve immediately in small cups.

Spiced Honey Milk. Add a tablespoon of mild honey and some mace or nutmeg to a cup of cold milk. Shake or stir thoroughly. Pour over shaved ice if desired.

Tropical Cooler. Blend the juice of 1 orange, 1 cup of unsweetened canned pineapple juice, and 1 pint of lemon ice cream in an electric blender. Fill four 8-ounce highball glasses. Garnish with thin slices of lemon dipped in granulated sugar.

Hot Beverages

Café au Lait. Into a half cup of hot milk pour an equal amount of hot coffee. Serve at once. To be really traditional, have hot milk in one pot and hot coffee in another and pour simultaneously into the cup.

Café au Lait from the Pantry. Combine a rounded teaspoon of instant coffee and a rounded tablespoon of powdered cream in a large cup. Add boiling water.

Café Borgia. Serve equal parts of fresh hot coffee and hot chocolate topped with sweetened whipped cream and garnished with grated orange peel.

Café Internationale. Serve in the living room after an elegant dinner party. Put 1/2 lump of sugar and a twist of orange peel in a demitasse. Heat cognac in a chafing dish or pan and light. Pour, flaming, over the peel and sugar and let it burn a few seconds. Then slowly fill the cup with boiling hot coffee.

Cambric Tea. Mix 1/3 part of hot tea and 2/3 part of hot milk. Sweeten to taste with honey or sugar.

Half and Half. Hot chicken broth mixed with unsweetened pineapple juice and served hot with a clove-studded lemon slice is delicious.

Hot Calypso Cider. Heat 2 quarts of cider with 1/4 cup of light brown sugar. Add 3 slices of orange and 3 slices of lemon. Simmer for 10 minutes. Add 2 tablespoons of Angostura bitters and serve.

Hot Tea Garnish. Place 3 or 4 cloves in the rind of lemon slices. Serve with hot tea.

Mexican Chocolate. Add 1 stick of cinnamon, 1/2 teaspoon of vanilla, and 2 tablespoons of instant coffee to 4 cups of hot, rich cocoa. Top with sweetened whipped cream.

Mint Cup. Add 2 teaspoons of mint jelly to a cup of hot tea. Serve with a lemon slice. To dress it up, scallop the edge of the lemon slice and top with half a maraschino cherry.

T-Tea. Pour leftover coffee or tea into ice-cube trays and freeze for use later in iced tea or coffee. Do not boil or reheat coffee.

Village Brew. Serve hot apple juice in a champagne or sherbet glass with a whole cinnamon stick as a stirrer.

Winter Mary. A wonderful cold remedy is hot canned tomato juice served with a dash of lemon juice and a dash of onion salt. Vodka or gin may be added.

Spiked Beverages

California Champagne Cocktail. Chill champagne glasses thoroughly and dip rims in powdered sugar. Fill each glass with California champagne and float California brandy on top. Splash with a dash of passion fruit juice concentrate. Serve with a spear of fresh pineapple. No bitters and no sugar added.

Calypso Freeze. Blend one 10-ounce bottle of quinine water, 1 pint of coffee ice cream, and 2 tablespoons of rum. Fill 3 glasses. Top each with a dash of nutmeg.

Continental Cooler. Fill a tall glass halfway with red table wine. Add cracked ice and sparkling water to fill. Spear 4 or 5 grapes, kebab style, on a stirrer. Claret or burgundy are particularly good for this. Or, if you prefer white wine, use a sauterne.

Grand Coupe à la Gaston. Place one small very ripe peach in the bottom of a chilled twenty-ounce glass (soda glass). Prick peach well with fork to extract juice. Add a jigger of peach brandy and fill the glass with champagne. Decorate with a sprig of fresh mint.

Holiday Ice Circle for the Punch Bowl. Place a few maraschino cherries and juice in the bottom of a ring mold. Set in freezer and fill slowly to top with water. When frozen, turn out, bottom side up, in punch bowl.

Margarita Cocktail. Pour 1 ounce of tequila, a dash of Triple Sec, and the juice of 1/2 lime over cracked ice. Stir as you would a martini, and serve in a martini glass. A real, before-dinner cocktail for those who think the vodka martini is old hat. Before pouring, dip the rims of the glass in lemon juice and coarse salt (may be done ahead of time).

Orange Cooler. Mix equal parts of sauterne or other white wine and fresh orange juice. Pour over ice cubes in tall glasses. Garnish with a sprig of fresh mint and an orange slice.

Pimm's Number 1. English in origin but made in England with "lemon squash," which is really lemon soda. This is a simpler, less sweet version, made with a man-size jigger of gin and Seven Up or Squirt. Serve in copper or pewter tankard, chock full of ice cubes and garnished with a slice of lemon and a slice of crisp, cool, peeled cucumber.

St. Louis Champagne Cocktail. Mix 50% champagne, 20% orange juice, 10% pineapple juice, 20% cognac.

Strawberry Sophisticate. Scoop strawberry ice cream into a champagne glass. Fill with sparkling burgundy and garnish with a fresh strawberry.

Venezuela, The Cocktail Chama. Make in an electric blender. For two, blend 2 cups of finely cracked ice, 1 cup of diced very ripe honeydew melon, 1/2 jigger of Cointreau, 2 jiggers of light rum, and 1 scant bar spoon of confectioners' sugar. Blend quickly and serve in chilled champagne glasses.

Instead of Meat

Canned and Packaged Meat Substitutes

Fantastic packaged meat substitutes other than canned, which are hardly distinguishable from the best, most tender meats, are now available in most health-food stores and many select super-markets: Loma Linda frozen meatless roast beef, meatless chicken, meatless turkey, meatless salami, and other items in 2-lb. or 5-lb. rolls; Morningstar Farms Breakfast Strips (like bacon), breakfast slices (like ham), links and patties (like the best sausages). Make cold or hot meatless roast-beef sandwiches on whole wheat bread; meatless meat submarines on whole wheat hoagie buns; club sandwiches with meatless chicken slices and the cooked breakfast strips, and breakfast slices and natural cheese sandwiches on stone-ground sourdough rye bread to eat plain or grilled.

Mock Chicken Pie. Put chunks of canned mock chicken cutlets or meatless chicken roll, diced cooked potatoes, frozen peas, and quarters of hard-cooked eggs in condensed celery soup to which you have added the well-beaten yolk of 1 egg. Add minced parsley and a bit of freshly chopped onion to biscuit dough. Place soup mixture in a buttered baking dish and top with small biscuits. The Roman Meal biscuits available in some supermarkets are great for this dish.

Mock Sausage Bake. Boil and peel sweet potatoes or yams. Cut into wide strips lengthwise and place in a buttered baking dish. Mix brown sugar with sliced apples and place on top of potatoes. Then brown Yum, a canned meat substitute, and place the browned slices on top of the apples. Pour hot water, 2 tablespoons of soy sauce, and 3 tablespoons of melted butter over all. Bake in a covered pan in a moderately hot oven for 45 minutes or until apples are done. Uncover for at least 10 minutes to brown.

Protose Goulash. Cube 1 can of Protose, a canned meat substitute. Mix with 1 cup of cooked kidney beans, 1 cup of cooked macaroni, and some well-seasoned marinara tomato sauce. Heat thoroughly. Serve with a green salad and whole wheat French bread.

Protose Hash. Dice Protose, a canned meat substitute, and brown onions, parsley, and finely chopped green pepper. Add to the Protose some coarsely shredded cooked potatoes and some minced pimento. Press mixture down with spatula. Brown on one side over high heat. Turn and brown on the other side. Do not stir or mix.

Protose Steak With Onions. Place 1/2-inch-thick slices of Protose, a canned meat substitute, in an oiled baking pan. Cover slices with slightly sautéed minced onions and parsley. Bake in a hot oven for 1/2 hour. Serve with broiled tomatoes seasoned with choice of herbs and butter and a pinch of raw sugar.

Savory Loaf and Potatoes. Mix equal parts of diced Savory loaf, a canned meat substitute, potatoes, and hard-cooked eggs. Scallop as you would plain scalloped potatoes.

Stake-Lets "Birds." Make a moist, well-seasoned bread stuffing. Put a spoonful of stuffing on each strip of Stake-Lets, a canned meat substitute. Roll up carefully and skewer with toothpicks. Brown in butter and transfer to casserole. Add pan drippings moistened with a bit of vegetable broth, and bake until brown. Serve with watercress and sliced tomatoes.

Vegetarian Chop Suey. Mix equal parts of bean sprouts, diced cooked celery, sliced sautéed mushrooms, sliced water chestnuts, and chopped sautéed onions (or any combination of these vegetables and fresh Chinese vegetables), and an equal part of diced Zoyburger, a canned meat substitute, or other meat substitute toasted in the oven without grease or oil. Hold together with a cornstarch-thickened sauce, seasoned with soy sauce, a pinch of ginger and a pinch of sugar. Serve on steamed rice with extra soy sauce.

Vigorost Swiss Steak. Flour and brown thick (1-1/2 inch) slices of Vigorost, a canned meat substitute. Add sautéed sliced onions, sautéed thin long slices of green pepper, 1 cup of tomato juice, salt, and freshly ground black pepper. Cook uncovered over low heat for about half an hour. Garnish with chopped parsley. Serve with mashed potatoes.

Zoyburger Filet. Lay 1/2-inch slice of Zoyburger, a canned meat substitute, in an oiled baking dish. Make a sauce of vegetable soup stock thickened with a *roux* of butter and flour and seasoned with grated onion and 1 tablespoon of lemon juice. Pour sauce over the Zoyburger slices. Sprinkle with coarse, buttered, whole-wheat bread crumbs (the prepared herbed, seasoned ones, dampened a bit are very good). Bake.

Cheese and Vegetables

Lentil Croquettes. Cook a pound of lentils in as little salted water as possible with 1 whole carrot, a large stick of celery, and a bunch of parsley. In regular meat grinder, grind the cooked lentils with 1 cup of hazel nuts and a large raw onion. Season to taste with herb sea salt or sesame sea salt and form patties. Dip in equal parts raw wheat germ and grated Romano cheese. Brown in natural oil or bake on an oiled cookie sheet.

Lima-Bean Pimento. Bake parboiled dried lima beans with chopped onion, salt, oil, paprika, and molasses until brown and tender.

Just before they are done, fold in a generous amount of chopped pimento.

Mock Cold Turkey. Mix equal parts of firm cottage cheese (sometimes called farmer's cheese) and ground mixed pecans, almonds, and cashews. Season with ground onion, ground green pepper, ground celery seed, a bit of sage, and horseradish. Mold, chill, and slice. Garnish with watercress and slices of jellied cranberry sauce.

Mock Veal Parmigiana. Dip gluten cutlets in cracker and egg and bake on an oiled baking sheet until brown. Cover with marinara spaghetti sauce. Place a slice of mozzerella cheese and some grated Parmesan cheese on top. Place under broiler until cheese is melted and bubbly. Serve at once with a tossed green field salad (rugelo, French endive, watercress, and lettuce).

Onion Cakes. Mix equal parts of sliced onions fried in butter and smooth, salted, fairly dry cottage cheese. Bake spoonfuls of the mixture in rich pastry squares folded over once to form triangles, the edges pressed together to seal. Slit the top. Bake in a very hot oven for about 15 minutes or until brown. Serve with brown gravy or a sauce made of condensed mushroom or celery soup.

Soy Cheese Croquettes. Add grated onion, sieved hard-cooked egg yolks, and 1 well-beaten egg to a cup of mashed or grated soy cheese. Season with salt and a tiny bit of sage if desired. Form into croquettes. Roll them in cracker crumbs and fry in oil or bake in a pan oiled with a vegetable or nut oil.

Nuts

Carrot Roast. Mix 2 parts of cooked brown rice, 3 parts of finely grated California carrots, 1 cup of peanut butter with milk and egg to hold the mixture together. Season with grated or ground onion, a pinch of thyme and basil, some minced parsley, salt, and freshly ground black papper. Bake in loaf pan. Let set a few minutes after removing from the oven. Serve with a green pea sauce made by heating condensed cream of pea soup, and adding a few fresh-cooked peas.

Elegant Japanese Vegetables. Cook frozen Stir and Fry Japanese Vegetables, allowing one package for each person. Serve topped with whole toasted almonds and walnut halves, or chunks of warmed frozen meatless chicken. Use rice as a side dish. For dessert, fortune cookies and Red Zinger herb tea.

Gluten Roast. Grind 2 cups of gluten fine in food chopper with 1 medium-size onion and 1 cup of English walnuts. Add 1 beaten egg. Mix thoroughly. Salt to taste. Place the mixture in a flat, buttered baking dish. Scatter several bay leaves on top. Pour some vegetable bouillon over it. Cover tightly to retain flavor and bake for about 1 hour. Remove bay leaves and brown a bit. Serve with a creole tomato sauce: tomatoes, onions, green pepper and oil seasoned with chili powder and some creole gumbo filé powder (pulverized leaves of sassafras).

Mock Hamburger. Mix 1 cup of cooked, steel-cut oatmeal (sometimes called Irish Oatmeal) with 1/2 cup of ground walnuts, and a small onion, ground. Season with salt and a tiny bit of sage. Add enough toasted whole wheat bread crumbs to make soft patties the consistency of hamburger. Fry in oil until nicely browned. Serve plain or with mushroom sauce.

Pecan Loaf. Mix equal parts of finely minced, tender celery, fresh bread crumbs, chopped pecans, lots of minced parsley, and some chopped onion. Moisten with eggs and milk and melted butter. Put in an oiled loaf pan and bake. Serve with sautéed apple slices and brown-butter gravy made with vegetable broth.

Princess Timbales. Prepare custard mixture without sugar as for cup custard. Add boiled rice, chopped cashew nuts, minced onion, and parsley (about equal parts of the custard and the rice-nut mixture). Season to taste. Bake in custard cups or timbale molds. Serve with a mushroom or parsley sauce.

Walnut Roast. Beat 2 eggs until light. Add 2 cups of half and half and 1-1/2 cups of toasted bread crumbs. Let stand for 20 minutes. Add 1 cup of ground walnuts or peanuts, 1 teaspoon of salt, and 2 teaspoons of grated onion. Bake in a moderate oven for 30 minutes. Serve with any preferred sauce and some red currant jelly.

Mineral-Rich Salads

Calcium Salad. Serve equal parts of grated fresh coconut, shredded cabbage, and cottage cheese topped with broken English walnuts, on a bed of lettuce with a honey cream dressing.

Chlorine Salad. On salad plate, arrange equal parts of chopped fresh spinach and shredded head lettuce. Put a large mound of chopped raw sauerkraut on the shredded greens. Top the sauerkraut with grated raw apple and crushed pineapple. Sprinkle with chopped chives or minced green-onion tops. Dribble on a little French dressing or olive oil. Unusual and delicious.

Fluorine Salad. Serve shredded cabbage and finely grated raw beets on watercress with a fresh garlic French dressing.

Hydrogen Salad. Serve fresh pineapple and melon cubes, or balls, mixed together, on a mound of shredded head lettuce. Garnish with grapefruit and orange sections. No dressing necessary. Whipped cream, sweetened with a bit of honey or brown sugar, may be used.

Iron Salad. On a bed of curly chickory, place a mound of finely grated raw beet, seasoned with 1 rounded teaspoon of frozen orange juice concentrate and a dash of powdered cloves. No salt or pepper is necessary. Top the beets with a generous dollop of sour cream or thick yogurt.

Phosphorus Salad. Use equal parts of chopped celery, grated raw cauliflower, chopped tomatoes, and coarsely shredded head lettuce. Toss with French dressing and top with ground sunflower seeds and ground tender prunes.

Potassium Salad. Toss equal parts of chopped watercress, minced parsley, chopped endive, and tomatoes with Roquefort or blue cheese dressing.

Silicon Salad. Toss equal parts of chopped raw spinach, cabbage, and cucumber. Sprinkle with whole almonds. Serve with your choice of dressing. For most green vegetable salads I prefer equal parts of lemon or lime juice, and olive oil, highly seasoned with vegetable salt, pepper, paprika, dry mustard, and fresh crushed garlic.

"16" Salad. Put a large sweet green pepper, a small bunch of parsley, and 4 large, raw mushrooms through the food chopper. Add 1 or 2 green onions minced very fine. Add 1/2 cup of steamed seedless raisins. Moisten the mixture with 1 tablespoon of salad dressing or mayonnaise and 1 teaspoon of horseradish. Halve and peel 2 avocados. Place peeled avocado on several leaves of Boston lettuce. Fill avocados generously with the vegetable mixture. Garnish with peeled tomato wedges.

Sodium Salad. Prepare equal parts of chopped celery, cucumbers, and apple, and 1/2 part of chopped spinach. Dress with equal parts of mayonnaise and yogurt or sour cream, sweetened with a bit of honey or maple syrup if desired.

Sulphur Salad. Toss equal parts of ground onions, green pepper, radishes, and cucumber mixed with finely grated raw turnip and minced celery. Serve on a leaf of lettuce. Top with a sweet-and-sour dressing made of equal parts of honey or maple syrup and lemon juice, flavored with vegetable salt and white pepper.

Vitamin A Salad. Serve finely grated carrots tossed with minced celery hearts and chopped seeded raisins with a cream-cheese dressing.

Cook's Dictionary

ACIDULATED WATER. Water with vinegar or lemon juice added. Use 1 tablespoon of acid to 1 quart of water.

À LA GRECQUE. Vegetables cooked in an oil and vinegar liquid with herbs added.

À LA MODE. In America, à la mode usually means topped with ice cream. In France, the term means "the way it is done."

À LA RUSSE. In the Russian style.

AL DENTE. An Italian term used to describe food, especially pasta but also vegetables, cooked so the food is still firm to the bite.

ASPIC. Jellied broth used to make molds of cold vegetables, meats, or fish, as a mask for cold foods, or chopped as a garnish.

AU GRATIN. Any food baked with bread-crumb, butter, and cheese topping.

AU JUS. In the natural juices. Meat *au jus* is meat served in its own pan juices, rather than with other sauce or thickened gravy.

BAKE. To cook in an oven with dry heat.

BAKING TEMPERATURES. Very slow, 250° F; slow, 300°F; moderately slow, 325°F; moderate, 350°F; moderately hot, 375° F; hot, 400°F; very hot, 450°F.

BARBECUE. To cook over an open fire or by direct heat, basting with a highly seasoned sauce.

BASTE. To pour small quantities of liquid, melted fat, or oil over food as it cooks. Basting keeps food moist and gives it a glaze. Roasted turkey or baked ham are improved by basting periodically during the cooking.

BATTER. A mixture of flour and liquid with other ingredients added. Thick batter is the consistency of whipped potatoes; medium batter is the consistency of sour cream; thin batter is the consistency of gravy.

BEAT. To stir vigorously and thoroughly with a spoon or beater.

BIND. To hold a mixture of foods together with a semiliquid ingredient such as mayonnaise or cream sauce.

BLANCH. To pour boiling water over food and then drain it almost immediately; or to parboil in water for a minute or two. Fruits, chestnuts, shelled almonds, and tomatoes are blanched to loosen their skins.

BLANQUETTE. A light stew; one made without browning the meat first.

BLAZE. See Flambé.

BLEND. To gently mix two or more ingredients until thoroughly combined.

BOIL. To cook in liquid at the boiling or bubbling point.

BOIL DOWN. To reduce volume by boiling.

BONE. To remove the bones from meat or fish.

BONED AND ROLLED. The method the butcher uses to remove the bone from a meat cut and then roll it up and tie it with string or fasten with skewers for roasting.

BOUILLON. A clear broth made by cooking meat, fish, or vegetables in liquid and then straining the liquid. Packaged bouillon cubes may be used as a substitute.

BOUQUET GARNI. A selection of whole herbs placed in a small cheesecloth bag or tied together and put in a broth or stock to flavor it while cooking. The bag or bunch is removed and discarded when the broth is done.

BRAISE. To brown meat or vegetables in fat or oil and then add a small amount of liquid and finish cooking, tightly covered, at a low temperature on top of the stove or in the oven. This is a cooking method which tenderizes tougher cuts of meats.

BREAD. To bread meat or fish means to roll it in fine bread crumbs.

BREAD CRUMBS. Soft bread crumbs used for stuffing and for some puddings made with day-old bread or stuffing mix (moistened a bit); fine bread crumbs are made from bread that is dried out and rolled or grated. Fine bread crumbs are sold in supermarkets.

BROCHETTE. Small skewer on which pieces of meat, fish, or vegetables are cooked (usually broiled).

BROIL. To cook under or over direct heat. This can be done in the broiler section of the oven, directly under the heating unit; over a wood, coal, or charcoal fire; or in a portable electric or gas broiler.

BROTH. A thin soup, or the liquid left after simmering vegetables, meat, fish or other foods.

BROWN. To cook in a little fat until brown.

BRUSH. To daub the surface of food lightly with some liquid, fat, or oil, applying it with a pastry brush or dribbling it on with a spoon.

BUTTERED CRUMBS. Fine crumbs cooked with melted butter or rubbed lightly with soft butter with the fingertips. Use for *au gratin* dishes. Soft bread crumbs can be rubbed lightly with the fingertips with soft fat, butter, or oil and used for stuffing poultry or meat.

CANAPÉS. Small pieces of fried or toasted bread spread with highly seasoned toppings and usually garnished elaborately.

CANDY. To cook in sugar or in a syrup, or to dip in egg white and then in granulated sugar and let dry (as mint leaves or grapes).

CANDY MAKING TEMPERATURES. Soft-ball stage, 234-240°F; firm-ball stage, 244-248°F; hard-ball stage, 250-265°F; soft-crack stage, 270-290°F; hard-crack stage, 300-310°F.

CARAMELIZE. To heat sugar or food containing sugar without liquid until it is light brown in color. To make caramel syrup, add water *after* the sugar is caramelized.

CHARCOAL-BROIL. To broil with the heat of a charcoal fire, directly over or in front of the coals.

CHILL. To place in refrigerator or other cold place until thoroughly cold.

CHOP. To cut in small pieces. Can be done with a sharp heavy knife (French style), a sharp paring knife, or a food chopper. Chopping cannot be done by a meat grinder. Chopping leaves the bits separate and distinct, whereas grinding mashes them slightly. Using the proper method for the particular dish involved is very important for correct flavor as well as texture.

CLARIFY. To clear a liquid of bits of food or cloudy substance by adding egg white and egg shell and beating them over heat. The broth is then strained; the food particles cling to the egg and are separated from the liquid. Also to melt and skim butter.

COAT. To cover thoroughly with a dry ingredient, such as flour or crumbs.

COMPOTE. A mixture of fresh or cooked fruits.

CONDIMENT. Seasoning or flavoring, including prepared sauces such as Worcestershire, catsup, mustard, or chili sauce.

CONFECTIONERS' SUGAR. Powdered sugar.

CONSOMME. A clear, strong, highly seasoned broth made from meat. The broth is strong enough to become jellied when it is chilled.

COOL. To allow to stand at room temperature until no longer warm to the touch.

CORE. To remove center fleshy part of fruit or vegetable including seeds, if any. (As pineapple or apples.)

CORNED. Cured by soaking in a salt solution or brine.

CORNSTARCH. A starch, made from corn, used to thicken puddings and sauces, used for thickening in many Oriental dishes.

COURT BOUILLON. An herb-seasoned broth used for poaching fish.

CREAM. To mix shortening and sugar with a spoon, electric mixer or blender, or the hands until the mixture is the consistency of whipped cream.

CROUTONS. Small toasted cubes of bread.

CUBE. To cut ingredients into uniformly square pieces.

CUT IN. To cut one ingredient (usually shortening) into another ingredient (usually flour or meal), using a wire pastry blender or 2 knives.

DEEP FRY. To cook in enough fat or oil to float the food. To assure a crisp crust, lower food slowly into the hot fat without crowding the pieces to prevent lowering the temperature and causing the fat to soak in. Drain on absorbent paper after frying. Keep hot, and serve immediately.

DEEP FRYING TEMPERATURES. Doughnuts, thin batter fritters and potatoes, 375°F; meat croquettes, nuts, meat and fish, 365°F; thick fritter batter and patty shells, 350°F.

DICE. To cut ingredients into very small, uniform cubes.

DISJOINT. To cut a fowl into pieces at the joints.

DISSOLVE. To stir a solid such as sugar, salt, yeast or softened gelatine in a liquid until a solution is formed. Gelatine may be dissolved in the top of a double boiler by mixing it with a small amount of the liquid called for in a given recipe.

DOT. To cover with small bits of butter, fat, cheese, or other semisolid ingredient.

DREDGE. To cover thoroughly with a dry substance, such as flour, cornmeal, or crumbs. A paper bag containing the dry ingredient can be used to shake the food to cover it evenly.

DRESS. To mix with some sauce or flavoring just before serving, as to dress cooked vegetables with butter, or salad greens with salad dressing.

DRIPPINGS. The residue in a baking pan after roasting.

DUST. To cover the top of a pastry or other food very lightly with a dry ingredient such as sugar or flour.

FILLET (ENGLISH) OR FILET (FRENCH). A cut of meat or fish without bones. Used as a verb, it means to cut such a piece of meat or fish.

FINE HERBES. Mixed herbs, chopped together very fine and used for seasoning. Usually includes parsley, chives and tarragon or sweet basil.

FLAKE. To break into small pieces with a fork.

FLAMBÉ. To pour alcoholic liquor over food and set it alight. To be sure liquor will flame, heat it or even light it before pouring it over the food, unless the food itself is very, very hot.

FOLD. To combine two ingredients by turning one over into the other, using a folding motion.

FRICASSEE. A stew. The meat or fowl may or may not be browned and then cooked in a liquid. The liquid is thickened and served over the meat.

FRY. To cook on top of the stove in a medium amount of very hot fat or very hot oil.

GARNISH. To decorate with a food of contrasting color or texture.

GLAZE. To give a glossy finish to food. This is done in different ways: fish or vegetables may be covered with a sauce or grated cheese or both, and glazed under the broiler flame; vegetables or fruits may be steamed in butter and glazed with some sugar added the last minute or so of cooking.

GOULASH. Hungarian meat stew, which is usually seasoned with paprika.

GRATE. To rub food on a grater until the food is in minute pieces. The food will be grated fine or coarse depending on the size and shape of the perforations in the grater.

GREASE. To rub lightly with butter, margarine, shortening, or oil. A paper towel dipped in the grease makes an efficient applicator for greasing pans.

GRILL. To brown, with some pressure, on a greased or oiled griddle, pan, or electric grill. If ordinary pan or griddle is used, food is pressed down lightly with a spatula while browning on one side, then turned and pressed down gently again. An electric grill browns both sides at the same time, the weight of the top griddle supplying sufficient pressure.

GRIND. To put through a grinder, cutting the food into tiny particles. Grains, coffee, nuts, meat, crackers, and dried or candied fruits are often ground for added flavor or a particular texture.

HORS D'OEUVRE. Appetizers, served with cocktails or as a first course.

JULIENNE. To cut into thin, long strips.

KNEAD. To work dough with palms and heel of the hands, by pressing, turning and pressing again. Sometimes done with an electric mixer at slow speed.

LARD. To insert thin strips of fat (usually salt pork or bacon) into the flesh of lean meat, using a special larding needle; also, the rendered fat of pork.

LEGUMES. Dried vegetables such as lentils, dried beans, split peas.

MACÉDOINE. A mixture of vegetables or fruits cut fairly fine.

MARINADE. A seasoned sauce in which meats or other foods are soaked.

MARINATE. To soak food in liquid, such as to soak in a marinade.

MASK. To coat or cover thoroughly with a sauce or aspic.

MELT. To liquefy or dissolve by applying heat.

MERINGUE. Stiffly beaten egg whites sweetened with sugar and used as a topping for pies and other desserts. A stiff meringue is sometimes baked separately in shell or cuplike shapes in a slow oven until firm. The baked shell or cup is then served filled with fruit or ice cream.

MINCE. To chop into very tiny bits.

PAN-BROIL. To cook in a skillet with little or no fat added. The pan is sometimes rubbed very lightly with fat or oil, but the food is not fried.

PARBOIL. To boil in salted water or other liquid until the food is just partially cooked.

PARE. To cut off the outer skin of fruits, vegetables, or cheese.

PASTA. The Italian term for all foods made of flour and liquid and then dried and cut into shapes such as spaghetti or macaroni.

PÂTÉ. A paste usually made of meat or fish, often molded. A pâté is used as a spread for toast or crackers or it can be cut in thin slices and served with a garnish as an appetizer.

PEEL. To cut or pull off the peeling of fruit, vegetables, or cheese.

PETITS FOURS. Small, rich cookies or tiny, fancy cakes.

PILAF. Rice cooked with flavorings, nuts, or meats or other ingredients.

PINCH. As much as you can hold between the thumb and first finger.

PIT. To remove seed or pit, as from prunes or cherries.

PLANK. To heat and serve food, usually meat or fish, on a wooden plank or platter, garnished with fruits or vegetables of contrasting color and texture.

POACH. To simmer gently in enough hot liquid to cover.

POWDERED SUGAR. Confectioners' sugar.

PREHEAT. To heat the pan or the oven before placing the food in it to cook.

PUREE. To put through a sieve or food mill until the food is a smooth paste.

RACK. A rib section of meat; a roast containing several ribs.

RAGOUT. The French term for stew.

RAMEKIN. Individual casserole; one that will hold enough food for a single portion.

REDUCE. To boil liquid until some of the water has evaporated. This makes a richer mixture, since the seasonings and flavorings are more concentrated in the reduced liquid.

RICH MILK. Half and half, or half milk, half heavy cream.

RICH PASTRY. Dough that has more shortening than usual.

RENDER. To cook solid fat slowly in a skillet or in the oven, until the fat melts.

ROAST. To cook in an oven with dry heat.

ROASTING TEMPERATURES. See Baking Temperatures.

ROLL OUT DOUGH. To use a floured rolling pin to press dough into a flat shape, or to press dough into a flat shape by rolling between two pieces of waxed paper without flour.

ROUX. A mixture of hot melted fat, oil, or butter and flour and used to thicken liquid. The hot shortening and flour are stirred together in a hot pan until bubbly before adding the liquid. Add the liquid cold and all at once to avoid lumpiness.

SADDLE. A cut of meat including the entire center section of the animal; that is, both loins.

SAUTÉ. To cook gently on top of the stove in a very small amount of fat, oil, or butter.

SCALD. To heat liquid to just below the boiling point; or to plunge solid food into boiling water for a minute.

SCALE. To scrape scales loose from a fish.

SCORE. To slash with a knife. Usually this refers to making light gashes in the skin or outer surface of meats, vegetables, or fruits.

SEAR. To cook quickly at high heat to seal in the juices. This can be done by starting a roast in a very hot oven and then reducing the temperature to cook; or it can be done by browning food quickly and at a high heat in a pan on top of the stove.

SHISH KEBAB. An eastern Mediterranean skewer of broiled meat, usually lamb. Sometimes vegetables are added to the skewer before broiling.

SHORTENING. Fats or oils used in cooking. Solid shortening means rendered and then congealed fats such as lard or tallow, hydrogenated vegetable fats, butter, or margarine. Liquid shortening means oil, melted butter, or other melted shortening.

SHRED. To cut into thin slivers with a sharp knife or coarse grater.

SHUCK. To take the shells off certain seafood, such as clams and oysters; or to remove the husks from corn.

SIFT. Shake through a flour sifter or through a fine sieve.

SIMMER. To cook gently in liquid below the boiling point.

SKEWER. Small, thin wooden or metal rods used for spearing foods for cooking or serving; or very small metal pins used to fasten foods together or to close a fowl after filling it with stuffing.

SKIM. To spoon off the fat or scum forming on the surface of a liquid, or to remove the cream from the top of milk.

SLIVER. To cut or shred into long, thin pieces.

SOAK. To cover with liquid and allow to stand.

SOUFFLÉ. A dish made with beaten egg whites folded in with other ingredients so the mixture rises and puffs when it is baked.

SPIT. A metal rod with a sharp end used for holding meats or fish while they roast over an open fire.

STEAM. To cook over (not in) boiling water in a tightly covered kettle. Bungalow cookers, kettles fitted with racks, are made especially for steaming. A large food such as a whole fish is placed on the rack of a large oven-roasting pan, water is put in the bottom of the pan so as not to touch the food, the pan is covered and the oven kept to moderate heat.

STEAMING VEGETABLES (ORIENTAL STYLE). Using a wok, electric skillet, or heavy covered skillet, cook vegetables gently in a little oil and just the water that clings to the vegetables after they are washed and drained.

STEEP. To add boiling liquid to a dry ingredient and allow to stand in order to draw out the flavor from the dry ingredient into the liquid, as in making tea.

STEW. To cook slowly in liquid for a long time until tender.

STIFF, BUT NOT DRY. Egg whites are beaten stiff but not dry when they are used to make a mixture light and airy. Beat them just until they stand in peaks. They should still be glossy and moist-looking and not too fine-grained. For chiffon cakes, it is recommended that the eggs be beaten longer until dry. For sponge cakes, the eggs are beaten stiff but not dry.

STIR. To blend ingredients with a circular motion with a spoon.

STIR FRY. To toss in a small amount of very hot oil.

STOCK. See Bouillon.

THICKENING AGENT. An ingredient or mixture of ingredients used to thicken liquid. It may be shortening and flour, cornstarch, egg yolks, finely grated potato, or various other agents.

TIE. To tie boned meat with string so it will hold its shape while cooking.

TRUSS. To tie a whole fowl with the wings and legs held tightly in place so the bird holds its shape while cooking.

TRY OUT. To heat or render fat or fat meat until the fat melts.

WHIP. To beat an ingredient quickly and vigorously until puffy and light. This can be done with an egg beater, wire whisk, fork, electric mixer, or an electric blender, depending on the ingredients.

WOK. A Chinese cooking utensil similar to a deep covered skillet used for steaming vegetables in a bit of oil. Our electric frying pans are very good substitutes.

Index